Dedication

To Anthony,
Alec and Louie Harris' grandson,
who was told by Spirit that he would
continue in his grandfather's footsteps,
but on the mental plane.

Alec Harris 1897 ~ 1974

ALEC HARRIS

~

The full story
of his remarkable
physical mediumship

by

Louie Harris

Published by
Saturday Night Press Publications
York. England

snppbooks@gmail.com

ISBN 978-0-9557050-4-5

Printed by
Lightning Source
www.lightningsource.com

Contents

A Note on the Illustrations

I have taken the opportunity to include in the book the drawings and paintings of some of our guides, which my father made in the 1950-60s and the pictures are as I remember the Spirit Guides when they materialised.. My dad was not in trance when he painted or pencil-crayoned these pictures. When we asked him how he did them he said that he had a strong impression to do them at that moment, and as he was doing them, it was as if he was being guided with his hand movements.

Amongst them are two different ones of Ginger but it is as the young man in the hat that I remember his materialising. The other picture of him as a boy, in a composite of four of our Spirit children, was probably one of the first to be drawn in 1950. Because of cost we have had to print them in black and white but we hope that you can appreciate their colours on the back cover of the book. -

Bradley Harris

The photographs of Helen Hughes, Maurice Barbanell and Ernest Oaten are by courtesy of 'Psychic News'.

Preface

'Alec Harris – the full story of his remarkable physical mediumship' by Louie Harris sees the light of day over 30 years after it was written, and as the result of a very fortuitous set of circumstances. An abbreviated version of the book, under the title *'They Walked Among Us'*, was first published in 1980, but the full version has languished in yellowing manuscript pages from the day it was written. I first read *'They Walked Among Us'* some years ago, and was impressed both by the transparent sincerity of the writing and by the quality of the phenomena described. It was clear, on the evidence presented in the book, that Alec Harris belonged in the very front rank of physical mediums, and the many accounts of his work that I came across subsequently served to confirm this conclusion. My own experience of physical mediumship, in particular during the two years I was privileged to visit and observe the Scole Group (Robin and Sandra Foy and mediums Diana and Alan Bartlett) and during the sittings I was fortunate to have with Stewart Alexander and with other physical mediums, has demonstrated to me the importance of this form of phenomena.

When observed under conditions that effectively rule out normal explanations, physical mediumship offers objective evidence for the existence of so-called paranormal abilities, and strong support for the belief in the survival of consciousness after physical death.

I had no expectation of learning very much more about the life and work of Alec Harris. Alec died in 1974 and there was no chance of meeting him, at least in this world. However, I knew that he had been associated with Cardiff, and on impulse I called in one afternoon at Park Grove Spiritualist Church in the city with the intention of enquiring about him. The result was that not only did I learn of the great affection in which he is still held by older church members, I was even shown – in a small room off the main body of the church – the chair in which he used to sit during his demonstrations of deep trance mediumship. This aroused my interest in Alec still further, and consequently I asked Clare O'Connell, a senior lecturer in psychology at the University of Wales, Newport, who knows virtually everything worth knowing about Cardiff, if she had ever heard of him. Not only had she heard of him, it turned out that she knew both his son Bradley and his grandson Anthony, who both live in nearby Caerphilly, very well. With her usual kindness she arranged for me to meet them, and she and I spent a fascinating afternoon interviewing them about Alec and his wife Louie. Meeting Bradley and Anthony was an enormous pleasure, not only for their readiness to talk about Alec and Louie and their experiences when sitting in séances with them but for their total conviction of the genuineness of Alec's mediumship and of Louie's own strong psychic abilities. Bradley had years of observing the extraordinary physical phenomena that manifested during his father's lifetime, while Anthony had many memories of the gifts of his grandfather. During the course of the interview we were also told that not only did a manuscript of the full version of 'They Walked Among Us' still exist, it was actually in their possession and we were welcome to borrow it if we wished. Naturally we were glad to accept this kind offer, and took the manuscript away in some excitement. Before leaving, we assured Bradley that we would think of possible ways of having the full version published, as it seemed clear that it contained additional information of great interest to all those concerned to know more of Alec's life and of his extraordinary mediumship.

Shortly after this I fulfilled an invitation from my old and deeply valued friend, Eric Hatton, former President of the Spiritualists' National Union, to be guest speaker on the psychological evidence for survival of death at a six-day course he was running at the Arthur Findlay College. Eric is a veritable mine of information on the work of the great mediums of the past, and while lunching with him, soon after my arrival, he mentioned Alec Harris and asked if I knew that a full manuscript version of '*They Walked Among Us*' was in existence. Intrigued by the coincidence, I replied that not only did I know it existed, it was now in my possession and I was hoping it might be possible to arrange for publication. Eric, who has seen far too many marvels in his life to be in the least surprised at this coincidence, immediately turned his attention to the practical question of publication. He agreed with me that no commercial publisher would be likely to take on the book knowing that a shortened version was still in print, and that the only way forward would be to find the financial support to publish it privately. Predictably, he then thought of a solution, namely the J.V. Trust, which gives generous financial assistance to worthy causes in survival research and mediumship, and which might well be interested in seeing the book published. As a Trustee he undertook to support me if I submitted a formal proposal to the Trust.

Accordingly I put together a proposal indicating the importance of the book and supplying estimates for some of the costs involved, and Eric contacted me shortly afterwards with the welcome news that the Trustees had agreed that the publication of the full version of the manuscript is long overdue, and that consequently the Trust would underwrite the costs of publication. Margaret Neville, the Solicitor for the Trust, kindly provided further confirmation of this fact. Two other encouraging developments quickly followed. Firstly, Ann Harrison, who runs her own publishing imprint, Saturday Night Press, devoted to producing books on mediumship and survival, readily agreed to my request that she see the book through the complex process that takes a book from manuscript to publication. Ann is an expert on the ins and outs of private publishing, and we first worked together when she arranged for publication of a book by one of my Ph.D students. Secondly, Bradley told me that the day after Clare and I visited him he heard out of the blue from Chris Watkins that he also had a copy of the full manuscript, given to his father by Louie Harris on the strength of his many sittings with Alec. Bradley and Chris had not met since 1956, and Bradley was unaware that Louie had given away a copy of the manuscript and that it was still in Chris's possession. Even more surprisingly, Chris reported that he had recently spent two years typing out and editing the manuscript, and now wondered if Bradley would like to have the finished result. The upshot was that at Bradley's suggestion Chris and I contacted each other and Chris sent me an electronic copy of his edited version, which proved an enormous help to myself (since it relieved me of much of the task of editing), to Clare (since it relieved her of the job of making an electronic copy of the manuscript and of many related chores) and to Ann (since it made her task of preparing the manuscript for printing that much easier). As a boy of 11 and 12 Chris had had sittings with the Harris Circle, and informed me that Alec's mediumship was so incredible that it has permanently affected him throughout his life. He also informed me that his parents were the Grahame and Marjorie mentioned by Louie Harris in the manuscript.

Psychic Press, who are the current publishers of the shortened version (with the help of a grant from the Noah's Ark Society) intimated that they had no objection to the publication of the full version. So here at last, all these years after it was written, is the complete text of Louie's book, setting out in greater detail the remarkable life she and Alec shared together, and the extraordinary gifts Alec possessed. It is evident from what I have already said that we have some happy coincidences to thank for its appearance, and some very special people:

Clare O'Connell without whom the whole project would never have come into being and who has worked with infectious enthusiasm and creative energy on it throughout; Eric Hatton for his wise understanding of the extraordinary manner in which things fall into place and for his quiet confidence that a way would be found to publish the book; the Trustees of the J.V.Trust for their ready acceptance of the value of the project and for their generous agreement to provide the vital financial support; Ann Harrison for her skill and hard work in surmounting all the difficulties associated with seeing the book through the press and for her missionary zeal in agreeing to take on the job; Chris Watkins for retaining for more than 50 years the memory of his experiences with the Harris family and for his long and committed work on the editing; and two dedicated women, Sheila Raymond-Jones and June Souter, who encouraged Louie to write her book all those years ago and who painstakingly took down her every word and then typed up the full manuscript for her. And above all, Bradley and Anthony Harris for keeping the memory of Alec and Louie so vividly alive, and for the strength of their ambition to see the book published. And not forgetting, of course, Alec and Louie Harris, wherever they may be. The book, under its new title, is a fitting tribute to these two very special beings, who devoted their lives to demonstrating the reality of survival, without media attention and without seeking fame or publicity or even thanks. Gifts such as those possessed by Alec and by Louie are extraordinarily rare, as is the total commitment they gave to every aspect of their work. They touched the lives of many thousands of people through their compassion for all those suffering bereavement and for all those interested in the deeper mysteries of life, and it is hoped that through the publication of this full version of the manuscript they will continue to touch the lives of many thousands more.

Both Bradley Harris and Chris Watkins have agreed to write their own forewords to follow my contribution, and these stand as excellent eye-witness testimonies to what will surely endure as one of the finest examples of physical mediumship in the long history of the subject.

Professor David Fontana
March 2009

The Mediumship of My Father,
Alec Harris

I was very fortunate indeed to have parents who brought me up
with the knowledge and experiences of life after death. From as
far back as I can remember it seemed quite natural for me to see
my father in trance and to hear the different voices of people
speaking through him. My mother explained to me that these
people lived in the Spirit World, the world to which we go when
we die, a world that we could not see with our eyes but that
nevertheless surrounds us. When I had measles and felt very sick
I can remember asking my mother to please let my father's Spirit
Guide, Adoula, come through and make me better, as I had seen
Adoula give healing to people at our home in the past.

In this book my mother has given a very good insight into all
aspects of my father's amazing physical mediumship. All I can do
is to fully endorse what she says. I sat in nearly all the circles we
held in our house in Manor Way, Cardiff and I can remember how,
on many Sundays, I had to help my mother tidy the house because
a bus-load of Spiritualists from a church somewhere in Wales
would be arriving in the afternoon to experience a materialisation
séance. Even at the time I can remember worrying about my dad
who willingly sat in the cabinet for usually two to three hours
allowing his body to be used for the materialisation of loved ones
and guides. Years later, when someone grabbed a materialised
Spirit and nearly cost my father his life, I realised how very
courageous my father had been in exposing himself for so many
years to this constant danger. It was my mother's faith in the
Spirit Guides for protection that helped give him this courage,
together with the fact that the sittings were being given to church
members who understood the risks that physical mediums run.

At this point I must be quite frank and say that, even if I had inherited my father's physical mediumship, I would not have the courage to expose myself to the life-threatening situation to which my father surrendered himself for all those years - a life-threatening situation that actually became a reality towards the latter part of his life.

It seems that there are so very few voice and materialisation mediums about today that when they do appear great care should be taken to see that only the most trusted Spiritualists are allowed to witness the phenomena. Yet even with such safeguards it has to be said that it was actually the secretary of a Spiritualist church who, for monetary gain offered by a local magazine, instigated the life-threatening plot to try and expose my father as a fraud. So what is the answer to such behaviour?

If people are searching for proof of life after death, then mediums like Colin Fry with the gift of clairaudience can prove to them beyond all doubt that we can communicate with our loved ones who are in the afterlife and do so without real danger to the medium. It is true, of course, that you have the ultimate proof of life after death when you can actually see your materialised loved ones face to face and speak with them and gently hold them and take part in the wonderful reunions that I have witnessed so many times in my father's séances.

In conclusion, I would like to say to any person who, like my father, is told that he or she is potentially a powerful physical medium, the road to developing the gift is not an easy one. It requires patience, total dedication and the sacrifice of your time if it is to be developed fully. However, if you do decide to dedicate your life to the service of Spirit, then the rewards are well worth-while.

Bradley Harris B.Mus.LSRM
March 2009

A Memoir of Alec Harris

How is it possible to write a true tribute to Alec and Louie Harris, who were the most remarkable people I have known? I am now 64 and my memory of them is primarily from when I was aged 11 and 12 during 1955 and 1956 just before Alec and Louie emigrated to South Africa.

I had become a regular sitter and the youngest at their materialisation and healing circles, along with my father Grahame and occasionally my mother Marjorie, who are mentioned in this book. I had first attended a children's Christmas Circle when I was aged 7, and 3 years later started attending more circles, which were to me so amazingly enjoyable although I never at the time fully realised the wonderful privilege involved.

Alec and my father, like so many people 50 years ago, were always full of humour and able to crack jokes. Louie and Alec had become best friends of my parents in the late 1930s through a love of music, when Louie, a concert violinist, and my mother, a concert pianist, would perform together in local cafés in central Cardiff and with the BBC Welsh Orchestra.

Everything experienced by me was just as Louie has written. Materialised Spirit forms were exactly like those in real life. The Spirits would usually fully materialise behind the small cabinet curtain and emerge from the cabinet by pulling aside the curtain and stepping out in front of everyone. Occasionally, as if to demonstrate the proof of materialisation, ectoplasm would build up in front of Alec to create a fully materialised Spirit form with whom we could shake hands or hug as appropriate and fully communicate just as if the form was really alive as in this current life.

When the power was waning the Spirit would usually return to the cabinet, sometimes re-emerging after receiving more power, but quite frequently would simply dematerialise by sinking to the floor in front of us. Often the cabinet curtain was drawn aside so that Alec could be seen in deep trance along with the materialised Spirit. I must emphasise that the manner in which the circles were conducted by Louie meant that there was never any question of fear of anything that happened. On the contrary it was simply a matter of great interest to witness the manifestations with much talking, laughter and singing. Being a musician and having been brought up as a Baptist, Louie knew many old Baptist hymns which were frequently sung to raise the vibrations.

At the age of 19, the year before our marriage, my wife Jan and I experienced one circle held in my parents' home when Louie and Alec were staying with them during their visit to Cardiff in 1963, a visit not mentioned by Louie. Following the dreadful treachery in 1961, as described in the final chapter, the materialisations were poor by Alec's previous standard, but were still incredibly strong and sufficient to convince everybody, including my wife and others who were present for their first and only materialisation séance. The return of materialised relatives is so convincing that it is impossible to have any doubts about the continuance of life. One's life is beneficially changed and there can then be no fear of death. Physical death is realised to be a pleasant release from an often depleted physical body. Knowledge of the afterlife was frequently brought by the guides and deceased relatives and friends.

Louie has covered only a very small percentage of all of the amazing séances that have been held for materialisation and healing. I experienced, at age 12, the materialisation of my grandmother, an uncle, a deceased circle member, and my American Indian Guide, with all of them talking and taking hold of me by shaking hands or hugging me. My wife experienced, at age 19, the materialisation of her father whom none of us, including myself, had ever met. Jan also spoke with her Spirit Guide, a North American Indian. He gave her his name, having fully materialised to his natural height of 6ft. His conversation with her indicated that he would never impose himself upon her in life, but she could always at any time think of him and he would be around as he was interested in her development in this life.

The circle guides and other helpers occasionally gave Spiritual philosophy, but were primarily involved with running the circles to ensure that everything proceeded smoothly. I expect that I am one of only a handful of people still alive who regularly experienced Alec's brilliant materialisation and healing circles. Alec was a former sceptic on any psychic matters, who changed to become possibly one of the greatest materialisation mediums ever known to the world. Louie and Alec devoted their lives to their Spiritual work. It is such a great pity that there are not now many more materialisation mediums of Alec's calibre throughout the world.

Christopher Watkins M.Sc. MICE
March 2009

Life Changing Experiences through the Mediumship of Alec Harris

Over the last few years, when speaking with people who are a little older, or a little younger, than myself, it has been significant to notice how the conversation has invariably moved to events which took place and shaped their lives so many years ago.

Many of these reflections are mundane, and though interesting, are of little importance in the scheme of things. How often have I noticed, that they are bemoaning the fast pace of life nowadays, the lack of reverence for religion and how belief in one or other aspect of religious life no longer pertains. Just a few people go on to say how certain unusual and inexplicable events took place, say, half a century ago.

The advent of physical phenomena was occurring throughout this country and indeed throughout the world. As one experiences the loss of a loved one and grief eventually gives way to questions of why they had to leave us and where they have they gone, orthodox beliefs then, no less than nowadays, fail to answer those questions.

Such was my case when I embarked upon my quest over sixty years ago. As a consequence, I travelled considerable distances to meet and listen enthralled to those who could see psychically and had the gift of mediumship. How fortunate I have been to witness in my search some remarkable revelations of the Spirit World, as a result of which my life was changed.

There is no doubt in my mind about which experiences were so exceptional as never to be forgotten. These were the occasions when Heather, my wife, and I were allowed to witness the closeness and unity of our worlds.

At a house in Manor Way, Cardiff, we were privileged to be part of the portrayal of eternal life, through the mediumship of Alec Harris. This humble man who had no academic background, and whose sole purpose was to serve others, allowed himself at great personal sacrifice to be used for physical phenomena which equated to any recorded in biblical times.

It was absolutely mind-blowing to witness, after the state of trance was entered, the many aspects of physical mediumship which were portrayed. Amongst these was the manifestation in red light of one spirit guide after another, in ectoplasmic form, which upon inspection were as tangible and solid as we who were present. Not only were there guides, but also spirit friends who embraced loved ones in the room. To witness such touching moments was the greatest of privileges. As the séance drew towards a conclusion, to see spirit friends walk amongst us, with Alec Harris clearly visible in the cabinet, almost defied belief. Yet it was so.

Before the séance commenced, Laurie Wilson, who was a barrister, and Geoffrey Wilson, a renowned scientist, under the watchful eye of their respected father, Percy, minutely examined the séance room, as well as the medium, to be sure there could be no question of doubt should any manifestation take place.

Even today, after all these years, I feel so indebted to Louie and Alec Harris for allowing me to see things which were equal to, if not surpassing, the recorded events of two thousand and more years ago. This answer to my prayers, and those of other bereaved people, provided a factual basis for my belief in the continuity of life, which until then had been a matter of faith. The answers to my questions concerning the philosophical implications and purpose of this life were in no small way provided through the mediumship of Alec Harris. They are answers which our world needs today, no less than then.

Eric Hatton
Honorary President, Spiritualists' National Union
July 2009

Introduction to the Original Edition*
by family friend, Rev. George May

In life's journey there are times when a great experience comes as a shining light to brighten the way, something to bring new hope, comfort and enlightenment to our lives.

Such was the experience of Peter, James and John when one day Jesus led them up the slopes of Mount Hermon to pray.

Suddenly, the Bible tells us, there was a bright light. From this materialised two figures, Moses and Elijah, who had passed many hundreds of years before.

At first the disciples were afraid. When they heard the kindly, loving voices of these two great prophets gently informing them that they had come from the spirit realms with a message for Jesus their fear turned to wonder and joy.

The communication for Jesus was to inform him that soon he would join them in the spirit world. The message for the disciples was that here was the complete evidence for Jesus' fundamental teaching that what we call death is simply the change to a new environment.

Many years later, Peter wrote his Epistle. He recalls this great experience as the highlight of his life and the ultimate evidence that being on earth is but a short journey leading to eternal existence. It prepared Peter and the other disciples for the return of their beloved master in materialised form following his passing at Calvary.

Many may say that these events happened 2,000 years ago. Can they happen today? The short answer is 'Yes'. History proves that in the intervening centuries there have always been faithful servants of God blessed with the priceless gift of mediumship.

Such a servant of God was Alec Harris. With the loving and faithful help of his charming and gifted wife, Louie, he brought hope, comfort and enlightenment to countless people who mourned a loved one.

Over 30 years ago I met Alec and Louie in Cardiff when they kindly invited me to a circle in their home.

That wonderful night was for me the highlight of my life.

When I entered the room where the materialisation séance was to be held I felt I was on sacred ground.

One by one, long-lost friends, now in what is beautifully described as the Summerland by them, fully materialised.

They came forth to speak to their loved ones. One such reunion deeply touched us all. A father and mother who had 'lost' their only son in the Second World War and were in deep sorrow suddenly saw their beloved boy come forth to greet them. Yes, there were tears - but tears of joy!

It is a great joy to me that the record of the wonderful work for humanity freely given by my dear friend Alec Harris is now published. It is not only a tribute to his sterling qualities as a medium, but to an upright and kindly soul who gave the essence of his life as a servant of the Holy Spirit to comfort all who mourn.

Rev. George May DD, PhD

1980

Printed with permission of Psychic Press

Chapter One

Meeting Alec Harris

❖ *Childhood reminiscences* ❖ *My meeting with Alec Harris*

Early one morning in the summer of 1909 I awoke with a strange feeling of excitement - it was almost exhilaration - as I recalled my visit, with my father the previous night, to the Palace Theatre in Porth, South Wales. Strangely, it was not so much the performance on the stage which enchanted me, although I had enjoyed every minute of it, but the accompanying orchestra which filled my childish heart with such delight. The thrill of it still lingered when I woke the following morning. I could picture Tommy Morris, the conductor, expertly leading his musicians as he swayed, caressing his violin with his chin while his sensitive fingers coaxed one lovely melody after another from his precious instrument. Something stirred deep down inside me. I knew when I grew up I wanted to be a violinist. I, too, would make the strings sing sweet music. I, too, might lead a similar orchestra. The decision was surprising. I was only nine years old and had never played a note of music on any instrument. Nevertheless I knew that was what I would one day be.

At that time I could not possibly know what my destiny held in store for me: how Fate had already decreed that my path should cross that of Alexander Frederick Harris of Cardiff, South Wales. Though then totally unaware of his extraordinary psychic powers, he was destined, it seemed, to become one of the most outstanding materialisation mediums of our time.

This is our story, that of our meeting, marriage and eventual mutual involvement in developing his quite phenomenal Spiritual gifts and giving them to the world. Alec's dedication to the work of Spirit and his selfless service to the sick and the bereaved are well known. Countless Spiritualists and non-Spiritualists flocked to our home to witness and marvel because when Alec was in trance, the Two Worlds, apparently so far apart and inaccessible to one another, could and did meet. The manifestations from the Spirit World were as solid and as real as physical ones.

On that morning after my theatre visit, I had a mind only for music, indeed, only for the violin. I dressed in a dream and wandered into the small garden in front of our home.

Our house was one of many similar dwellings, double-fronted and neat, with a small garden at front and back, which clustered together in friendly neighbourliness in High Street, Cymmer, a small village near Porth, South Wales. We considered ourselves to be country dwellers, for Cymmer nestled at the foot of a mountain in the Rhondda Valley. In springtime the daffodils spread a carpet of gold over the meadows and the surrounding woodlands. The busy, bustling city of Cardiff was only an hour or so away, near enough to be easily accessible, yet far enough to leave Cymmer to carry on its leisurely way of life undisturbed by progress.

At that early hour the people of the village were still wiping the sleep from their eyes. I strolled slowly down the garden path kicking the small pebbles underfoot, still lost in my musical reverie, when I saw at my feet two thick sticks, dried branches of a nearby shrub. As I gazed at them my childish imagination transformed them into a glorious violin and its bow. Delighted, I picked them up, placed one beneath my chin and sawed happily away with the other, humming a melody to myself, imitating the conductor of the previous night.

My daydream was broken when my mother's voice called to me cheerily from the doorway: "Louie," then louder, "Louie. Come child. Your breakfast is getting cold now and your father is waiting. What on earth are you doing with those sticks? Be careful of your dress, dear."

"They are not sticks, Mam," I corrected. "They're my violin."

"Violin? Bless you, child, what an imagination you have!" But she smiled in understanding, her Welsh heart aware of the importance of music and song to our people. "Well, just leave your violin there while you have your breakfast, dear. Come along, hurry now."

"Yes Mam," I said obediently, grateful that she had not ridiculed my plaything. She patted me lovingly as I joined her and we went through to the kitchen where breakfast was waiting. But I did not feel like eating; my mind was still miles away.

The door opened and the tall figure of my father, Tom Bradley, entered. He greeted me in Welsh and then switched to English, "Why so silent, my girl?" When I did not answer; "Not like you at all." Then turning to my mother he enquired, "Is the child sickening for something?"

Mother smiled, her eyes twinkling. "Not she," she said. "She's just indulging in her daydreams again. She's got a violin out in the garden and she's a wonderful musician, did you not know?" she teased.

"A violin in the garden? What's that you say, Mother?"

I could stand the strain no longer. It was now or never and I blurted out the question; "May I learn the violin Daddy? Oh, may I? Please?"

Father stroked his black moustache thoughtfully, while his hazel eyes considered my anxious face. Then he asked seriously, "Are you sure this is what you want child - quite sure?"

"Oh, yes, yes!" I pleaded, "More than anything, Daddy."

He looked severely at me and remarked: "You'd have to work hard at it, Louie girl. We haven't money to waste on whims, you know."

"Oh, I will, I will. I promise I will," I said, never taking my eyes from his.

After a moment's thought, he nodded and his face creased into one of his lovely warm smiles. "Well, in that case," he said, patting my head, "we had better be finding you a teacher then. And he'd better be a good one. And of course, a violin!"

I threw myself on him and exclaimed, "Oh, Daddy! Daddy! I do love you." Then more seriously, "Thank you. I will work very hard - very, very hard."

Four weeks later, clutching the small, inexpensive violin my father had bought for me, I stood in the home of my hero conductor, Tommy Morris. Now that I had achieved my objective I had an acute attack of 'butterflies in the stomach' and 'cold feet'. But Mr Morris turned out to be sympathetic and understanding and we soon began our weekly lessons. It transpired that I had talent and he seemed impressed. However, our association was short-lived. After only 12 months he had to leave the district and my lessons were discontinued. I was heartbroken. Mr Morris advised my father not to let my tuition lapse, as he considered that I was gifted and had the makings of a good violinist. Father persuaded a music-teacher friend of his to continue my tuition. But this association too was short lived. Being a delicate child and the climate of Cymmer, Porth, not being conducive to my good health, I was sent away to Seaforth, just outside Liverpool, to stay with an aunt for 6 months. Of course, another tutor had to be found for me. After much searching, it was finally decided that I should become a resident pupil of Professor Cunningham. This was a most fortunate decision for me. The Cunninghams proved to be a delightful couple, who made me very welcome and very soon I was regarded as one of the family and accepted as such by their six children.

There followed six happy years with the Cunninghams, at the end of which I emerged as a qualified violinist. I was now fifteen and a half and my dream had come true.

It was then 1916. Britain was in the throes of war. Our family had been disrupted when the younger of my brothers, Ted, was sent away to serve at the front in France, while the elder boy, Tom, was kept back to work in the coal mines. Quite unexpectedly, my father's health gave the family cause for grave concern. He contracted an incurable ailment and became seriously ill. Very soon he had to give up his job and with that his income promptly ceased. I could no longer rely on Dad for financial assistance and I realised that I would have to find some means of supporting myself. But the question was, how?

Professor Cunningham came up with the answer. He was in the process of forming an orchestra to play at the Prince's Theatre in Bootle, Liverpool. Due to the war, most musicians were serving at the front and there was an acute shortage of orchestral personnel. He managed to get together a small group of seven musicians and to my delight put me in charge as conductor and violin lead. Being so young, I felt that his faith in my ability was unfounded.

Louie Bradley ~ the young violist

However, it was the opportunity I had longed for and I gladly commenced my first professional job playing nightly and grappling for the first time with a new form of musical manuscript, that of ragtime and syncopation. Previously I had only been concerned with classical music. I became known in that area as 'the child violinist' and we were all greatly relieved that the venture was a success.

My delight and pleasure in achieving success with this new orchestra was severely dampened when tragedy struck our family. Our beloved father ultimately succumbed to the malignant disease from which he had been suffering and in September 1917 he passed mercifully into Spirit. It was a bitter blow to all of us. He had always made home such a happy place, filling it with musicians and singers. I shall always remember the lovely musical evenings he arranged for us. But it was his passing and a message he sent to me through my mother, that set me thinking about life after death. The subsequent fulfilment of his prophesy proved beyond doubt that he lived on after his physical death. It was the first link in the chain of psychic events which indicated that this world and that of Spirit interpenetrate. Each is as real as the other.

None of us in the family had had any psychic experiences, except my father, who often spoke of hearing voices. Not being conversant with such matters at the time, we were inclined to treat such disembodied voices with a measure of jocularity, as a figment of imagination perhaps. But father's awareness of the Hereafter was greater than we realised.

On the morning of his passing, as he lay on his death-bed weak and unable to move, he whispered to my mother. "I have to leave you now. Sorry I can't see my boy, Ted, before I go and my little Lou." His voice was so quiet mother had to lean close to his mouth to hear him. Ted was still serving in France. Then came the message for me, barely audible.

"Tell ... tell little Lou that ... that I'll be the first to greet her from the Other Side." Mother nodded, too overcome to speak.

Father was quiet for some time, his eyes closed. Then, quite unexpectedly, he sat up unaided, his eyes open, his face radiant. He stretched out his arms and joyfully exclaimed, "George! Austin!" These were the names of his deceased brothers. A beautiful smile transformed his thin face. With a deep sigh of satisfaction he lay back on his pillows, passing peacefully into Spirit. Father kept his word and made himself known to me at a sitting some years later. Even before that, I often heard his voice calling my name.

When I told the Cunninghams of my experience they frowned in disapproval and advised me not to let my imagination run away with me. So, although I still continued to hear my father calling me, I told no one. But I often wondered about it.

After my father's death, my mother gave up her home in the

Rhondda Valley and came to live with me in a house in Waterloo, a suburb of Liverpool. My experience of orchestras began to grow as I applied for and got, a variety of violinist engagements, which included playing at the Winter Gardens in Waterloo. But, in 1919, my mother began to yearn for the Rhondda Valley with all its old associations and she said she wanted to return. I decided to give up my job and go with her. Now that my father had gone, I felt my responsibility towards her keenly and could not possibly let her go alone.

Once back in our home territory I sought and obtained the job of leading violin at the Hippodrome, Tonypandy. Once more we were financially secure. This engagement had far-reaching consequences for me and might be considered the turning point in my life. It was at the Hippodrome that I became friendly with the pianist Peggy Gunter, later to become Mrs Phillips and, as such, the aunt of the man I was destined to marry, Alexander Harris.

Peggy and I were very close friends. We had lovely musical evenings together when we were not playing at the Hippodrome and later at the Empire. But we both had to leave the Empire when a dispute erupted between the Musicians' Union and the Theatre Management. The Union called us all out on strike and Peggy and I found ourselves without employment.

After kicking our heels in frustration for a time, Peggy suddenly came up with a suggestion. "Hey, Lou! How about attending that audition for that summer job at Ilfracombe?" she asked. "If we don't get it, it would be nice to go over there just for the day, wouldn't it?" The idea appealed to me. "What about going next weekend?" I said.

"All right. We'll take the day excursion on the boat. It will be fun!" Peggy was enthusiastic. "And we might land the job into the bargain."

So the following Saturday two excited young ladies caught the early boat from Cardiff bound for Ilfracombe. We attended the audition, which was successful, but we declined the job because of the poor remuneration offered. Feeling that nothing was lost as we had had a lovely day, we boarded the boat to return to Cardiff. And this is where Fate took a hand in shaping my future.

A thick black cloud descended upon our boat. This worsened until it became a generalised fog, making visibility practically nil. As a result, our arrival in Cardiff was delayed three hours. To our dismay we missed our train connection and could not get home. I suggested to Peggy, that we spend the night with a friend of mine, Lily Bristow. I knew she would gladly help us out of our dilemma. I did not think that mother would be unduly worried, as we had an understanding that should I, at any time, be in difficulties I would immediately go to Lily for help. So, within an hour, two weary, dejected girls were knocking at her door pouring out their tale of woe. Lil was understanding and gladly offered us shelter for the night. As Peggy got into bed and turned out the light she sighed: "It has been a grand day, hasn't it? Pity it had to end like this."

"Yes," I yawned, "and I'm sorry about the job, too; I would really have liked to have gone to Ilfracombe for the summer."

The next day was Sunday. It is one I shall always regard as my special day, for that was the day when I saw Alec Harris for the first time.

Peggy woke me early. I was surprised to see that she was already dressed as it was only 6.30am. "Lou, I've just thought," she said, "I can't go home without first seeing my husband's sister and brother-in-law and their children."

"Oh," I said, still half asleep. "Where are they?"

"They live in Malefant Street. You've heard me speak of Fred and Edith Harris, surely? She's my husband's sister. Would you like to come along with me? I'd like you to meet them."

"But Malefant Street is a long way from here," I said. "Remember it is Sunday. There's no transport."

"Never mind," said Peggy. "We can walk there." She was insistent. "Oh come on Lou! You'll really like them. Fred Harris is such a scream! He's the well-known comedian, you know, been in pantomimes, variety shows, the lot! He always has us in 'fits'." She laughed as she thought of him, "He's just as funny off the stage as on."

"What's so funny about him then?" I asked.

"Oh, just everything he says is funny. It's always like that in the Harris' home, such a happy place. And you'll like the family too. There's never a dull moment."

I threw my legs over the edge of the bed and sat up. "When do you want to go?" I asked.

"Right now," said Peggy.

"Now?" I gasped, "But it's only half past six. You can't visit people at this time of the morning!"

"Oh, the Harrises aren't just people, they're family," exclaimed Peggy. "Anyway, if we've got to walk and you still have to dress, we won't get there much before eight."

"All right," I sighed, "we'd better tell Lily we're going then."

I dressed hurriedly and we set off in the direction of Malefant Street. After what seemed ages, my violin case feeling more cumbersome every step, Peggy stopped suddenly and said: "Ah! Here we are. This is it, 123 Malefant Street." Then with a grimace, "Hmm! Not much sign of life yet, is there?"

We were standing in front of a long terrace of houses and there seemed to be nothing to distinguish No.123 from any of the others. It was a neat, double-storied, dwelling; its bay windows, sparkling clean, were draped by spotless net curtains. There was a tiny, well-kept garden in front and I knew there would be another at the back, there always was! We went through the gate, up the path and knocked on the door. There was no answer.

"Like I thought! They're all still asleep," said Peggy.

She tried the door and found it latched. Then she knocked and we waited. I held back, nervously.

Presently footsteps could be heard. The door was opened by a beautiful girl no more than sixteen. She was still in her night attire. Her light brown hair curled softly around a face that could not conceal its surprise at being confronted by visitors so early on a Sunday morning. Her eyes lit up with pleasure as she recognised Peggy.

"Oh! It's you, Aunt Peggy!" she smiled. "I'm afraid we are all still in bed but please come in. I'll just go and call them." Peggy kissed her and then turned to me. "This is Connie Harris, one of the seven children I told you about." Then, having introduced me, she followed Connie inside, calling over her shoulder to me, "Come on in, Lou. Make yourself at home." Connie excused herself and started up the stairs. Peggy closed the door behind me and I followed her into the Harris' sitting room. Suddenly an idea struck her. She said, her eyes narrowed and twinkling with mischief, "Let's wake them all up and give them a surprise."

"How?" I whispered, fearful that they might hear.

"I'll show you," said Peggy. She walked over to the corner of the room and opened the piano, sat down and started to play a rousing march, thumping the keys with all her might, laughing all the while at her own prank. She winked at me and I caught her mood. I grabbed my violin and gleefully added my talents to the cacophony.

It had the desired effect. Soon, there was a thumping overhead as people fell out of bed. Voices were raised, calling to one another: "What's going on? Who's that downstairs? Who's making that racket at this hour of the morning?"

Then came the resonant baritone voice of Alec's father, Fred Harris. "Has everyone gone mad in this house?" he asked. "It's only eight o'clock! And it's Sunday!"

A young girl's head peeped over the banister and she gasped, "Why, it's Aunt Peggy at the piano! And she's got a little girl with her and she's playing the violin!" I suppose that was all I appeared to be, a little girl, for being very small, my looks belied my twenty-one years.

Within minutes they were all streaming downstairs and into the living room; first Father Fred, then Mother Edith, closely followed by the children, in various stages of dress, amazement plainly visible on each face. The last to come in, still pulling on a pair of trousers over his striped pyjamas, was a sturdy, well-built young man of twenty-four, about 5ft.8ins. tall. He was extremely handsome; his hair, still tousled from sleep, was the colour of burnished gold; his eyes were of a deep shade of blue, so very blue! He stopped dead in his tracks as he caught sight of me.

I ceased playing in the middle of a bar, bow in hand, violin still tucked under my chin, mouth gaping like a goldfish. I couldn't move. I felt that a hand had grabbed my heart and the fingers were squeezing so tight that I couldn't breathe. For what seemed a very long moment we stood still and stared at one another. Peggy broke the spell as she said: "Good morning, Fred! Hello, Edith! Please forgive our little practical joke. We just wanted to wake you up and surprise you."

"Well, you certainly did that!" boomed Fred. "Thought the roof was coming down, indeed! Anyway, nice to see you, Peg. What brings you here at this unearthly time of a Sunday morning?"

"We got caught in the fog yesterday, on our way back from Ilfracombe," exclaimed Peggy. "Our boat was delayed three hours, so we had to spend the night with friends down town."

"What took you to Ilfracombe?" asked Fred.

"We went down for an audition, but didn't take the job. I couldn't go back home without calling on you, so I said to Louie .. Oh! Lou, forgive me!" she gasped, as she suddenly remembered she had not introduced me. Peggy then presented me to each member of the family, finally saying, "This charming young lad who seems transfixed in the doorway, is Alexander Harris. We all call him Alec."

We smiled at each other awkwardly, he suddenly aware of his state of undress, realising that it was too late to do anything about it! I was conscious, for the second time in my life, of a stirring deep down inside me. It was a feeling I could not comprehend, yet somehow knew that it was concerned with my meeting Alec! This encounter was later to weld our lives together in a life-long partnership of love and service to the inhabitants of two worlds.

Chapter Two

Our Marriage

❖ *A proposal of marriage* ❖ *My acceptance* ❖ *Birth of our son*

Alec Harris' path and mine did not cross again for two long years. In 1923, mother and I moved from the Rhondda Valley to Cardiff. Alec later explained that, although we did not meet, he had frequently stood on the opposite corner of the street outside the Theatre where I worked and watched me being escorted home by the same gentleman every evening. He naturally assumed that there was an association and we were going steady, so made no approaches. The gentleman in question happened to be a fellow musician who, because he was going my way, offered to see me home safely each night at that late hour. It was an act of courtesy, nothing more, and I regret that it kept me apart from Alec. We finally met again one cold December night as we were both taking our respective mothers home after a show. The four of us were on the same tram, but unaware of each other.

Mother nudged me and whispered in my ear; "Look at that boy sitting over there. He looks just like Theophilus, Peggy's husband."

Peggy had married Theophilus Phillips, who was the brother of Alec's mother; so it was no wonder there was a family resemblance.

"That's the Harris boy I was telling you about," I whispered, excited at seeing him again.

"He's nice," said mother, appraising him thoughtfully. "I like his looks, I do indeed." Then turning her attention to the lady beside him, she enquired, "Is that his mother with him I wonder -

he looks very like her?"

"Yes, it is. Come, mother, this is where we get off."

The tram had stopped and I saw that Alec and his mother had also alighted. My heart gave a little somersault as I realised he was coming over to speak to us, his hand in his mother's arm.

"Good evening, Miss Bradley," came the soft, rich baritone voice. "Nice to meet you again." The Welsh lilt made music of his speech.

"Oh, hello," I said shyly. "Good evening to you, Mrs Harris."

"My child, we haven't seen you in years," she replied.

"Two," I said and hastily bit my lip. It sounded as if I had been counting them; which of course I had. "This is my mother, Mrs Bradley," I said quickly to cover up.

"I'm pleased to meet you Mrs Harris," said mother. "Louie has told me about how she met you all after the fog. And she's told me about Alec, too," she added with a knowing smile that made me want to scream. I glanced quickly at Alec and caught him stifling a smile.

"You going our way?" asked Alec. "We live in Malefant Street."

"Oh, we live close by there ourselves," replied mother. "Let's walk together awhile and chat, Mrs Harris," she suggested.

So the two mothers went on ahead, chatting amiably, while Alec and I walked behind, shyly making small talk, awkward and very conscious of one another.

When we parted company Mrs Harris remarked, "We're having a party on Christmas Day. Why don't you and your daughter come along? We'd love to have you Mrs Bradley."

"That's a good idea," said Alec cheerfully. "Why don't you come? We always have a lot of fun. You'll meet a lot of nice people."

Before mother could reply, I interrupted: "I'm afraid I can't. Thank you very much though, it's nice of you to ask us." I glanced quickly at Alec to see his reaction and was gratified that he looked crestfallen. "I'm going to a theatre party on Christmas Day." I explained.

"Well then," replied Mrs Harris, undaunted, "what about

Christmas Eve then?" Alec looked anxiously at me.

"Yes, I'm free on Christmas Eve," I said.

"Very well then, we will have our party on Christmas Eve. And we shall look forward to seeing you both there."

Mother and I offered profuse thanks, bade them goodnight and went our way.

"What nice people!" said mother. I didn't answer. I was already counting the days to Christmas Eve!

That first party at the Harris' home is one I shall always remember. The music, the singing, the games, the dancing; there was so much laughter and fun. Fred Harris was keeping us all in fits, as Peggy had said, with his jokes and patter. He was a really professional trouper. But most of all I recall it was during that evening something deep, warm and lasting was born between Alec and me. He had unwound sufficiently to talk about himself a little.

He told me that he had been born in Treherbert, in the Rhondda Valley, in 1897. I mentally made a note that he was three years older than I. "Just right," I thought. Alec spoke of how, at the age of three, his family had moved to Cardiff, where he went to Marlborough Road School, leaving at the age of fourteen to take up a job. By way of explanation he said: "I wanted to help contribute to the family's upkeep. There are a lot of us, you see. Father, being a painter and house decorator and that, doesn't bring in all that much money. That's why he makes a bit on the side as a comedian in pantomimes and shows and things." And then, as an afterthought, he added, "He's really clever, is Dad. He can do almost anything with his hands. He paints stage scenery some- times." His filial pride showed in his face.

"I'm sure," I said. "And you?" He smiled: "Oh, I suppose I inherited some of his talents. I like painting and making things, too."

"You're handy round the house, then?"

"Sure thing. I'll make someone a good husband some day," he said pointedly. I smiled and dropped my eyes shyly and changed the subject. "What sort of job did you do when you left school so young?"

"Well," he thought back, "for a while I worked in the office of a paint firm down at the docks." Alec smiled in reminiscence. "It made me feel very important, being a working man. Then I was offered the job as projectionist at the Gaiety Cinema."

"That must have been fun," I enthused.

"Yes, I could see all the films for nothing," he laughed. "I liked the work there. Being good with my hands, I could keep everything in order."

I nodded, but kept silent, for fear of interrupting his story.

"Then, when I was a lot more experienced, I got what you might call promotion." He emphasised the word and smiled. "I obtained another job as projectionist and later became manager of a small cinema in Gilfachgoch. Good for my ego, it was."

I laughed with him. "And the war?" I asked. "Were you called up?"

"Oh, yes," he said, "I joined the Royal Engineers and quick as a wink was over in France. I had my eighteenth birthday over there. King and Country and all that! Singing 'Tipperary' and 'Keep the Home Fires Burning', very patriotic. Four long years I was there; terrible years they were."

"Tell me about them," I said.

Alec shook his head. "Best to forget about them. I was one of the lucky ones." His eyes clouded: "I was in those terrible battles of the Somme and Passchendaele. A lot of the fellows, my friends and comrades, didn't make it. I did."

He sighed and shrugged his shoulders. "I had some narrow escapes but I'm here to tell the tale. Just lucky, that's all." Alec smiled suddenly and changed the subject. "But I don't want to bore you any longer. This is a party and you're looking sad."

"Oh, I'm not bored," I said hastily and added shyly, "Alec, I'm glad you made it." Our eyes locked for a moment; then, without speaking, he took my arm and led me back to join the dancing inside.

We met frequently after that and one Sunday afternoon he took me to Roath Park in Cardiff, where there was a pretty lake. One could hire rowing boats and spend a lazy afternoon on the water.

We decided to do just that.

After rowing about for a while, Alec pulled into the bank and rested on his oars. He looked at me seriously. I had that breathless feeling again; but tried my level best to look calm and collected. A voice inside me said, "This is it!" Slowly he leaned forward.

"I love you Lou," he said simply, "I've known for a long time. I want to marry you." He paused, assessing my reaction. "Well, what do you say? Will you?"

Panic seized me. "I can't," I said. "I promised my father I would look after mother. I can't marry anyone, not for years."

He looked bewildered and very disappointed. "But why ever not?"

"Because ... well, it's my music. It's my career! I can't give it up to marry."

"But you won't have to Louie! You can be married and still have your music. You won't have to stop."

I felt I was being squeezed into a corner; and I had to get out before I weakened. "Well ... you see it's ... er ... ," I began lamely; and his face clouded.

"Oh," he said, crestfallen. "I understand. You don't love me?"

"Oh, but I do, Alec, I do. I ..." and I bit my lip. The words had slipped out before I could stop them and I saw his shoulders relax. He smiled his lovely smile and my heart once again did a somersault.

"What's your answer then?" he asked softly. "Is it 'Yes'?"

"No." I had to fight hard not to weaken. "I can't .."

He laughed and his blue eyes twinkled with mischief. "Oh, it's still 'No', is it? Well then...." and he shifted his weight suddenly, tilting the boat violently. "It's into the lake you go, my girl!" He gave me a playful shove.

I screamed, struggling and fell against him. Alec's strong arms were about we and there was a moment of breathless anticipation. Then, slowly, he bent his head and kissed me gently. "Say yes, Lou," he whispered, "Please."

I was silent, thinking hard. My musical career meant much to me. I had worked hard to achieve it. "Give me a year to think about it, Alec," I pleaded.

"A year?" He gave me a twisted smile. "That's a long time when you're in love," he said wistfully.

"If you are in love, you won't mind waiting," I teased, "will you?"

He squeezed, my hand. "No. I'll wait until you're good and ready, no matter how long." He looked very serious. "That's how much I love you, Lou."

Alec sighed in resignation, picked up his oars and said, "It's getting late. We'd best be making tracks for home." And in silence he began to row.

Not one, nor two, but four years passed, after that afternoon on the lake, before we finally decided to name the date of our wedding. It was to be a quiet family affair. So, when we emerged from the church as man and wife, one fine day in June 1928, we were greatly surprised to see Lionel Faulkman, the well-known conductor and radio personality and sixteen members of his orchestra grouped together at the church door, forming an archway with their instruments.

A wonderful surprise as the orchestra pays
tribute in June 1928

I was the seventeenth member of that orchestra, which was then playing at the Capitol Cinema, and the only woman! Lionel was a very fine violinist and he had been a wonderful friend to me. So, when they started to play 'Ain't She Sweet' especially in my honour, I was moved to tears at the warmth of their wedding tribute and I clung to Alec who patted my hand understandingly. I was now 28 years old and Alec was 31. A wonderful new life of love, work and service together lay ahead.

Above :- Alec with Louie's mother, Mrs Bradley

Left:- The Happy Couple, Louie and Alec Harris.

We soon managed to buy our own house at 31 Manor Way, Whitchurch and settled down to marital contentment. My mother continued to live with us and we were glad to have her in our home.

On the 1st November 1932 our home was blessed by a happy event. A baby son was born to us. Inspired by my maiden name we called him Bradley. We felt that now our cup of happiness was filled to overflowing.

Their house in Manor Way, Whitchurch, Cardiff.
Louie and her niece Phyllis are at the gate

We spent 25 exciting, eventful, happy years in Manor Way. Many wondrous things were shown and explained to us by Spirit friends.

Chapter Three

Our Spiritual Journey Commences

❖ *We are drawn into the Spiritualist Movement* ❖ *Our first Spirit Guides make themselves known*

In 1934 a dreadful thing happened. My sister, May, told us that our brother, Ted, had not only become a Spiritualist, but was also a medium. We were all greatly shocked. There were gasps of dismay all round.

"That's nonsense, May!" exclaimed mother, looking worried. "Ted doesn't know anything about Spiritualism!"

"He does indeed, mother." May's voice was hushed, as if she feared someone might hear. "He's preaching in the Spiritualist Church and describing 'dead' people." Her voice trailed off, as if she felt that these things were best left unsaid.

"Don't be silly!" I laughed. "Ted? Preaching? He doesn't know his Bible well enough."

"But it's not Ted that's doing the preaching, he says, but some- one speaking through him, someone," her voice dropped to a shocked whisper, "someone who's dead, he says!"

"Dead?" We all gasped and fell silent, as we contemplated the terrible fate which had overtaken our Ted.

I was the first to recover. "There's only one thing to do," I said. "I'll have to go down and see Ted and put a stop to all this nonsense."

Soon, I was confronting Ted in his small Rhondda Valley home. Pulling my small frame up to its full height, I shook an admonitory finger at him.

"Now, look here, Ted," I scolded, "what's all this about you being a Spiritualist medium? We are all good Baptists. Shame on you, Ted!"

My brother smiled tolerantly at the ferocious little figure in front of him.

"Thank goodness," I breathed, "you still look all right." Though Heaven knew what I had expected a Spiritualist medium to look like! "But why, Ted, why?" I asked. "You've always been such a sensible person."

"I still am," he laughed. "And so are you."

"Me? What's that got to do with it?" I snapped.

"Just that you will be in the movement yourself very soon, Lou girl."

"Me?" I was flabbergasted. "No! Alec would never agree to it."

"Oh, he's coming into it, too, but he doesn't know it yet!" Ted was positively beaming. "And shall I tell you something else? You will both do far greater work together than I could ever hope to do. It's something special you've got, so be happy, Lou."

"Nonsense!" I retorted. "That's ridiculous, Ted! How can you say a thing like that?"

"Oh, it's not me. I'm not the one who's saying it. It's Michael."

"Michael?" I enquired, looking around me and seeing no one. "Who's Michael?"

"He's a Spirit Guide and he's never been wrong yet," said Ted with conviction.

I felt bewildered, distrustful of Ted's words. Nevertheless, I experienced a vague stirring of interest. It prompted me to put many questions to him about Spiritualism, often arguing volubly. Ted always answered me tolerantly and patiently. I asked him how it was that he had become interested in the subject. He chuckled, as if at some private joke, so I pressed him further for an answer.

Still smiling at the memory of it, Ted told how he noticed that his wife Annie and a friend always went out together on a Monday evening. They never said where they were going and seemed rather secretive about this regular outing. So he had decided that on the next Monday's excursion he would follow them.

Keeping well out of sight, he saw them enter a house which was unknown to him. The door stood open and several other people came up and just walked inside without any preliminary knock or invitation. Ted followed them in and found himself in a large room, with rows of seats and a platform at one end.

"It's a meeting," thought Ted. He seated himself at the back of the room, well concealed from his wife's vision and that of her friend, who were sitting at the front.

A man stepped on to the platform. He started to address several of those present, giving them messages from departed friends or loved-ones.

Understanding dawned on Ted. This had something to do with what was called Spiritualism, something one usually spoke of in hushed tones.

Not wishing to have any part of this, Ted had slid down as far as possible in his seat to make himself less conspicuous. Alas, his movement had attracted the attention of the man on the platform who promptly, to Ted's dismay, stepped down and walked straight towards him. All eyes turned in his direction.

"You, sir!" began the man, pointing a finger at Ted, who squirmed uneasily. "There is a young Frenchman here, a soldier named Pierre. He says that you served together in the war; working with horses, lorries, transport. Do you know this man?"

Ted disliked the attention he was attracting and was fearful that Annie would discover his presence. He kept his voice low. "I met many people called Pierre in France. How am I to know which one this is?" Ted was being difficult, trying to trip the medium who, nevertheless continued undaunted.

"This Pierre is now showing me a scene," he said. He spoke slowly as he described what he saw. "You are both standing under some trees alongside your lorries. It is a battlefield; there is a bridge. Pierre is saying, 'You stay here, I will go over first.' He leaves you to cross the bridge. As he does so, there is a great explosion. The bridge is blown up and he is killed."

Ted was astounded. He recalled the incident very well and now remembered his friend. He was further taken aback when the medium remarked that he, Ted, could contact the dead and bring messages of hope to the living. "I suggest you join a circle and develop this gift," the medium urged.

Meanwhile this conversation had been overheard by Annie. Needless to say, she was delighted.

"Annie persuaded me to form our own circle," smiled Ted. "After only three sittings I was controlled by my Spirit Guide, Michael." He shrugged: "So that's how it happened. There was nothing I could do about it, really. But now I'm glad, Lou, very glad. It has changed my life." I asked him if he had seen Dad. He replied, "No. I haven't seen him, but he has been described to me." Ted paused, as if listening, then continued: "Michael is saying that you will see Dad before I do. Lovely thought, isn't it?" Somewhat shamefaced, I took my leave of him, begging him not to mention the subject to Alec and mother when he came to see us. "Alec is sure to object," I said, "and it will only cause trouble."

Ted did not take umbrage at my rudeness. He merely put an arm about my shoulders and smiled. "Don't worry, Lou, I will hold my tongue," he promised. "But you mark my words; Michael is never wrong!"

I did not discuss this conversation with anyone, least of all Alec. So he was quite unprepared for what happened two months later. Alec had to make a business call on a Mr Hewitt, whose house was across the road from us. Finding he was not yet home from work, Alec fell into conversation with his wife, Mary. A chance remark she made, apropos of nothing that they were discussing at the time, caused Alec to beat a hasty retreat.

According to Alec, Mary seemed to look through him, rather than at him, as she remarked: "You have a lot of lights around you Mr Harris. Do you know you are a very powerful medium?"

Alec had stammered, "What kind of a medium do you mean?" Mary replied, "Why, a Spiritualist medium, of course."

This caused Alec to take his leave with undue abruptness, much to Mrs Hewitt's amusement. As he burst through our door he gasped the story out breathlessly to me, ending with the observation: "Fancy, Lou! A nice, sensible woman, like Mrs Hewitt, being a

Spiritualist."

However, it was this chance meeting with Mary Hewitt, herself a medium, which set our feet on the path of Spiritualism, where they became firmly planted, never deviating for the rest of our lives.

Two weeks after this meeting the Hewitts invited us to spend a few days with them in their caravan at Llantwit Major. Needless to say, the conversation was mostly about Spiritualism. I was fascinated by Mary Hewitt's many psychic experiences.

Seeing my interest, she invited me to go with her the following Sunday to Park Grove Spiritualist Church. To my surprise I found myself accepting happily. Alec would have no part of it.

As soon as I arrived at the little church a sense of peace and contentment descended upon me. Mrs Hewitt whispered to me, "You belong here, dear." Somehow, I felt that I did.

The simple service appealed to me. I was most impressed with the impromptu address given by one of the members of the congregation. It seemed to answer most of the nagging questions that had been troubling me.

On my way out of the building I had to pass through the church library. Pausing to browse around, I came across a book entitled simply 'Raymond' by Sir Oliver Lodge. I had heard that he had been the Professor of Physics at the University of Liverpool and a scientist of some repute. Being a well-known and respected member of society and a scientist, I felt that I could rely on the words of such a man. So, I selected the book and prepared myself to be further enlightened about communication with the world of Spirit. The book proved to be so absorbing that I was unable to lay it down until I had read it from cover to cover.

One facet of Spirit communication which had intrigued me was table-moving. At our next meeting, I asked Mary Hewitt if she had experienced this phenomenon. She had and suggested that if I was interested, we should try it out that afternoon. I was delighted and a little nervous, wondering what Alec would say if he found out.

Mary pointed out that the table moved with more facility if it was light in weight. As hers were of the heavy variety she asked if I could bring along a lightweight one from my home. After lunch, I was creeping softly downstairs, my little table clutched under my arm, when to my dismay the door was flung open and Alec came into the hall. He stopped in his tracks, puzzled by my antics. His eye alighted on the piece of furniture I had under my arm. "Where are you going with that table, Lou?" he asked suspiciously.

Overcome with confusion I blurted out: "To Mary Hewitt's. We are going to try a table-moving séance."

Alec's mouth fell open. When it snapped shut he looked angry. I thought he would explode. "That you are NOT!" he said. Then he called: "Mother! Your daughter's going to a séance. Come and tell her she's not to go. I don't want her mixed up in that sort of nonsense."

Mother came hurrying into the hall and saw us. Alec's face was dark with anger. I stood on the stairs, holding the small table, now looking very determined.

"Look, Alec," said mother reasonably, "she's a wife and mother. She should know what she's doing." Alec turned on his heel and left the house.

I felt upset that I was going against Alec's wishes, but I felt a great urge to pursue the séance. I left the house, still clutching my small table and went across the road to the Hewitt's house. Mr Hewitt opened the door. He smiled in amusement when he saw the table, but made no comment. He was a tolerant man and, though not interested in Spiritualism, did not interfere with his wife's participation, or with her friends who came to the house in this connection. He invited me in and took me up to Mary's bedroom, where the séance was to be held.

"Now," said Mary, "I'll explain. This may seem a little strange to you, this method of communicating, I mean. Certainly, it is a very slow procedure, but perhaps a good way for you to begin."

"Yes, I understand," I said, "and I would like to know more about it."

"We will sit for only an hour." said Mary. "If nothing happens we will try another time. And we must always open with a sincere prayer for protection and guidance. One must never omit such prayers. To do so would be courting trouble," she said seriously. I nodded nervously. She then began to pray most beautifully. We joined in singing hymns together and waited. Nothing happened. Not a movement of the table. I experienced a feeling of acute disappointment.

"We will try for a little while longer," said Mary. We sang a few more hymns, but still there were no manifestations. The hour passed quickly. "I'm afraid we shall have to close," Mary announced. "We can try again next week."

At this juncture there was a knock on the bedroom door. Mr Hewitt entered, ushering in a strange gentleman who, it appeared, had just called at the house to see him on business. On hearing the singing emanating from upstairs, he enquired about it and was informed that a séance was in progress. The visitor was most interested, saying he, too, was a Spiritualist. In fact, he had been impressed by his own Guides to go upstairs and give power to the circle. Would Mr Hewitt, he wondered, permit him to assist the ladies? With a smile Mary's husband agreed and led him upstairs to where our unsuccessful séance was about to close.

Introducing him Mr Hewitt explained, "This gentleman is a Spiritualist. He has been directed to help you. May he join you?"

"Yes, certainly," invited Mary. "Come in. Sit down and place your hands with ours on this table." He did so. To my astonishment, in a very short while the table moved! It rose slowly and lifted itself right into my lap. As we recited the alphabet it would rock, coming to an abrupt halt when the required letter was called. This way it spelled out the name TOM. Mrs Hewitt then asked, "To whom do you wish to speak, Friend?" The table spelled LOU.

"That's my name!" I cried excitedly. "And my father's name is Tom." "That's interesting." commented Mary. "Ask him any questions you wish to confirm his identity."

This I proceeded to do and all were answered correctly by my father.

There now seemed to be a lot of power available. The table had no difficulty in moving. Our hands were barely touching its surface. The strange gentleman withdrew his entirely and sat back with his hands on his knees. Yet still the table continued to move. I asked my father what his second name was and the answer came back JOHN. I was disappointed as I thought this was incorrect; it should have been RICHARD. However, I consoled myself with the fact that all the other information had been accurate. We then closed at Mary's suggestion and the stranger took his departure downstairs. I told Mary that I felt quite sure that I had found my beloved Dad. As I said this, there came three loud knocks on the wardrobe, which was some distance from us. Mary said, "That is your Dad saying 'Yes'." She added, "My dear, I feel strong physical mediumship emanating from you. There is great work ahead for you to do." She smiled.

When I recounted my experience later to mother, commenting on the only error being Dad's second name she said: "No, dear, that was no mistake. Your father's other name was John. Richard is your brother's second name." I was greatly relieved to hear this.

Alec was furious when I told of the knocks that had occurred. "Playing around with that nonsense you'll end up in Whitchurch Asylum!" he snorted. "You are just fooling yourself with your own thoughts! I'm coming over next Sunday to prove to you that it is all a lot of nonsense." I was filled with misgivings. Fortunately he did not carry out his threat.

Later, I accused him of not having the courage of his convictions because he had not turned up to justify his words of condemnation. I flounced off to bed without telling him what had transpired at our second sitting, again a very successful one. The table had been very active, without the assistance of the stranger this time.

Alec remained downstairs, obviously deep in thought. Around midnight, he came upstairs and woke me. "I will not let you go to sleep until you sit with me," he said. "We'll soon see that this whole thing is ridiculous nonsense." I was afraid to sit without Mrs Hewitt for fear that nothing would happen. I would never live it down. I protested; "Not now Alec, it's midnight! Tomorrow perhaps?"

"You are afraid," he taunted. "You know I can prove that it doesn't really happen. It's all in the mind." Alec pointed at my forehead.

Incensed, I retorted: "You are the one who should be afraid, ridiculing something like this when it's true. It's true, I tell you!" He was looking very determined. "All right, we'll sit and you will see!" I said with a bravado I did not feel and I desperately hoped that something would happen to convince Alec.

We found a suitable small table in the bedroom and we commenced. Fortunately no light came into the room from outside. It was a new area with only a few houses and the street lighting had not yet been completed. Only a faint glow came from the gas fire, which had been turned down low. I told Alec that Mrs Hewitt was emphatic that no circle should begin without prayer and explained that we would sit for only one hour.

Having prayed we began to sing, 'to raise the vibrations and build power', I told Alec and he gave a twisted smile. Time passed and nothing happened; no manifestations, or movement of the little table took place. It appeared resolutely glued to the floor. Alec became restless and at the same time a trifle smug that he had made his point. My disappointment became an unbearable longing. I silently prayed, "Oh, God, please let something happen to convince Alec, please!"

Immediately I had a feeling of being lifted up and the whole room was illuminated by an unearthly blue light, which swelled gradually in luminosity as though someone had turned up a gas mantle and then, just as gradually, it diminished in brilliance. I was afraid; so was Alec. He said, "Heavens! What's that?"

"I don't know," I whispered. With that the table began to rock violently. "You are moving it yourself," accused Alec. "I am not, look!" and I removed one hand from the table, still holding the other lightly over it. When it continued to move Alec insisted that I was manipulating it with my legs. I was indignant and moved away, sitting right back from the table. Still it continued to rock. I asked nervously, "Is that you, Dad?" The entity acquiesced and gave a message. Alec was not impressed. He maintained he was already aware of the information proffered, having been told the same thing by me some time before.

"Well, ask it something yourself," I suggested. Hesitantly Alec asked if there was anybody there who wished to speak to him. Instantly, the table's movements ceased to be so violent and gently spelled out CON, the name of Alec's beloved sister, Connie, who was now in Spirit. She was the beautiful girl I had met with Peggy, all those years ago, a girl much loved by everyone and very dear to Alec. Tragically, she had contracted tuberculosis, passing away on 27th November 1923. Connie returned that evening, obviously aware that if anything could convince her brother of life after death it would be her Spirit communication. But Alec did not accept it. Her message was too similar to one that I had often spoken of before. Alec attributed it to the manifestation of my thoughts and not hers. The question of how the table came to be moving at all seemed to escape him! I reminded him that there must have been hundreds of incidents which had taken place between himself and Connie about which I knew nothing. I suggested that if he were to ask her about any one of these and receive a satisfactory answer, perhaps then he would accept that the Spirit of his sister was indeed present.

Tentatively he asked, "Con, do you remember, the week before you died, I read a book to you and you expressed a wish that I should hurriedly finish reading the book myself and tell you how it ended?"

"Yes," came the gentle reply. "Can you give me the name of that book?" Alec probed. Immediately the answer came back, 'Girl of The Limberlost'.

Alec was shaken. "But that's amazing!" he said. "Only Con and I could possibly know that."

"There!" I urged. "You must believe now that your sister is here." I quickly asked her a question, hoping for further proof of her Spirit presence. "Can you see us, Con?" I asked. She replied that she could. "And the baby," I added. She affirmed this, too.

"Where has he got his hands?" Without any hesitation she spelled out, "On his head." I had my back to the cot, so Alec asked me to have a look. I got up and peeped at the baby. Sure enough, as he lay peacefully asleep, his hands were on his head! What could be more convincing!

Alec was silent, unable to speak, so great was his amazement. Up to that point he had firmly believed that all Spirit communication was a well-handled hoax. Contact with his dead sister, Connie, had moved him greatly. Her loss had been a bitter blow from which he had not yet recovered. Naturally, we sat every night after that and received some truly remarkable messages. At times these were marred by nonsensical trivialities. Later we learned these were possibly the result of interference by mischievous entities who used the table as it was the easiest form of communication.

We found table-moving an extremely slow way of communication with the Spirits, so decided to improve on it. We cut out the letters of the alphabet and arranged them in a circle. Placing a glass or tumbler in the centre with our hands lightly over it, it would move quickly from letter to letter and spell out Spirit messages. This was a much more satisfactory method and we abandoned the table.

Things were going well when, quite suddenly, all messages ceased and only one kept repeating itself, 'Join hands!'

Mary Hewitt

Being novices, we could not understand its meaning. I asked my friend, Mary Hewitt, what she thought it meant.

"They want you to sit in a circle and join hands to build up the power," said Mary. "One of you is a trance medium obviously and I think it is Alec." I came back and told Alec, but we did not do anything about it at that stage.

Some time later, when I was going to church with Mary one Sunday, I could see that she was ill. After the service she had walked on ahead slowly, while I stayed behind to get a book from the church library. When I joined her she remarked: "Marie Therese (*her Spirit Guide*) has been here and she says that Alec can give me healing. I will come over this afternoon, if I may, and we will try it." She urged me not to mention the location of her ailment as it would afford further proof of Alec's mediumship if he located it for himself.

At 3pm sharp Mary arrived. The three of us, she, Alec and I, went into the lounge and sat with our hands linked. After a short while Mary said quietly, "Now, Alec, give me some healing, please."

Alec was embarrassed and stammered, "But I don't know how, or what to do!"

"Just pass your hands lightly over my body and you will find that you will be impressed by Spirit what you have to do," Mary told him.

Alec looked self-conscious as he tried to follow Mary's advice. Quite suddenly I sensed a Spirit presence and then had my first clairvoyant vision! I saw a small Chinese boy overshadowing Alec. His hands moved very quickly, as they passed over the exact spot on Mary's body where the pain was located. Afterwards, Alec confessed to feeling very strange during the healing session. He felt he could not control his arms. It was as if some other force was manipulating them. Mary attributed this to the little Chinese Spirit boy whom she too had seen with Alec. We were all very excited, feeling that we were making fast progress.

The following Sunday, Mary asked if she could bring her sister, Artie, for healing. She had been ill with a nasty dose of flu. It had left her with a persistent catarrhal and sinus condition. The pair arrived at our house, but Alec was not keen on treating any outsiders so refused to treat Artie. Mary then tried to give her sister healing. No sooner had she commenced than Alec was controlled by Spirit and went into trance. He began to administer healing to Artie, who immediately felt a marked benefit. The healing session completed, Alec sat down and started to sing a little Chinese song. I knew then that the Spirit controlling him was that of the little Chinese boy I had seen clairvoyantly at the previous circle. He told us his name was Toi-Toi and thereafter, he attached himself to our circle. It was thrilling to know that Alec had started his work with Spirit. I felt very happy.

At this time I was still employed as a violinist at the Theatre and did not get home until 10.30pm. This meant that we could have a proper circle only on Sunday evenings. As we were anxious to know more about this wonderful revelation, we sat most nights in meditation to help prepare the way for our Spirit friends to come through.

During one of our meditation sessions I looked up and, to my great astonishment, saw an elderly Chinese gentleman standing beside Alec. He appeared to be a physical being, certainly not merely a vision! He wore a beautifully embroidered Chinese robe and a small round black hat was perched on his head. His pale yellow skin was drawn tightly across high cheek bones, eyes aslant. The form stood scrutinizing me, his gaze penetrating, searching. So real did he seem that I was frightened. The figure must have realised that his sudden appearance had made me afraid for he disappeared as suddenly as he had come. I could not get that strange visitor out of my mind, nor he, us, apparently.

A few weeks later, as I sat quietly beside Alec while he slept on the divan, I glanced up at his face and noticed with bewilderment that his features were changing! As I watched, he slowly acquired a Mongolian appearance, with the unmistakable high cheek bones. Alec's eyes narrowed, becoming upturned at the outer corners. His mouth was drawn slightly downwards. "My Alec's being overshadowed by a Chinaman!" I gasped. I was dismayed, not knowing quite what to do. Then came a voice through the lips of Alec. It was oriental in inflection, high-pitched and nasal: "Little Lady," it said, "Chang come to help, not to harm you."

The calm words reassured me. I moved across to the divan and had a closer look at the face. At once I recognised the elderly Chinese gentleman I had seen previously. Alec's lips parted slowly and the Chinese voice intoned again: "You must make a time when I can come to speak to you. It is very important and concerns the development of the medium. There is great work to be done. Chang will look after medium always. I am his principal Guide. I will always be on hand to help him."

With these comforting words Chang quietly withdrew from Alec. His features returned to normal as he slept on. I felt a great flood of relief that matters were now under the control of a trustworthy Guide. Many had controlled Alec, but, somehow they did not belong; Chang did. We had acquired a valuable, life-long friend in Alec's Chief Guide.

We sat most nights in meditation and sending out healing, thereby giving the Guides an opportunity to develop Alec's mediumship. Little Toi-Toi was a frequent visitor and brought a lot of power to our circle.

One evening, a young man communicated. He had been one of the first to use the alphabet and glass. He said his name was Jolkim, a young Russian of about 25. He had died on horseback while trying to escape from the enemy in the first world war. Each time he came Jolkim would re-enact the circumstances which caused his death. This was traumatic, to say the least. Alec had to suffer boisterous and even rough treatment from him. Jolkim was generally difficult and appeared to resent having been sent to work with us. Often he was quite disagreeable. Complaining that our rooms were always too hot, he brought freezing cold winds which caused us to shiver in discomfort. I was far from happy about this state of affairs. I feared for Alec who, when controlled by Jolkim, was completely at this mercy. We were greatly relieved when this young Russian was removed from our circle for a period of six months. When he returned he was made to treat Alec's body with much more care.

In spite of this rough patch in their association, both Alec and Jolkim were told, first through the medium Helen Hughes, later through other mediums, that they would become 'closer than brothers and walk arm in arm'. How true this proved to be. Jolkim, eventually, became one of our band of trusted Guides. What a wonderful friend that lad has been to me and to hundreds of people over the years.

Shortly after Jolkim had returned to our circle, Alec and I were sitting in the lounge chatting, when my husband suddenly announced that he could hear a foreign language and had an urge to speak it. "Speak, then," I said. "Just do what you are being impressed to do."

Alec emitted a flow of quite incomprehensible words, which obviously had the pattern and grouping of intelligent speech. After a moment, the Spirit entity seemed to realise that I was completely at a loss to understand what he was saying. He promptly changed to English, projecting a beautiful, deep, rich and resonant voice. "My name is Ewonga," he said. "I come to tell you I am the medium's bodyguard. From henceforth, no one will control medium without my sanction."

I felt very relieved, realising that at last our circle was being properly managed and controlled from the Other Side. I expressed my gratitude to this gentle yet authoritative Spirit. What a source of strength he proved to be over the years. I came to love this Red Indian dearly and we both trusted him implicitly. Ewonga was always present at our séances, guarding Alec while he was in trance. We would have long and interesting talks with him about Spiritual matters. During one of these he told me that a Spirit who was greatly loved and respected, even revered, was being sent to take charge of our circle.

Alec's artistic impression of Ewonga - Alec's bodyguard while in trance. (Drawn 1954)

"Louie-One," he said, this was the name he always called me, "this advanced Spirit belongs to you. Many sit at his feet and listen, for he speaks words of wisdom. Already they are preparing the path by which he will come to you. So, be prepared to receive him."

Although Ewonga had not given us the name of this advanced Spirit who had attached himself to me, we were impatient to make his acquaintance. But patience was something we had to learn to cultivate while Alec was developing his mediumship. Things do not usually happen quickly in this field.

After Ewonga's coming, our circle was much better organised. We always followed any advice he gave. He told us to form a circle of regular sitters and always to hold our séance on a Sunday night. He stressed the importance of these two factors if we wished to make progress. I was only too eager to comply.

At one of these Sunday night sittings a deep baritone voice announced himself as 'Adoula'. Then he struck his breast and repeated, 'Adoula come'. He was an African, he said and he had a poor command of English. This improved greatly over the long years of his association with us; but Adoula never became fluent in the language. Often, when he was unable to find the correct words, some of his phrases were a delight to hear.

Adoula was a wonderful soul and became very closely associated with Alec as his Healing Guide. What a remarkable healer he was, with numerous cures to his credit. No! I correct that. Adoula never took credit himself for any of the miraculous healings which occurred while Alec was controlled by him. When many blessed his name and thanked him he would spurn such thanks saying with deep humility: "No thank Adoula. God give Adoula ... and Adoula just give you." It was his way of saying that all healing came from God, that he was just a channel directing healing to wherever it was needed.

At the healing sessions, Adoula always worked with an ordinary pocket handkerchief. Using it rather like an X-ray, he would hold up the unfolded handkerchief and view the patient's body through it, moving it about until he came to where the organs, bones or ligaments were out of balance. There was never any need to describe ailments to him or even indicate their situation. Adoula, with uncanny infallibility, could locate the complaint. Never, at any time, did he presume to diagnose. He knew what was wrong and where.

Without comment or discussion with the patient, he would proceed to administer Spiritual healing.

Placing the handkerchief over the affected part, Adoula would blow on to it a stream of healing breath. Sometimes he

Adoula - the Healing Guide

emitted a deep-throated humming sound, low-key and vibrant, which generated power and in turn, produced heat. More often than not, the patient almost immediately felt relief. Some spectacular cures took place instantaneously; while others required a series of treatments, sometimes over a long period.

On Ewonga's advice, we formed a healing circle. At these, Adoula was always present to administer to the sick through Alec, and Alec was always happiest working in this field of mediumship.

Chapter Four

Development of Voice Mediumship

❖ *A sitting with Helen Duncan* ❖ *Introduction to White Wing*
❖ *We are instucted to begin sitting for physical mediumship*

Though I was very pleased with the way Alec's trance mediumship was developing and was happy to meet the Guides who, one by one, were attaching themselves to our circle, nevertheless, I often thought of my brother's prophecy that I would 'see' my dead father before he did. I wondered when and how this could possibly happen. Needless to say it came about and in rather unusual circumstances. Although I did not know it, I was about to be introduced to a most astounding type of mediumship - materialisation. One not only heard, saw, touched and embraced lost loved ones, but they appeared as solid and real as any physical being. In appearance, they were no different from when they were on Earth.

My mother had a niece named Maggie but, because she was so much older than I was, I always called her Aunt Maggie. She was a very religious lady, attending every Pentecostal church service or prayer meeting whenever possible. The rest of the time she devoted herself to her large family of four girls and three boys who lived happily together, though a trifle cramped, in a small house in Porth. Of necessity, the three youngest girls Ethel, Doris and Janette, slept together in one bedroom.

Quite suddenly, Ethel, an extremely beautiful girl, with long golden hair reaching to below her waist, fell ill with tuberculosis. She quickly succumbed and passed into Spirit. Because of their cramped sleeping conditions, her sisters also contracted the deadly disease and died within 18 months of Ethel.

Poor Aunt Maggie was desolate with grief, overcome by this appalling tragedy which had struck at her close-knit family. Only her unswerving faith in God kept her sane. Despite her triple bereavement she had no desire to try to communicate with her beloved daughters through mediumship, believing that Spiritualism was the 'work of the Devil'. Anyway, she firmly believed that they would lie peacefully asleep in their graves awaiting the call of the 'last trumpet'!

My brother, Ted, used to visit her every week in an effort to bring her a measure of comfort. Naturally, he tentatively put out feelers to see what her attitude was regarding Life after Death. Ted suggested that he might help her to communicate with Ethel, Doris and Janette. Aunt Maggie was aghast! She chided him for being a Spiritualist, spitting the word out with distaste, accusing him of working with the Devil. Somewhat deflated, Ted tried to lend weight to his arguments by telling Aunt Maggie that Alec and I were in the movement. On hearing this, she threw up her arms and prayed aloud for our salvation. Ted deemed it wise to beat a hasty retreat!

Not long after this unfortunate encounter, mother and I held a séance, with Alec in trance. To our surprise, we heard Janette's voice. She addressed my mother saying, "Auntie Polly, please go and see my mother. She is very ill. Tell her we are with her and helping her. Tell her we love her very much." Mother promised she would do this. Next morning, though she rarely went out, she rose early, dressed and caught the Rhondda bus bound for Aunt Maggie's house. When she alighted at her destination she was surprised to encounter her son, Ted, getting off the bus coming from the opposite direction. Ted was flabbergasted at seeing his mother so far from home at that early hour and asked the reason. Mother explained that she was on her way to see Maggie. Then she related Janette's urgent request at the previous night's séance that she should call and see her mother.

Ted exclaimed in surprise: "But that's an extraordinary coincidence! Ethel came to our circle last night and she said the same thing. That is why I am here. I have not seen Aunt Maggie for a couple of weeks so I was not aware of her illness."

"That is very strange," mother replied. "Both girls bringing the same message at the same time, but in different places!" She pondered a moment, then said: "I fear there must be something very wrong with Maggie. Let's go quickly and see for ourselves." and she hurried Ted across the road to her niece's little house.

Sure enough they found Maggie gravely ill. Both Ted and mother passed on gently her daughters' Spirit messages which she found difficult to understand, believing that they had gone from her for ever. She smiled as she thought about it, then murmured, "Oh, if only I could believe that." Hope flickered momentarily in her eyes as she added, "How happy I should be." Then her face clouded as she remembered her firmly entrenched beliefs. "But that is not possible. They are in their graves," she added sadly.

"Listen, Maggie, my girl," mother spoke gently but earnestly, "I am telling you the truth. You must believe me. They did come to us last night, through Alec and Ted. They want you to know that they are not asleep in the grave as you believe awaiting a trumpet call or the second coming of Christ. They are alive and with you now. How else did they know you were ill? And how could they come to tell us if this were not so? We knew nothing of your sickness, dear."

Aunt Maggie seemed a little happier at that, though not entirely satisfied, as she sank back among her pillows. But a ray of hope had been given her. Within the month she passed into Spirit during her sleep. One can imagine the joy she experienced at being reunited with her three lovely girls again.

I have told this story because it had a sequel which gave irrefutable evidence that Maggie, Connie and my father were all still alive, albeit in another dimension. To prove it they were able to materialise with such clarity and physical detail that we had no difficulty in recognising them.

This physical manifestation occurred when famous materialisation medium Helen Duncan gave a séance at our Spiritualist Church. Mary, Alec and I were fortunate in obtaining three of the greatly coveted seats. Alec bought a bunch of violets, 'to give to Connie', he said. On arrival at the church he had placed these flowers inside the cabinet.

A word of explanation is perhaps necessary here for those who are not familiar with the term 'cabinet'. This is a term applied to the curtained off space in a room, behind which the medium sits in deep trance during a séance. It is usually a black cloth, or curtain, hung across one corner of the room, with a chair placed behind it for the medium. In either case, the enclosed area is very small, affording no room for fraudulent manipulations. These curtains are always made of black material because, against this dark background, the Spirit forms, particularly those who have had difficulty in building strongly, are more easily discernable. The Spirits can then make use of the ectoplasm emanating from the medium's body. The Spirit people wishing to materialise then clothe their finer Spirit bodies with this denser physical substance, this ectoplasm, thus enabling them to become visible to the sitters in the séance room. The cabinet structure is necessary to protect the ectoplasm from the harmful effect of light and to conserve the psychic forces emanating from the medium, as well as the power generated by the sitters themselves during their singing and conversations. The human voice is a powerful contributing factor in the production of the vibrations necessary for Spirit materialisation. These vibrations are referred to as power and become concentrated inside the cabinet, where they are prevented from dissipating by the Spirit scientists in charge of the sitting and made available for the use of any materialising Spirit entity.

The Helen Duncan demonstration began with the usual procedures. Prayers were recited, followed by a few hymns. Very soon phenomena began to happen!

A cultured male voice, with a strong Cambridge accent (the medium was a Scot), announced himself as Albert Stewart, Mrs Duncan's personal Guide. Albert welcomed us to the circle, giving explicit instructions on how we should approach the materialised forms. He also issued advice on conducting ourselves during the séance. This done, the curtains were parted, revealing the medium in deep trance. A tall figure of a man in a flowing white robe stood beside her, his hand on her shoulder. I was utterly fascinated. It was my first experience of materialisation. Alec and Mary were equally enthralled. After Albert materialised many others came to show themselves and bring messages. Though it was a marvellous experience, we were somewhat detached from those Spirit communicators who were not known to us. We waited anxiously for one of our own loved ones to bring the evidence we needed.

We were not to be disappointed. After a while, a beautiful young girl stepped right out of the cabinet. It was Connie. Every feature was as it had been when we last saw her. To Alec's joy she held his violets in her hands! "Thanks, darlings, for the violets," she said softly, but quite distinctly. Then she handed the posy to Alec. The extraordinary thing was that after they had been handled by Connie, the violets lasted for weeks without withering.

As we left the church, after the conclusion of the circle, I was conscious of a certain disappointment that my father had not shown himself; but I consoled myself by acknowledging that what I had seen was very rewarding.

I wanted Ted to witness these marvellous manifestations. He did such good work around the valleys of South Wales, giving so much, taking church services, always rendering very convincing clairvoyance. Ted was a popular medium. When he demonstrated the churches were filled to capacity. I felt that a sitting with Helen Duncan would help and encourage him further. I also thought that father would most certainly materialise for Ted. Ted was excited at the idea and a sitting was arranged.

Afterwards, I anxiously enquired if he had seen father. He replied that he had not. "But guess who did come? Maggie!" Knowing Maggie's antipathy to Spiritualism, I was most surprised. "Maggie!" I exclaimed.

"Yes," Ted affirmed: "Maggie! She came out of that cabinet looking just as she had on Earth. She put her hands on my shoulders and said, 'Teddie!'. She was the only one in the family who ever called me Teddie." Ted's voice was full of excitement as he underlined this piece of evidence. Then he continued, "She said, 'Teddie, I've come to tell you that you are right about

Spiritualism; I was wrong. You must carry on with this good work." Ted laughed delightedly. "Aunt Maggie said that, can you believe it, Lou?"

"But what about father?" I asked. "Did he come?"

"I asked Aunt Maggie if he would come. She said; 'He's here, Teddie. He helped me to come. He thought it would be more convincing for you if he did it that way.' Good heavens, Lou! This Mrs Duncan's mediumship is something fantastic!"

Which of course it was.

We had to wait several months before Helen Duncan returned to our Church. Once more, mother, Alec and I were in the front row beside the cabinet, anxiously awaiting father's materialisation. This time we felt certain he would come. The previous night he had come through at our circle and said that the Guides were busy preparing him. They would help him to show himself at the Duncan circle. Father said that he would build strongly and that we would be able to recognise him. It was with bated breath we waited for the Guide Albert to conclude his usual preliminaries. This done, he paused, looking around. His eyes came to rest on our little group. I could scarcely breathe!

"There is a gentleman here," he began and I squeezed mother's hand tightly, "who wishes to come to the lady in the front row." I could barely contain my excitement.

"For me?" I gasped. "Has he come for me, Friend?"

"He has come for the lady next to you," came the reply, "but for you, also."

With that the curtains parted and my beloved father stepped out of the cabinet! He came forward, his arms outstretched to mother. "Poll," he said gently, "I am with you."

Mother went to him. There followed a quiet conversation between them, too personal to relate. There was no doubt in our minds it was Dad. Before father appeared, Albert had instructed us to remove the handkerchief shading the red light used at materialisation séances. He explained that this Spirit had built up so strongly that he would be able to tolerate the increased light and added, "He is anxious to show himself clearly to his loved ones."

We looked closely at Dad, hardly believing that he was there before us. Every feature was clear. His eyes, the texture of his skin, every line and detail of his face, were there for all to see. Apart from the visual proof, he appeared to be as solid as I was when I took his hand. He bent and kissed me lightly on the cheek.

A week or so later I was browsing round the library when I came across a book entitled 'Towards the Stars' by Dennis Bradley. The title intrigued me, so I took it home with me. It was a very comprehensive report of the investigations undertaken by the author into the direct voice mediumship of George Valiantine, a well-known American medium. Every time I picked up the book a voice said, "You can get that." Puzzled, I dismissed the suggestion from my mind as probably imagination. However, the voice was so persistent I decided to discuss it with my medium friend Mary Hewitt. She took the matter seriously. She did not think it was imagination, but someone trying to impress me that we should sit for direct voice.

At our next circle, I asked Ewonga if we should try to obtain direct voice. Without any hesitation he replied, "Get a cone, Louie-One and wait." He was, of course, referring to a megaphone-shaped séance trumpet.

Every time we attended the Spiritualist church the demonstrating medium would single out Alec or me and tell us about 'the great work' we had to do or that there were great plans for our future in Spiritualism. It was all very well, but, up to that point, nothing had been made clear as to what these were to be. Our circle seemed to be following the same pattern with no change. It is understandable, therefore, why the controlling Guides sent a gentle Spirit to encourage me, through the entranced Alec. Softly spoken, saying her name was 'Patience', she came to bring me patience, of which I was sorely in need. She told us to persevere and we would ultimately get what we were striving for. We were greatly heartened by her words and after that we were better able to endure the delays encountered.

Time passed. We tried to wait patiently for those on the Other Side to move when they were ready. Then, quite unexpectedly, a new, important Guide made himself known to us. Through Alec, in trance, came a deep resonant voice, "I am White Wing!" Alec, controlled by the new Spirit, rose to his feet, seeming to gain in stature as he came towards me. "I belong to you, Faithful," he said, taking my hands in his. "There is much work for you to do."

"I repeat," came the rich voice, "there is much work for you to do. Your world needs the help we will bring. We look to you to

Alec's artistic impression of White Wing - He was Louie's main Guide and head of all the Circle's workers in Spirit

help us carry it through. I will speak simply for you to understand. Your man is like the engine. You are the power which makes the engine go."

"White Wing not promise riches, but you will have sufficient for your needs. Now, the path is narrow and difficult, but White Wing say, one day, it will be a long, wide road and hundreds will travel along it with you."

I was quite overcome by his words. I felt so close to this wonderful soul that I was prepared to do all I could to help him in his work. I even offered to give up my music if it was necessary.

"White Wing," he answered seriously, "may even ask that of you, Faithful." This was a sobering thought, as I loved my music dearly.

I was touched by the beautiful name he had given me and wondered why he had called me that. As if picking up my thoughts he said, "My name for you is 'Faithful' because White Wing know you will always be faithful even through difficult times. One day," he prophesied, "when you come over to White Wing, there will be a reward for your faithfulness. May the Great White Spirit bless you."

The Guide withdrew, promising to come again. We were to become very close over the years. He tutored me in all subjects relating to Spirit matters. I found out how little I really knew. I became his eager and diligent pupil, trusting him completely. Never once did I find him to be wrong.

We bore in mind White Wing's injunction, given at a subsequent circle, 'to sift and question all that purports to come from the Other Side. Never accept anything if your better judgement indicates that it is unacceptable'. He told us that so many people accepted wholeheartedly and unquestioningly every single utterance from a medium. They did not realise that, in the developing stages particularly, things could go wrong, permitting interference and distortion to take place. This warning made us cautious of any manifestation we encountered.

At this time, we started to experience quite a lot of physical phenomena in our home, even in comparatively bright light. Objects moved for no apparent reason; teaspoons were lifted by unseen hands and tapped against saucers and so on. Alec disliked being in trance as he was unable to witness anything that took place. To conciliate him, so that his interest would not flag, I agreed to sit for automatic writing after I came home from the theatre, so that he would be able consciously to participate in the

Spirit communication. One particular evening, Alec said he had an urge to put the pencil in his left hand. It was only a small stub and difficult to hold. I was surprised to see him insert it between the first and second fingers of the left hand. Being right handed, this would make writing a difficult undertaking. No sooner had he grasped the pencil between his fingers than it began to write quickly on the blank piece of paper before him.

Though it commenced at the left hand margin of the paper, the script started with the last word at the end of the sentence, finishing on the right of the paper with the word beginning that sentence. In other words, the communication was back to front. And to make things even more complicated, the script was upside down! The finished message, written in this manner, was legible to me, sitting directly opposite Alec, but not to himself. The letters were written at great speed. This convinced me completely that it was some Spirit person and not Alec, who was the writer of the message.

Three times the pencil wrote the same message; and always back to front and upside down. It was 'Tell Mary - keep away from London'.

"Which Mary?" I asked. 'Hewitt - your friend,' wrote the pencil. "Who is it who is writing this?" I asked. 'Bert,' came the reply.

At this juncture we suddenly noticed a strange acrid smell. I sniffed and turned to Alec. "Can you smell something? It's like sulphur burning."

Alec's nostrils twitched. "It's like the smell left after a shell has exploded. I remember it only too well."

No explanation was forthcoming, either about Bert, or the strange odour. A few weeks later we learned that Alec Hewitt's brother, Bert, had been killed by a shell-burst in the first world war. It was Bert's first contact with us, but he subsequently communicated frequently after that for many years, during which time he gave his sceptical brother all the proof of survival that he needed.

After receiving Bert's warning, it was too late to deliver it to Mary. Early the next morning I made a point of doing so, knowing that sometimes Mary drove to London at weekends.

As she read the message Mary's face showed her amazement and she was visibly upset. She told me it seemed inevitable that she would have to go to London. Her husband had mentioned, only the night before, that he intended to operate his business from the capital and wanted to reside in London. "But we shall have to have second thoughts before moving, won't we?" she said gravely.

* * *

I had read that it was absolutely essential to sit in complete darkness to achieve Direct Voice mediumship with only the séance cone or trumpet edged with a band of luminous paint round its wider end to make it visible to sitters. I was disconcerted, having no desire to sit in the dark. Alec and I continued to meditate in red light, an ordinary white globe covered with a red cloth, in our dining room. The Guides apparently decided to condition me to sitting in the dark, because no sooner had we commenced our meditation than the light would go out. Afterwards we would discover that the globe (*light bulb*) filament had been destroyed. Time and again this happened. I felt a growing annoyance as the pile of broken globes increased.

As usual when in difficulties I consulted Mary Hewitt. I told her about this new problem, explaining that the Guides were being fractious, if not a little destructive, in their efforts to persuade us to sit in darkness. She smiled, amused at the battle of wills that was taking place between the two worlds, and offered to attend that night and observe what took place.

Sure enough, the same phenomenon happened again. As soon as our sitting commenced, out went the light. Mary chuckled and shook her head wisely: "I'm afraid, Lou dear, you will have to learn to comply with the Guides' wishes. They are in charge and will brook no interference with their arrangements. Try sitting in darkness, otherwise I don't think you'll get what you are looking for."

I sighed and grudgingly agreed. To our surprise, thereafter, the Guides were able to put the light on and off at will without manipulating the switch and I made no move to interfere.

Mary and her husband did eventually leave our district to live in London, despite Bert's warning. I felt her loss keenly. Where would I go now, I wondered, when I encountered the inevitable problems?

The Spirit people, always aware of our thoughts, were quick to console me and allay my fears. I received a message through a visiting medium at the Spiritualist church. "You must not be upset. One friend has left you, but two more will come later to help you in the work you are undertaking."

Alec and I now continued our evening meditation sittings in the dark. Before we sat I placed the luminous trumpet on the mantelpiece. Here it would remain, resolutely immobile, apparently disinterested in the proceedings.

One night, quite unexpectedly, just as we were about to close, to our amazement, the trumpet moved! It rose up, glided silently across the mantelpiece and came to rest on the opposite side, carefully avoiding two vases which stood in its pathway.

Simultaneously, a loud rattling sound could be heard, as if pebbles were being thrown against the door. The sudden noise startled us, but we were very excited and waited expectantly for further manifestations to occur. The trumpet made no more excursions. We closed the sitting. To say we were pleased with what had taken place would be a gross understatement. We were both thrilled.

The exciting possibility of future phenomena so unsettled us that when we finally went to bed sleep eluded us. We lay awake into the small hours, contemplating the wondrous things which might lie ahead for our circle. Uppermost in my mind was a deep sense of gratitude to those dedicated Guides who were working so tirelessly to help us achieve our objective.

The following Sunday, I invited a friend, Betty, to join us in the séance room. She was the young daughter of a friend of my mother. Betty's mother had passed into Spirit not long before. The previous Sunday I had received a message from her through the church medium to relay to Betty. I thought it would be nice for

Betty to speak to her mother herself, hence my invitation.

Just before we commenced sitting, Betty's cousin, Murdo, arrived asking for Betty. He had locked himself out of the house accidentally. Murdo was staying with Betty and her family and came to borrow her key. Murdo was such a personable young man I felt drawn to him and asked him to join us. Alternatively, I said he could wait in the lounge until the circle was ended. Alec approached Murdo and tried to persuade him to join the sitters, saying, jocularly: "You are a canny Scot, Murdo. I would be grateful for your unbiased observations on what takes place at our circles. I would like to know what really goes on. I can't believe half of what they tell me. I'm unconscious all the time." Seeing the puzzled expression on Murdo's face, Alec hastened to explain: "I'm in trance during the whole proceedings. I don't know a thing about what takes place."

Murdo nodded his understanding and agreed to accompany Betty into the séance room. It was their first experience of Spirit communication, so I gave them a short explanation of what to expect. Alec then went into trance and the circle began.

Ewonga was the first to come through with this advice: "The time is right for you to sit for voice, but Ewonga say who shall sit. Ewonga know best."

Each sitter was expectant, hoping to be chosen for the voice circle. Ewonga's deep voice resumed. "First, Alec and Louie," and addressing Betty and Murdo, "perhaps this lady and gentleman would be kind enough to help us by giving their time each week. If, of course, they are interested," he added.

They indicated that they were most interested and willing to join the small circle. Then, with characteristic courtesy, Ewonga begged the remaining sitters not to be disappointed because they had not been selected. "These four that I have chosen," explained Ewonga, "have what is necessary in their bodily emanations to obtain direct voice from Spirit. If they sit alone, quite apart from your present group, voice will come quickly."

Noticing some of the sitters seemed a trifle downcast, he added a word of comfort: "Afterwards, you will all benefit from their efforts. Once they have been successful, voice will then come to your Sunday circle." This relieved their despondency and Ewonga continued: "White Wing will give you your instructions next Sunday. I suggest that you start sitting for voice the following Tuesday. I wish you success, Louie-One. May God bless your efforts." He withdrew, leaving us greatly encouraged, anxious to start the new Tuesday circle.

Betty lived very near the theatre where I worked, so we decided to hold the voice sittings at her house. I could go there between shows. We would be able to sit for one and a quarter hours weekly.

At the Sunday circle, when White Wing gave us our instructions he stressed the importance of regularity. "Never miss one sitting," he urged. "It is essential that the link is not broken." We all complied with his instructions to the smallest detail. Even Murdo, a traveller, made sure that he never left Cardiff on Tuesdays.

After sitting for nine Tuesdays we had a setback. On the tenth, Alec inexplicably failed to appear for the circle! Feeling hurt and disappointed that he had let us and the Spirit people down, we realised that he had probably grown tired of sitting week after week for the past two and a half months with nothing to show for his pains but negative results. But we remembered White Wing's injunctions regarding the importance of 'regularity' and 'keeping the link unbroken'. Rather than cancel the sitting, we held the circle with just the three of us, Murdo, Betty and me. We decided to place Alec's empty chair in position in the circle, as if by this gesture he would be present in Spirit.

White Wing had instructed us to sit around a table with our hands resting on it. The little fingers of each hand were to be in contact with those of the sitters on either side of us and thumbs were to be kept apart. No explanation was given for this. He also advised us to let water flow through the trumpet before laying it down on the table. The instructions carried out, we commenced, opening with a prayer followed by singing. Very soon we were amazed to see the trumpet start to roll around the table. It slowly crept up on to my hands, remained there for a moment, then returned to the centre of the table where it became stationary again.

We were more than pleased with our progress. As we closed

the circle, each of us experienced a feeling of achievement. At last, something positive had happened. We were getting somewhere, we felt, if the trumpet moved at all. Our weeks of patient sitting had not been a waste of time.

I got home to find Alec waiting for me, looking somewhat sheepish. "Well, how did the voice circle go this evening?" he asked. "Anything spectacular happen?"

Still feeling hurt by his deliberate boycott, I retorted angrily: "How dare you ask that? You should be ashamed of yourself, letting the Guides down like that. Have you forgotten what White Wing said about 'not breaking the link'? Anyway," and I looked smug, "you needn't bother to come again if you don't want to."

"What are you talking about?" said Alec. I could see he was curious. "Just that the trumpet moved without you, that's all."

"It moved?" He looked incredulous. "I don't believe it!"

"Well, it did," I said simply. I then told him that White Wing had insisted that he was not to allow himself to go into trance at these voice circles, as it was intended that I should be the voice medium. I asked Alec if he would be willing to help me develop in that field. To my relief, he readily agreed, only too happy to be able to witness the proceedings himself for a change.

The following Sunday, White Wing told us that the room we were using was not satisfactory as it was too large. He asked us to sit in a smaller one if possible. Betty had a small sewing room which seemed ideal for our purpose. So, having blacked it out satisfactorily, we used this the following Tuesday.

We commenced the next circle with the new format, Alec remaining conscious throughout. The prayers and preliminaries completed, we were greatly surprised to see the trumpet rise from the table and move swiftly about the room. It was suspended eerily in mid air and obviously directed by unseen hands. Later, we learned that to perform this feat, psychic rods were used, fashioned from ectoplasm drawn from the sitters and the medium.

No one was more surprised than Alec himself, this being his first experience of the trumpet circle and he expressed his amazement aloud. While we were all congratulating the Spirit friends and ourselves on the degree of success attained, the trumpet suddenly fell to the floor with a clatter that brought gasps of dismay from the four of us.

Thinking that the power had diminished, we sang the bright Sankey and Moody hymn 'Bringing In The Sheaves' at the top of our voices. This was to raise the vibrations. It had the desired effect. The trumpet began to creep along the floor slowly. It edged itself along until it reached my feet. It then crept up my leg and moved up the side of my body to my shoulder keeping in close contact with me all the while. I sat motionless, scarcely able to breathe, lest I should impede it in any way. It then descended again by way of my arm, returning to the table where it came to rest. As I closed the circle the trumpet moved again and came to me, laying itself upon my clasped hands, as if to indicate that our friends in Spirit were joining with us in prayer. It was a reassuring gesture.

Shortly afterwards, I was grateful for Spirit comfort received from the trumpet. There had been an unfortunate incident at the theatre which had left me hurt and bewildered. None knew of my distress, for I had spoken of it to no one, least of all to the other sitters in our circle. What took place, therefore, convinced me of the concern that our Spirit friends have for our wellbeing. We had gone into the sanctuary as usual and were singing one of our favourite hymns, when the trumpet crept up my arm, stroked me gently with caressing movements and then lifted up my chin, as if to say; 'Be of good cheer. All is well. We are here every step of the way'. The thought that our Spirit friends knew of my hurt and were offering what comfort they could through the trumpet consoled me greatly.

Chapter Five

Development of Physical Mediumship

❖ *More Spirit companions join us* ❖ *Alec is a powerful physical medium*
❖ *Helen Hughes predicts that Alec will be a materialisation medium*
❖ *We encounter remarkable physical phenomena.*

Those in charge of Alec's mediumship now planned to take his development a step further. Chang, speaking through the medium in trance, announced, "Little Lady, Alec must go in cabinet."

"But, Chang," I protested, "Alec says he will never sit in a cabinet; he doesn't like being confined."

"Little Lady," the oriental voice intoned firmly, "when Chang say medium go in cabinet, in cabinet he must go!"

Disconcerted, knowing Alec's aversion to cabinets, I asked White Wing for an explanation. If I was the voice medium, surely it was not necessary for Alec to sit in the cabinet.

"Faithful," came the calm, rich voice, reassuring in its warmth: "you are the voice medium certainly, but Alec is a very powerful physical medium. We have decided that instead of developing you separately, we will endeavour to blend the power. Alec will go into trance and you, Faithful, must be the conscious half. It is essential that a physical medium has a conscious counterpart to take care of him. But, I say to you, Alec will only have voice manifestation if you are present."

I was quite happy with this new arrangement and felt greatly thrilled! Alec was far from pleased. "Why do I have to go into trance?" he complained. "And why in a cabinet for Heaven's sake?"

I did my best to explain what White Wing had said: that he, apparently, had a very special power that the Guides could use for physical mediumship. I told him that he ought to be overjoyed at the prospect of this new development. Alec sighed and grudgingly consented to do as Chang asked.

We had taken the first step towards the production of direct voice and the materialisation of Spirit entities in our own séance room. I was thrilled, excited and overwhelmed that we should be privileged to participate in this work. White Wing, however, warned us, "Keep your counsel and do not speak of this abroad until we are ready." I was disappointed, but we respected White Wing's command, not discussing what took place in our circle with anyone.

Now that Alec's physical mediumship had been launched, a new Guide joined us. Christopher became an important member of our band of Spirit helpers. He was an intermediary between circle members and beings on a higher plane who gave information and instructions to us regarding the handling of the circle in general and the medium in particular.

Christopher received these instructions and relayed them to us. The advice was wise, helpful and invaluable at all times. We accepted what he said without question, always believing that 'Christopher knew best'.

He never materialised, but usually spoke in what is known as independent voice. His lisping, gentle, light baritone voice, with its slow presentation, would be heard either from above the cabinet, or from high up in any other part of the room. Occasionally, Christopher used the trumpet. Sometimes he would be heard conversing with Alec in the cabinet. He always came with advice, never indulging in trivial remarks. Christopher was a very important cog in the materialisation machinery in the Alec Harris circle. There were many such cogs, some big, some small, but all of them important, having their own specialised work to do.

One by one, these cogs, in the shape of friendly Guides, began to operate smoothly in our circle. As each appeared, he politely introduced himself, explained the reason for his presence and methodically applied himself to developing Alec's mediumship. Each step was guided into its proper channel at the appropriate time. Never was anything ever hurried. Naturally, with the advent of each new and trusted Guide, confidence in our Band of Helpers grew.

When, one evening, a calm gentle voice announced 'I am Rohan' we were very happy to welcome yet another Spirit friend. I was impressed by the warm timbre of this new voice, which seemed to pour out so much love, peace and harmony. I asked him what he had been during his Earth life.

"What I was," came the gentle reply: "is of no account. It is what I am and the work I come to do that matters. This is my greatest concern. I come to assist you to give the world the truth about life after death. My work is to help mankind to a better understanding of what is known as death. From henceforth," he continued, "I shall always be close to the medium, to help and protect him and to guide his efforts and yours along the path ordained."

Rohan promised to be present at every circle from that time forward. It was always he who came first to greet and advise sitters at the commencement of every circle. I felt that Rohan's beautiful voice must be accompanied by beauty of form. Later when we achieved full-form materialisations this proved to be the case. Rohan was a dearly loved Spirit Guide and greatly respected by all of us in the physical circle.

In deference to Alec's aversion to sitting in a cabinet, he was allowed to sit to one side of it, a little away from the rest of us. Christopher told us to place the trumpet outside the cabinet. We did exactly as told, firmly believing that voice phenomena would surely take place. We were to be disappointed. For several weeks, the cone declined even to move, let alone produce the faintest whisper.

While we debated what to do, we suddenly received a change of instructions. We were told to place the trumpet inside the cabinet at the next Tuesday circle. Unfortunately, I forgot and set it outside, as before. No sooner had we commenced when the trumpet rose in the air and went into the cabinet of its own accord! Later I received a reprimand from White Wing: "Faithful, you ask for voice. You must carry out all our instructions if you want success."

It was clear that the Guides never forgot what had taken place between us at previous sittings. They liked to be obeyed. Thereafter, I became a veritable sergeant-major, so meticulous was l over procedures pertaining to the circle.

About this time a visiting voice medium came to Cardiff. I was anxious to revive Alec's waning interest in this type of mediumship and thought I could achieve this by letting him have first-hand experience. I took a night off from the theatre. Murdo, Betty, Alec and I attended one of the voice sittings that were being arranged.

The procedure seemed no different from ours, except that as well as the trumpet, there were various toys, bugles and tambourines lying around, marked with luminous paint. Obviously, these were all to be moved, jangled or blown by Spirit entities during the circle.

Not having been to such a séance before, we were all intensely interested. However, it was not as spectacular as we hoped. Hardly any direct voices spoke, only those through the lips of the medium. Quite a lot of minor physical phenomena were in evidence. I found this quite fascinating since the medium could not have been responsible for it. He was securely tied up by Murdo and several others prior to the séance.

Then the medium's Guide said that he wanted to speak to the lady by the window. Since I was the only female so positioned, I was amused to see many of the women in the hall acknowledge his call. "No," said the Guide, "I repeat, I want the lady by the window." I then responded and he intimated that I was the person he wanted.

"Lady," he said, "you have in your home someone with far greater power than the medium I am using today." I thought, "He must mean Alec, but can I trust him?" As if in answer to my doubting question, the Guide continued: "I have here with me a great Chieftain, a North American Indian. He gives you this message. He is looking to you to see that the work begun is carried out. He asks, 'Will you promise, Faithful, to do this?'."

Amazed that White Wing should be present at this circle, I gave my ready assurance. We were impressed at the manner in which he identified himself. By using the name that he had given me, 'Faithful' there could be no doubt in our minds that it was he. Also by returning through a medium other than Alec was further proof, if we needed any, of the reality of his existence, particularly as this medium was unknown to us and we to him.

There now followed a demonstration of physical phenomena. Bells rang, tambourines rattled, objects floated in the air about us, we were touched by unseen hands. It was a wonderful experience for me. I hoped the same for Alec, but he was quite unimpressed by 'all this nonsense'. He insisted that nothing had taken place that could not quite easily be performed without the aid of Spirit intervention.

"Alec!" I gasped, shocked at his disbelief. "How can you say that? What about the message from White Wing? How could that medium know that he always called me Faithful? Come on, what have you got to say about that?" I challenged. Alec could not explain that part, but insisted the phenomena could be duplicated by physical means. Betty and Murdo entered the fray, protesting at Alec's attitude. The argument became quite heated, but Alec would not relent.

"All right!" he snapped. "Tell you what: you tie me up and I'll show you I can do all that. It won't be Spirits moving the things about cithcr!"

Without any warning, Alec suddenly fell into trance. The high-pitched voice of our oriental Guide, Chang, addressed me. "Little lady," he said, "do as the medium says. At your next circle, tie him up. He will have big surprise. You all have big surprise, big shock." Chang seemed amused, then continued seriously: "Do not be angry with Alec. He pick up other people's thoughts and speak them as his own. Not his fault. This is not what he thinks himself." He paused, as if thinking something, then continued: "You do as he says. Tie him up and see what happens."

As if by the snap of a switch, Alec came out of trance. Conscious once more, he continued heatedly with the argument which had raged just prior to Chang's announcement. He was totally unaware that there had been a break in the conversation and knew nothing of Chang's remarks. "I'll show you," he said. "Just give me a chance and I'll show you." He looked defiantly at the three of us.

With Chang's recent advice in mind, we all agreed to give Alec an opportunity of demonstrating how fraudulent mediums operate. "All right, Alec," I said smugly, "next Sunday, instead of our usual circle, we will tie you up good and proper and you can show us how it is done." He stopped short at that, looking, I thought, a trifle alarmed, but he endeavoured to laugh it off with a shrug. I think he hoped we would all forget about it. But we had no intention of doing so.

Early on Sunday we prepared the séance room for Alec's demonstration. We placed a curtain across the corner of the room to serve as a cabinet. As it was Christmas, we decorated the walls and ceiling with streamers, tinsel and balloons and the like. We found some toys, drums, bugles, tambourines etc. and placed these, together with my baby son's reins, which were heavily hung with bells, on a table inside the impromptu cabinet. We used anything that could be moved or make a noise. The chair for Alec was placed outside the cabinet.

When evening came we went into the séance room, followed by a somewhat downcast Alec. Much of his bravado had evaporated since his heated assertion that given the chance he could produce Spirit phenomena by physical means. Here was his chance; we intended to hold him to his word. After all, had not Chang said we should?

Glumly Alec took his place in the chair set aside for him. Murdo tied him securely with yards of stout rope. Perhaps he was a little too enthusiastic about this. Alec called out in alarm: "Ah, Murdo! Not so tight, man. The rope's biting into me."

"It's the way I tied the other medium, you know, the faking one," he teased and chuckled as he tightened another knot.

We all laughed at Alec's discomfort, feeling absolutely certain that he would not be able to move his hands, let alone anything that lay in the cabinet, so thoroughly had Murdo performed the tie-up job.

Sitting in red light, we opened the circle with a prayer and prepared ourselves for a long wait. This proved to be unnecessary. Almost immediately and to our astonishment the bells were being shaken vigorously in the cabinet. Their tinkling was loud and clear. Quickly we glanced at Alec to see if he had achieved the impossible and freed himself from Murdo's ropes. But no! He sat, still securely bound hand and foot, looking decidedly scared. Alec realised that this was no physical manifestation engineered by one of us. We were all linked hand to hand. Murdo looked across at me and I nodded. He got up and extinguished the light and then things really began to happen!

Something, a strange object, was dropped into Murdo's lap. The piping Chinese voice of the little Spirit boy Toi-Toi could be heard angrily denouncing the medium: "Alec, him plenty bad man! Give him back that 'thing' he bring with him. We not need it." Being dark, we were unable to see what it was that had so angered the little fellow. We had to wait until the end of the circle, when the lights would be switched on, before we could inspect it.

What a wonderful circle that proved to be. The balloons were supernormally removed from the ceiling and burst with loud bangs. This delighted the Spirit children, who were all having great fun. In their childish enthusiasm they pulled down all the decorations. Tambourines were played with gusto. Little hands excitedly wound up toy cars, popped toy guns, played mouth organs and beat drums. They generally had themselves a wonderful Christmas party, showing that Spirit children were no different from Earth children. It was all so unexpected. We could hardly credit that all this physical phenomena had occurred in our circle.

There were 12 sitters and dear doubting Alec. We then recalled Chang's words about letting Alec try for physical mediumship and we would all have a big surprise. Surprise? What an understatement! We were all astounded.

During the circle, Ewonga spoke to us in his gentle baritone voice, expressing gratitude to Alec for making it possible for them all to manifest in this way. What an achievement it had been for those on both sides of the cabinet. Ewonga added that this was the first of many such circles. In the future even greater happenings could be expected.

Before leaving, he urged us not to be angry with Alec. Angry? How could any of us feel anger towards him? We were thrilled with what had occurred. It was now obvious that Alec had very special mediumistic qualities.

At last I began to understand the earlier repetitive prophesies regarding the 'great work' that lay ahead for both of us. I regretted the irritation I had always felt when told about this.

As soon as the light went on, we hastened to inspect the object Toi-Toi had so disdainfully cast into Murdo's lap. At first, we were puzzled to discover that it was an expanding rule, the type generally used by artisans. Then, understanding dawned. Alec had apparently slipped this instrument into his pocket with the intention of retrieving it during the séance. By extending it, he had hoped to simulate Spirit activities by touching us or moving objects, however inexpertly. This, felt Alec, would prove undoubtedly his point about fake Spirit manifestations and gullible sitters. The Guides however had other intentions. By taking a strong hand they had proved that Alec was a very powerful physical medium. Not that this in any way pleased him. He would rather have left the whole business of mediumship in abeyance, or preferably given it up altogether. But Alec realised that having got this far in his development, he was committed to continuing with the work Spirit had assigned to him.

Thereafter frequently on Sundays we held special circles. Amazing things happened. For instance, a sitter would be tied to Alec by a strong cord which was secured by a variety of complicated knots, police knots, naval knots and those improvised by various circle members, which would be difficult to untie at the best of times, let alone in the dark.

Sometimes we were told to tie a thread of cotton between Alec's thumbs, making hand movements impossible without severing the thread. This we were advised would convince us that the medium had not had any part in the fantastic demonstration which followed. Having been securely tethered, Alec would pass into trance.

Within a moment Alec's pullover, worn under his jacket, would be Spirit-removed, leaving intact knots in the cord and the thread between his thumbs. This was a physical impossibility.

Strangely, whenever it happened to be my turn to be tied to Alec, I would experience a sudden drop of bodily temperature at the precise moment when the pullover was withdrawn from his body. A strange coldness enveloped me as the garment was dematerialised. This indicated to me that a large amount of power was necessary for this demonstration.

Another demonstration was designed to give us an insight into Spirit perception. All members of the circle would place a personal article on a table inside the cabinet prior to the sitting before Alec came into the room. Then at the end of the séance each article was found to have been accurately returned to its rightful owner. Never once was there a mistake. It was a means of proving to us that there was a supernormal intelligence at work.

Of course, there will always be doubting Thomases. I remember on one occasion, a Mr K in Cardiff remarked, 'The medium always sits in his own house and uses a special chair'. What type of chair this was he did not enlarge upon. One of our sitters heard this remark. Feeling that it denigrated Alec's mediumship, relegating it to fraud, he hotly retorted that wherever Alec sat and whatever chair he sat in made no difference to the phenomena. Remarkable phenomena always took place.

"But could he do this in my home?" challenged the sceptic. "I will only believe it if the same manifestations happen at my place," he added with an air of belligerence.

So Alec was obliged to give a séance at the doubter's home. On the appointed day, Mr K had invited a number of his own friends to form a circle. To ensure that we had nothing to do with preparing the séance room, we asked if he would do all the preliminary arrangements. The sceptic readily agreed. Earlier in the day we left with him a small suitcase containing the black curtains for the cabinet, rope for tying up Alec and various toys painted with phosphorescent paint to make them visible in the dark. At the agreed time we arrived to find everything in order and everybody ready to start. We each put a personal article on the table in the cabinet before Alec came into the room. Before going into trance, he was securely tied up by Mr K and his friends; we had nothing to do with this. Of course, the same phenomena happened as before, with the same measure of success. Each member received his or her own article before the end of the circle.

At this point we were disturbed by the sound of children crying. Some of the sitters had placed their sleeping babies in an upstairs bedroom while the séance was in progress. On waking up in a strange room they had proclaimed their fright vociferously. I realised that we could not continue with such a distraction, so I asked Toi-Toi if perhaps he could put the children back to sleep. He said that he would try. In a matter of minutes there was silence from the floor above. All the babies were fast asleep once more!

A piano stood to one side of the room. Mr K seated himself in front of this. Still endeavouring to test the extent of Spirit capabilities, he asked, "Will someone knock on the piano?" Immediately there came a loud thumping sound on the wooden instrument. Not content with this piece of evidence, he pressed for still further proof that Spirit beings were present. "I meant play the piano," he demanded. Immediately unseen fingers were running up and down the keys.

"That's quite amazing!" he exclaimed excitedly, convinced at last, "because the piano is locked!" He needed no further proof after that.

The Spirit people were in a musical frame of mind, it seemed, for now they switched their attention to pitch forks. We could hear one fork being struck which gave off a humming tone in the key of 'A' tuned for the violin which belonged to me. Then another tuning fork was struck which gave off a lower tone, which belonged to a cellist who was also one of the sitters. Both forks had been placed in the cabinet before the circle had begun. Quite extraordinary was the fact that each fork was returned to its correct owner later in the séance, though they were identical to the eye.

Mr K left the séance firmly convinced now of the authenticity of the phenomena he had witnessed and generally gave the impression that a good time had been had by all. I felt our work was not to provide entertainment for casual sitters, nor to be at pains to convince those disbelievers who were so blind they would not see. However, the Guides were tolerant of the difficult and incredulous ones; and to keep Mr K and his friends interested and happy they put on what must have seemed a good show. I realised that all the while they were building up the power, testing and experimenting, trying to assess the degree of development achieved.

We now had an addition to our group of workers, two delightful Spirit children, Sunny and Kitty. They became close associates of our small son, Bradley. Growing up with them as he did, he came to regard them as part of the family. If he was in difficulty at any time, or lost something, he would always ask their assistance. They never failed to come to his aid.

Alec's artistic impression of four of the Spirit children who often visited the Circle. This drawing, done in 1950, shows Toi-Toi, Kitty and Sunny and a young Ginger, which is not how he materialised, (see p116 for his materialised appearance)

Park Grove Spiritualist Church in Cardiff was fortunate at this time in receiving a visit from famous, much-loved medium Helen Hughes. I immediately arranged a personal sitting with her. Helen's Red Indian Guide said he knew that we were sitting for Spirit voices and that we would soon get it. "You will," he added, "also have full-form materialisation before very long." This seemed hard to believe. He explained, "This will be so because Alec is a very powerful physical medium."

Medium ~ Helen Hughes

When Helen came out of trance she heard clairaudiently about the production of fully materialised forms through Alec's mediumship. She smiled and said: "If my Guide has said this then it will come to pass. Materialisation is to be Alec's forte. There is great work for you both. One of these days, I shall be asking you and your husband for a sitting!" Ten years later her prophesy was confirmed. Helen sat in one of our materialisation circles.

At about this time, my niece, Phyllis, came to live with us. She asked to join our Tuesday development circle. We were delighted to have her. She was a lovable and affectionate girl, with a sweet musical singing voice, which was a great asset to our circle. It was fortunate that Phyllis came to us when she did, for quite unexpectedly we suffered a setback in our circle. Betty and Murdo had to leave Cardiff for personal reasons. Had it not been for Phyllis joining the circle we would not have been able to continue with the voice sittings. Phyllis and I decided to continue with just the two of us giving what power we could to Alec in trance. We held the circles in our own home now, upstairs in my bedroom. That anything would come of this seemed a forlorn hope. But one night, as Phyllis and I were singing, the trumpet left the cabinet and to our amazement my father spoke. He called my name through the trumpet. It was only a whisper, but it was my father's voice; of that I was absolutely certain. Again I remembered his promise to be the first to greet me from the Other Side, but I had hardly dared hope to hear his voice again.

On another night I was singing 'The Indian Love Call'. When I sang the closing words of the verse 'You belong to me', a deep baritone voice from the cabinet completed the song, singing beautifully, 'I belong to you'. Later I learned my beloved White Wing was responsible. There was no doubt now that the Spirit communicators were beginning to speak and sing quite independently of the medium. Though it was many months before they could converse with us at any length, when they did their voices were strong, recognisable and quite distinguishable from Alec's. It had taken two years of dedicated and diligent sitting to achieve this. Very much encouraged and thrilled by our progress, Phyllis and I continued the sittings each week when I came home from the theatre and continued to get good results.

During the winter months it was bitterly cold. As we held our circles in the bedroom, Phyllis and I sat up in bed with the eider-down over us. Poor Alec meanwhile languished in trance in a corner of the room behind a curtain hung to form a cabinet. He always insisted that he be tied up, as he feared that he might be accused of manipulating the trumpet himself. This was ridiculous because there were often as many as three trumpets in operation at the same time. There were also a luminous plaque and a cross which we always placed on the floor beside the cones before commencing the circle. These floated round the room, gently touching the sitter whom the Spirits wished to address.

One night, feeling sorry for Alec, we decided not to bind him in the usual manner. We left him sitting relaxed and comfortable in his chair behind the curtain. No sooner had we started than the two Spirit children, Sunny and Toi-Toi, came through saying that they wanted to tie up Alec.

They took the case containing the ropes, etc from under the wardrobe and set about the job with determination. We could hear the rope going back and forth as the binding-up was in progress.

Once the job was completed the séance went into full swing.

We had a real party that night! We were sprayed with perfume. Pictures were removed from the walls and placed on the bed. All my clothes were taken out of the wardrobe and gleefully laid on the bed by the children. They were simply full of pranks! Then there was silence. I strained my ears to hear what was going on and sensed, rather than heard, a heavy object being moved. Absorbed by my concentration, I was startled when a loud knocking occurred near my bed. It was made by a drawer handle in a tall chest which always stood far across the room. It was a heavy piece of furniture, impossible for one person to lift. Yet, here it was standing right next to my bed, quite ten feet from its original position. What was even more extraordinary was the fact that I had left a full glass of water balancing precariously on the edge of the chest. The glass was in the same position when we put on the lights to inspect the room and not one drop of liquid had been spilled! We then drew aside the curtain to inspect Alec. Poor man! There he sat, trussed up like a turkey. The Spirit children had put all the knots at his back where he could not possibly reach them. Sunny and Toi said afterwards that they had done this to show us 'how he should really be tied up'. It took us 20 minutes to release Alec.

White Wing now said that the time had come for him to keep his promise of sharing the voice with our other sitters. We should sit for this phenomenon on Sundays and make another day for healing. So on Thursdays we had the healing circle and Sundays the physical circle. This arrangement was apparently satisfactory, for both the healing and the voice developed rapidly. We witnessed some remarkable Spirit manifestations.

Despite being told of the wonderful things that happened through his mediumship, Alec remained difficult. He was not at all anxious to continue séances. I felt that it was not quite fair to make him do something he so obviously disliked doing. We talked it over and decided to discontinue the physical sittings and concentrate on his healing. This was something he really enjoyed doing.

Life put a strain on Alec at this time. He had great responsibilities at work, being in charge of a large number of men and working 12 hours a day. The only time we had together was on a Sunday and much of that was taken up by the circle.

White Wing, aware of Alec's feelings and anxious to restore his interest, asked me to place a pad and pencil near my bed. He said that when an opportunity arose he would control Alec. I was to write down what he said and show it to him. I did this and some nights later there were three loud knocks on the headboard of our bed. I knew it was White Wing. He tapped out that Connie, Alec's sister, wanted to speak. Immediately afterwards, tapping could be heard coming from underneath the spring mattress.

Tapping out her message, Connie said that we must not give up the circle. So much depended on keeping Alec to his mediumship. I replied; "Con, dear, nothing I say seems to do any good." Then I suddenly had an idea as I remembered the little pad and pencil I had placed on a chair at the foot of the bed.

"If only you could write on that pad, Con," I said, "I'm sure that would convince Alec." She said that she would try. We slept in a double bed and Alec had slipped from sleep into the trance state. He had one arm under my body, so I took hold of his other hand to link up with him for power.

Presently, I heard the pencil being picked up and tapped on the chair. Then it could be heard scraping on the paper as it wrote. There came the sound of the sheet being torn from the pad and I could sense a presence floating, it seemed, towards the bed. I felt breathless with excitement.

At this point Alec awoke and I joyfully exclaimed; "Alec! Con has been here!" and I put on the light. To my surprise, the piece of paper was lying on Alec's chest. I grabbed it and read; "Be good, Al ... Con." I was overjoyed, but my pleasure was soon dampened as Alec demanded, "How do I know that you didn't write it?"

At this point there commenced a loud rapping on the bedside lamp and I said: "It's your sister! She's here, Al! Now do you believe? Speak to her and ask her yourself," I urged him.

I quickly put out the light as I knew that it would be easier for Connie to rap in the dark as light always has a detrimental effect on ectoplasm and therefore diminishes power. Sure enough, the knocks were louder. I saw the dim outline of Connie's figure standing by the bed.

"Look," I whispered. "Oh, Alec, she's there. Can you see her?"

Obviously moved by renewed contact with his dead, dearly-loved sister, Alec gazed intently at the faint apparition. Then he said hoarsely, "If it is you, Con, touch me."

Another intolerable silence followed while I waited. Then Alec let out a joyful gasp; "It is Con! She has her hands on my head!" I could have cried out in relief. My gratitude to Connie knew no bounds. After that wonderful experience, which convinced him that his dear sister was alive and near him, Alec was only too happy to sit again and so the work went on.

One weekend in 1938, Mary Hewitt, my medium friend who had gone to live in London, came on a visit to Cardiff with her husband. She was still anxious to convince him about Spiritualism, so managed to persuade him to attend one of our physical circles on the Sunday. Mary came alone earlier in the afternoon to help us prepare the room. We were collecting some of my son's toys and Mary had in her hands a pair of Bradley's boxing gloves, saying, "I hope they give my husband a good biff on the nose with these, because he is so stubborn!"

Alec came home, the sitters soon arrived, the last being Alec Hewitt, Mary's husband. He hung his big overcoat on the hall stand and came into the room. We locked the door and placed a table against it to reassure Alec Hewitt that nobody could enter. As soon as the light was extinguished, something was dropped into Mr Hewitt's lap. While the séance was in progress he suddenly received a punch on the head with one of Bradley's boxing gloves.

Little Toi-Toi explained the reason for this action in his piping oriental voice: "Mary say do, so Toi-Toi do." Mr Hewitt was so startled that he roared with laughter.

When the lights were eventually put on, he found his keys in his lap. He was puzzled because he had left them in the pocket of his overcoat in the hall. Yet, there they were, transported through the locked and barricaded door. This left him with much to think about and no physical explanation to account for it.

Chapter Six

War and the Power of Spirit

❖ *Spirit communication becomes an even greater need* ❖ *Alec is removed from the circle room* ❖ *We meet the Spirits Alfré and Raf* ❖ *Alfré proves to be a remarkable seer* ❖ *We hear how Spirit friends protect us*

In August 1939, political conditions in the world had so deteriorated that it seemed that war with Germany would be inevitable. Appalled that such a catastrophe could again overtake the world, I asked the Spirit Guides about it at the very next circle.

"There won't be a war, will there?" I asked, hoping to be reassured; but Jolkim's reply left us all aghast. "Why should you think not, sister?" he said. "It is clearly apparent to all, of course there will be war and," he added gravely, "it will be a long and bloody one!"

There were sighs of dismay from our side. "I just can't believe it! Not again," I said and added, as an afterthought, "Oh dear! we've got no blackout curtains, nor any spare supplies in our store cupboard."

"Well then," Jolkim continued, "I suggest you go out first thing in the morning and acquire these things, for you are most surely going to need them."

How prophetic were his words, for war was declared on 3rd September 1939. In the dark years that ensued the world was more than ever in need of Spirit help and guidance. Spirit rescue work was stepped up as so many souls were precipitated into the Other World. Consolation and comfort became the dire need of those who were bereft and left behind to mourn their dead. Many of the distraught became firm believers in Spirit communication after contact with their lost loved ones. Their joy was our reward.

On Christmas night 1939 Phyllis and I suggested to Alec that we should have a circle, thinking it would be nice to exchange greetings with our many friends in the Spirit World. To our surprise Alec readily agreed. He usually had to be coaxed to give any extra circles. Being an unwilling convert to Spiritualism, he was never very keen on spending long periods in trance. Before he could change his mind, we hastily hung a curtain across the room to form a cabinet. Alec was placed inside and at his request we tied his hands and feet.

My mother had already gone to bed. The fire was very low and we screened its glow as best we could. In our haste, we had not darkened the windows completely and being a moonlit night the soft beams filtered into the room, so that we were able to see much better than usual.

No sooner had Alec lapsed into trance than Ewonga said: "We are going to try an experiment tonight. Please tie string around each of the knots in the cord binding the medium. Make them extra secure! We ask you to do this so that the medium, when he wakes, will have no doubts that what has taken place was indeed the work of Spirit and no one else. It will be a feat that no human entity could perform!" Then, with a note of amusement in his voice, he added: "Also, have your long coat ready, Louie-One! Please secure the knots now."

Puzzled, we set to work on the cord, making a very good job of it. This done, Phyllis and I took our places and began to sing carols. After a moment, Jolkim joined in with his beautiful deep musical voice; then the Spirit children added their voices in beautiful harmony; then two voices could be heard singing together. We had a lovely Christmas party. Jolkim and the children entertained us throughout the evening, making amusing remarks and keeping us in fits of laughter.

The moon later became very bright. By its light the trumpets were clearly visible in their entirety, not just the luminous areas painted round their edges. The curtains forming the cabinet did not quite reach to the floor. I saw beneath them a white, semi-transparent substance billowing along the floor. My stomach constricted with excitement as I realised that a materialisation was probably forming. Phyllis was sitting very still. She had also seen this substance and we waited expectantly for developments.

After a while, two Spirit arms projected from the cabinet holding a shoe in each hand. One shoe was placed on my lap and the other on Phyllis'. Next, Alec's belt and jumper were laid alongside the shoes. As this was taking place, I again experienced a feeling of extreme cold. My body temperature dropped to the point where I was shivering.

Then a deep droning hum could be heard from the cabinet and Adoula announced himself. He was producing the same powerful, resonant vibration that he emitted at the healing circles and I felt much relieved. Suddenly, we heard Alec, whom we had bound with cords, rise from his chair. The curtains parted and he stepped out of the cabinet, to be greeted by our shocked exclamations. He was now also minus his trousers. I promptly jumped up and protectively draped my winter coat around him, as it was cold in the room now that the fire was only embers. He came out of trance and glancing down at his state of undress, no trousers, belt, shoes or jersey, he wrinkled his brow in puzzlement and exclaimed: "What's going on around here? What's happened?"

We quickly switched on the light and drew aside the cabinet curtains. Phyllis, Alec and I stood in shocked silence, unable to believe our eyes. There, sitting in the chair just as if Alec's body was still inside them, with the ropes still securely binding them, were his trousers!

"Impossible!" said Alec. He glanced down at his lower torso to confirm that he really was without his trousers. "It's amazing!" he added, "I can't understand it."

It was the Spirit Guides demonstration of passing matter through matter, by the process of dematerialisation and subsequent rematerialisation. It served to prepare us for many such extraordinary happenings which followed later as Alec's physical mediumship developed.

In 1940 we heard the dreadful news of the fall of Dunkirk and were saddened by the tragic loss of so many young lives. Sitting with us at that time was a Mrs P who had two daughters whose husbands, Jack and Arthur, were in the Military Police and were serving with units engaged in the relief of Dunkirk. One of the daughters sat with us at the time of the fall of Dunkirk and she begged the Guides to take care of 'the boys'.

At the following voice circle we were sitting as usual linked by our hands, with the sitter at the end of each row sitting close to and touching the wall, so that nobody could possibly pass. We were all singing lustily to keep up the power, when we were told, unexpectedly, not to sing but to keep very quiet. This was most unusual. Singing was considered to be absolutely necessary to raise the vibrations and maintain them. However, we did as we had been instructed and waited in silence for what seemed a very long time for something to happen.

I began to experience a peculiar sensation; one that I could not explain or understand. I felt a kind of strange emptiness. I remarked to the others that I had a feeling that none of the Guides was present. Then an unfamiliar voice spoke from the cabinet offering a most unusual suggestion, "Wouldn't you all like to go downstairs and have a cup of tea?"

I was flabbergasted! What a ridiculous remark to make. Then there came a knocking at the door, which was always kept locked during a séance. And Alec's muffled voice filtered through from the other side of the door, coming from the direction of the landing outside, saying, "Haven't you finished yet?"

There was a prickling at the nape of my neck and my hair felt as if it were standing on end. Alec, I knew, should be inside the cabinet, securely bound to his chair, in the room, not outside, with the door bolted from the inside. How could he possibly have got out. I was really frightened. I feared that my husband would come to harm if he could be moved about by Spirits like this.

I sprang to the door and opened it. There stood Alec, well and in good spirits and fully conscious. We all plied him with the questions; Why? How? When? To everything he could only answer that, in some inexplicable way, he had found himself out on the landing, with Chang beside him. He could offer no explanation as to how he got there. It was 1.00am in the morning and so quiet that any one of us would have heard the slightest movement had there been any.

I was troubled about this incident. Chang, perceiving this, spoke to me later after the circle, when Alec and I were alone in our bedroom. Taking Alec in trance, he spoke through him saying: "You asked us to look after the boys, Jack and Arthur. They were in grave danger tonight. You will find out that what I am saying is true. They had need of us and we were being kept back from assisting them by your thoughts and desires for the circle. So we took the medium out of the room, knowing that you would then close the circle and leave us free to aid them."

He then administered a gentle reprimand. "You must have confidence in us and not worry about the medium, for we have promised to look after him." His explanation and his gentle words promising to care for Alec at all times, did much to relieve my fears.

When Jack and Arthur returned from Dunkirk, we asked them if it was true that they had been in grave danger on the night in question. One of them, Arthur, then referred to his diary to confirm the date. He had written of that fateful night: "It's Hell on the beach tonight! Jerry is flying low and dropping heavy stuff. I wonder if we will get out of this alive? I wonder if we will ever see our dear ones again?"

So Chang, it had been proved, had been fully aware of their dire predicament that night as they fought to survive on the beaches of Dunkirk; and once more I marvelled at Spirit.

A rather unusual Guide made his presence known to our circle about this time. His name was Alfré. I say he was unusual as he came solely to give clairvoyance from the Spirit side. Alfré always worked with a handkerchief, using it in the same manner as a physical clairvoyant might use a crystal ball. He would 'see' in the folds of the handkerchief the people, places and events about which he would give information and predictions.

The procedure was as follows. We would sit around a table, with a red light, and Alec would be entranced by Alfré. The person requiring clairvoyance would hold a large white handkerchief between the palms of his two hands for a few moments before handing it to Alfré, who then cast it on the table before him and gazed at it for a brief period. According to the lie of the material he would see pictures of forthcoming or past events. From these he would proceed to give forth his clairvoyant information. At times he would point out to us the pictures shown in the handkerchief and we often saw them for ourselves.

I remember a sitting given by Alfré to young Grahame Watkins who had been a member of our circle for a long time. Grahame had joined the Fire Service for the duration of the war, but was disappointed that he had been posted away from his home town of Cardiff to Newport, which was some distance away. He was particularly anxious about his wife, Marjorie and their baby, who had been left alone in a large house and who often had to spend nights sheltering under the stairs during many air raids. Grahame had a sitting with Alfré in 1942 and he asked if there was any hope of his getting a house in Newport where he could bring his wife and baby to be near him.

Alfré cast his handkerchief upon the table before him. After observing it closely for a time, he slowly shook his head and said, "Your wife will not be joining you in Newport, but you will very soon be returning to Cardiff." Grahame protested that this was impossible as there was definitely no post for him in that town. But Alfré remained adamant.

"Grahame, I say to you that a post is being made for you. And here," he pointed to the handkerchief, "is the house in which you will work." Grahame peered into the folds of the handkerchief as it lay on the table and to his surprise he distinctly saw a big house with a flight of steps leading up to it.

"It is in the country," explained Alfré, "just outside Cardiff." Still Grahame remained incredulous as it seemed so highly improbable that he would be able to return to Cardiff. Politely, he murmured his thanks to Alfré and went away disappointed. Two weeks later, however, he revised his opinion about Alfré's prediction.

Marjorie was startled, one day, to see a car drive up to her house and her husband pile out with all his luggage and books. He rushed up to her excitedly gasping out his story of a transfer from Newport to Cardiff, where a post had unexpectedly been made for him, just as Alfré had prophesied and his headquarters were to be in a large mansion just outside Cardiff, in country surroundings, which had been requisitioned for the purpose. To his amazement, when they went together to inspect the place, he saw that leading from the driveway up to the front door was a flight of elegant steps! The accuracy of the information contained in the handkerchief was uncanny to say the least.

One Sunday we had a visit from a friend who wished for a sitting with Alfré. She said she preferred to sit alone, so I retired to the dining room. It had always been necessary for me to be present as it added more power to the sitting. Before I had time to occupy myself in some other activity, the lady came out saying sadly that Alfré regretted that he had nothing for her; but he had sent a request that 'Louie should come to him instead'. I was surprised and not a little curious as I had never asked for a sitting for myself.

I went in to him and he said, "You hold handkerchief." This I did and after holding it for a few moments I handed it back to him. He threw it down upon the table, gazed at it and then turned to me and said: "Louie, you are going to have your heart's desire in .. and I see here a three. It is not three months, or three weeks." He hesitated.

"Is it concerned with material or Spiritual things?" I asked.

"It is material this time. Look," he said, pointing to the hand-kerchief, "here is your island of desire and here," his finger moved to indicate three elevations in the folds of the handkerchief, "are the three boulders to get there."

I was fascinated. The picture was so clear; I did not pretend to understand it, but I was prepared to wait three weeks, three months or three years if necessary, because I believed in my heart that if Alfré said it would come to pass, then it most certainly would.

Three days later, the following Wednesday to be precise, I was playing during the lunch hour at the Continental Restaurant when our cellist whispered excitedly to me: "Look, Louie! Over there! It's Mai Jones! You know, the brilliant pianist-arranger and producer for the BBC."

"Where?" I asked and she indicated a woman sitting with a group of people. "She's been staring over here for some time. I think she is interested in us."

I glanced perfunctorily at the group. Thinking that the party could not be particularly interested in us, I continued with my playing. Presently, I saw this lady rise from her chair. Leaving her table she approached the manageress and had a few words with her, then she returned to her table, but still continued to take an interest in our orchestra.

It was only after my lunch break that I learned from the manageress that Miss Jones had enquired if I was indeed Louie Bradley, the name I always used professionally. Having the answer in the affirmative she had requested the manageress to ask me to phone her as soon as possible.

Intrigued, I did so and I was thrilled when she asked me to audition for her that evening. She would like to include me in some of her programmes. The audition proved to be successful and I was engaged for a great many of Mai Jones' shows with the BBC.

So, once again, Alfré had been proved right! I had indeed attained what might be termed my heart's desire as far as my music was concerned and in only three days from his pronouncement.

Arthur and Jack, the two young men who had such a narrow escape on the beaches of Dunkirk and who managed to survive as a result of the intervention of our Spirit Guides, returned to their units after a brief recuperative leave to find that they had been posted to Cairo.

Jack's wife, Eileen, had a sitting with Alfré, in an effort to get further information. Again the handkerchief was cast upon the table and Alfré consulted its folds and patterns. After a few moments he shook his head and said sombrely: "I am sorry to have to tell you that there is a dark cloud over both Jack and Arthur. You will have disturbing news." Seeing the distress on Eileen's face, he quickly tried to reassure her. "But, do not worry," said Alfré, "all will be well with them eventually." Eileen made a mental note of the pause before his final word, but before she could comment on it, Alfré was again peering closely into the folds of the white material. "I can see these men with tanks," he observed.

"But that's impossible," said Eileen. "Both boys now work in an office in Cairo." Alfré shrugged, but did not comment. A little time elapsed after this sitting. Then one day, we were confronted by a very distraught Eileen. She had just received word that both Jack and Arthur were reported missing while on service. She immediately rushed to enlist Alfré's help.

The sitting gave her a measure of comfort. Alfré told her that they were not dead, but were prisoners of war in Italy. This was later confirmed by the War Office; they were in a POW camp somewhere outside Rome.

Months passed and all poor Eileen could do was wait and hope. Then, unexpectedly, Italy had a change of loyalties and decided to become our ally. Alfré was again consulted and he said that Arthur, the more impetuous of the two, would make a bid to escape from the prison camp, but that Jack would play it safe and remain in Italy until he was released by the British.

All this information was confirmed by the young men when they returned home to the UK. They told us that they had, in fact, been sent to serve with a tank corps in Egypt, where they had been ambushed and captured by the Italians.

The infallibility of Alfré's clairvoyance never ceased to amaze me and many others besides. He even predicted the massive air raid inflicted on Cardiff on 18th May 1943 as a reprisal by the Germans for the damage caused by the Dam Busters on their epic dam-destroying mission.

Alfré was unique. He would have played a very important part in Alec's mediumship had he been permitted to do so. It was a great pity that my husband was not anxious to co-operate more closely with him.

Phyllis had become very friendly with a charming young man named Trevor Cowley and she asked if he might sit with us one Sunday as he was interested in the subject of Spiritualism. I discussed it with Alec and as Phyllis vouched for him, we agreed to let him join us the following Sunday. At the circle, he had a piece of very convincing evidence of life after death when the trumpet moved over to him and a voice came through it saying: "I am your father, Jim. You may not remember me as you were so young when I left." Trevor was only three years old when his father, Jim, had been killed in the first world war. The voice continued, "But I have been looking after you, my son." Then, probably in order to give irrefutable proof of his identity, he spoke of material things.

"Ask your mother," he said, "why she removed the picture I always liked from the living room and placed it in the attic." Not comprehending, Trevor asked, "Which picture is that?" To which his father replied, "The one of the oak tree with a seat around it." Trevor knew this picture and promised to speak to his mother about it. On hearing of the conversation he had had with his father, she readily agreed to replace it in its former position in the living room.

The war was escalating and Trevor now found himself serving with the Air Force, but he still sat with us whenever he could.

During the period 1940 to 41 casualties among fighter and bomber pilots were high and it was at this time that the Spirit of a deceased RAF Squadron Leader, who became affectionately known to us as 'Raf', attached himself to our circle. He told us that he had been shot down earlier in the war over France. He said he was glad he had had his ticket, as he put it, because he was greatly disturbed by the fact that he was not always able to accurately hit his target. As a result, many innocent people had suffered. This had worried him very much and he felt that he had to come back to help others. In so doing he felt that he would, in some measure, be making amends for the havoc he had caused through the errors of his judgment.

He teamed up with Jolkim. The two of them did commendable work together, helping the boys who had lost their lives to come through with their messages to their families. These two Spirit lads often vied with one another in demonstrating their superior Spirit knowledge, Raf speaking through one trumpet, with Jolkim answering through another elsewhere in the room. One evening Jolkim boasted that he was as good as Raf at making prophesies, to which Raf responded laughingly, "Give us a demonstration then!" Jolkim then said to me, "Sister, when the snow is heavy on the ground, you will get your heart's desire." Then he chuckled, "But

Boy! What SNOW!" My curiosity was aroused. What I really wanted more than anything was a car.

Imagine my delight when the following Saturday after the matinée I found Alec and Trevor waiting for me at the stage door in a neat little car. As he opened the door, Alec proudly announced: "Lou, girl, it's ours. Trevor got it for me really cheap. Fantastic isn't it?" I clambered aboard feeling like a queen. "Our own car," I said. "Unbelievable." As we started for home it began to snow heavily. I suddenly recalled Jolkim's words, 'Your heart's desire and in what snow'. So heavy was the fall that for six weeks we carried a shovel with us everywhere to dig ourselves out when we got snowbound. Jolkim had certainly excelled himself as a prophet.

Raf took a delight in making prophesies, which sometimes scared me stiff. He kept us well informed about the progress of the war at the various fronts and his information was always proved correct later, when the facts would be blazoned across the newspapers. One evening we were all feeling very despondent as the war news had not been too good when Raf came along and said: "Cheer up, folks. Why so glum? There's good news on the way. The Germans are on the run. We'll drive them out of Africa, Sicily, Italy. You mark my words."

A week later came the news that Montgomery had won the epic battle of El Alamein, which proved to be the turning point of the war for the Allies.

Trevor had a surprise in store for him when he sat with us again while he was home on leave. The Guide, Alfré, came to speak to him through the trumpet. "You are going abroad." he predicted. "That's not likely," smiled Trevor, "My job is more important here, working on aeroplanes."

"Nevertheless," continued Alfré, "I can see you in a hot country and you are sitting on an elephant." Trevor did not argue, but dismissed the information as being highly improbable, not knowing that one should never take Spirit precognition lightly, especially Alfré's.

On another occasion, Trevor's Spirit father spoke to us when

Trevor himself was not present. He told us that he had been at great pains to protect his son who had very nearly come over to Spirit as a result of an accident. He begged us to warn Trevor to be more careful in future, which we promised to do

We were puzzled by this piece of information because we had no news of Trevor being involved in any accident and he had certainly not mentioned any mishap in any of his letters. When he came home on leave we told him of our conversation with his father. He admitted that he had a miraculous escape when he was struck by a large aeroplane propeller, which had left him unconscious for many hours. He explained that he had not written and told us about this for fear of causing us anxiety.

When he returned to camp he was informed that he would be going abroad. He had been issued with warm clothing, so he thought that it was to a cold country he was being sent; probably Canada, he conjectured.

I recalled Alfré's words earlier about his being sent to a hot country and of being seated on the back of an elephant. I said to Phyllis: "No. I'm sure it is not to Canada they are sending him. When has Alfré ever been wrong?" Phyllis waited months for word from Trevor clarifying his new posting. Then the long awaited letter arrived. She tore it open and read its contents avidly. Then she smiled and handed the letter to me. Trevor's squadron had been posted to Burma. He wrote that on their arrival they had seen some elephants standing nearby. Just for devilment, they had all climbed upon their backs and had a ride. So Alfré's prophesy had come true after all and Trevor remained in Burma for the duration of hostilities.

Chapter Seven

Materialisation Mediumship Commences

❖ *Alec develops materialisation and we at last see our Guides* ❖ *A practical aspect of Spirit guidance* ❖ *Spirits David, Grey Rock and Ginger make themselves known*

1940 was a year that stood out as a milestone on the path of Alec's mediumship. It was then that it took a great leap forward and never looked back, going from strength to strength.

White Wing had kept saying, "One day, Faithful, White Wing will walk, talk and mingle with you." So far, nothing had come of this promise. I was surprised, because everything he prophesied had always occurred. I assumed we would have to find a materialisation medium and have a sitting to make this possible.

I had heard that Helen Duncan the famous materialisation medium was visiting Barry, a small town only 12 miles from Cardiff. It would be only a simple matter for us to go there. At our circle, I put the question to the other sitters and asked if they would be agreeable. Before they could answer, Rohan spoke: "There is no need to ask this lady. You have the power in your own circle. But you must sit for materialisation on another night other than your usual Sunday circle. And I say to you, be patient!"

We were delighted at this news, but a problem presented itself. As I was working at the theatre every evening, the circle to develop materialisation would have to be held very late at night after I got home. Bearing this in mind we chose sitters who lived near us who were prepared to sacrifice their sleep. We decided upon Tuesdays for the new sitting. I explained that it would probably be a lengthy business. It had taken two years to obtain voice phenomena, I pointed out and would probably take seven for this. But they were undeterred.

The following Tuesday we assembled at 11pm. There were six of us, all rather doubtful that anything would happen. The circle commenced in total darkness. To our amazement a luminous ball began forming in the centre of the cabinet curtain. A face could be seen within this luminous mass, not very clearly, but still a face. While we pondered who this was, the head began to turn. The feathered headdress of a Red Indian could be discerned. I knew then who it was. "White Wing!" I cried out in joy. At the sound of my voice the head seemed to come alive. Slowly he turned to face me. His eyes gave me a long and searching look.

"White Wing, it is you, isn't it?" I said quite overcome. Slowly he nodded, then faded from sight. I was overwhelmed. Too full for words, I felt tears stinging my eyes. I had seen my beloved White Wing at last.

Another ball of luminous ectoplasm formed at the top of the cabinet curtains and another face could be seen. I knew from the oriental features that it could only be Chang. Then there was another face at my feet. This time it was Raf. We could see his laughing eyes and strong white teeth and he was wearing his flying cap.

"Oh, Raf," I exclaimed. "How lovely to see you!" and smiling, he too faded away. It was all so breathtaking, so marvellous to me, that I was up in the clouds for days.

I realised that it only remained for us to continue developing until we had full forms. White Wing told us to put a small red globe in the light socket, which we did. Thereafter we sat in the dull red light which enabled us to see better what transpired.

It was interesting to watch the formation of these wonderful Spirit phenomena. At first, only heads appeared, but we recognised many faces easily. Then, after some time, came full forms. What an achievement that was. Only now, in producing this, the faces became less clear, rather like those on a film that is out of focus. The curtains would part and the fully materialised form of the Spirit would stand before us.

One night, only Red Indians materialised. Many different types came, but each was quite distinguishable from the other as regards features, heights and individual characteristics. Yet, with all this, I noticed that the forms did not speak.

As the weeks went by the forms grew stronger and stronger. One night, a beautiful girl stepped out of the cabinet, her figure clearly visible through her gossamer robes of ectoplasm. She leaned over to us and whispered, 'Con', Just the one word, but she had spoken! I could hardly believe it. She was the first to be able to speak, even though only one word, while maintaining her materialised form. I was so excited I could hardly wait to tell Alec about his sister's return.

Afterwards many came who managed to speak a few words as the power grew stronger. Mostly these were Guides. They, it seemed, were better able to handle this power than loved ones, who often suffered from an excess of emotion. This detracted from their concentration. It was exhilarating to meet the Guides face to face and to feel the touch of their hands.

There came an evening of exquisite pleasure. It was the night when Rohan at last chose to show himself to us after years of communicating only through his beautiful voice. He stepped from the cabinet fully formed, draped in a flowing white robe of ectoplasm. Rohan was of Arabic origin in his earth existence and his robe and headgear were draped to resemble his national dress. Of medium height and slender; his thin face displayed remarkably refined features. A close-cropped black, curly beard covered his chin. This tapered to meet his hair on either side of the face at the temples. Rohan's upper lip was covered by a black moustache which was short and in no way concealed his lips.

There were two characteristics which made an indelible impression on my mind and through the years were always remarked upon by sitters and psychic investigators. These were firstly his eyes. They were of the darkest brown, almost black and they stared into one's own disconcertingly as if looking deep into one's own soul, but always with love and gentle understanding. Secondly, his hands were always noticed. They were extraordinarily beautiful, narrow and delicately shaped, with long slender tapering fingers. I discovered this as he took my own hands in his, as a welcome.

These two bodily characteristics were totally different from those of the medium. Alec's eyes were deep blue. His hands were broad and capable, with square spatulate fingers. There was absolutely no physical resemblance between my husband and Rohan, a point which gave credence to the whole concept of materialisation to those who were doubters and others who were on the border of belief professing to have an open mind.

Rohan was now in charge of the circle proceedings. As result of this we coined a name for him, affectionately referring to him as 'The Master of Ceremonies'. He was a lovely person, always so calm and gentle. When he came he radiated peace. One could feel the love and harmony he brought at all times.

When he first materialised we had been singing the song, 'If I Might Only Come To You'. He remarked on it, saying that he liked it. So thereafter we always sang it especially for him.

Having once obtained materialisation, we knew that it had come to stay. I began to understand about the great work it was said we had to perform. I could envisage the enormous possibilities this type of mediumship would open up for helping the bereaved.

Seeing for some is believing; and what came through now from Spirit would be far more convincing than anything we had hitherto had to offer the lost and lonely.

Each year, as the old year ended and the new began, we would spend this time with our Spirit friends in the sanctuary. In the early hours of the morning of 1st January 1941 we had come downstairs to celebrate, when White Wing unexpectedly took control of Alec. He spoke to us, with a serious note in his voice. "There have been many dangers in the past year," he said, "and I have come to warn you of a greater danger at hand, to prepare you for this. But have no fear. Know that we, on this side, will do all in our power to protect you. Only trust in the Great White Spirit."

Then glancing at my young nephew, John, sitting in the circle and looking decidedly solemn, White Wing asked, "John, why you look so troubled?" John replied that he had been called up.

Though he had hoped to go into the Air Force, he had been drafted to the Army. White Wing hastened to reassure him, "John, White Wing say you go into the Air Force and all will be well with you." Later, John was surprised when this did actually come to pass. And while he was in the Air Force he was made constantly aware of the great protection he received and continued to receive throughout the war.

For my part, I was very concerned about White Wing's prophesy portending great danger near at hand for us. Knowing, as I did, that whatever he said had always proved to be correct, I found I could not keep my mind off it. When I went to the theatre that night I told my colleagues about this Spirit message and felt put out at the obvious scepticism they showed. Admittedly, if it was something to do with the war, Cardiff had not had a really bad air raid up to that point. There had been only nuisance raids by German planes passing over en route to Coventry and other parts of Britain. We had not even had a single alert that night, so their attitude was not surprising.

On 2nd January 1941, however, we were in for a shock. We had just finished the overture for the play at our theatre when the Air Raid Siren wailed out its fearful warning, a sound to chill the heart of the hardiest! Our cellist ran to the stage door and looked out to see what was happening. He came back very shaken, to report that Leckwith Woods were burning, also the Paper Mills and that a vast quantity of incendiary bombs were being dropped in all directions. Fire fighters, he said, were battling to extinguish the flames outside the theatre. Amid all this havoc not one incendiary had dropped on us. Being a very old theatre it would have needed only a couple of these bombs to set it alight and turn it into a blazing inferno.

The management and cast decided to carry on with the play, but it was a nerve-wracking performance. Every time a bomb exploded the building shook terrifyingly, causing the scenery to hang precariously askew on its ropes. It needed a great deal of courage and self-control to keep the show going, but it seemed the best thing to do in the circumstances.

When we eventually went outside the sight that greeted us was one of complete chaos. The Germans had really strafed the town with incendiary bombs. All the shops and every building round about us, with the exception of our theatre, appeared to be blazing furiously and the city was cordoned off. My thoughts went immediately to Alec and home. I had told him that in the event of a raid such as this he was never to go out and look for me, but was to stay with our son and my mother. I only hoped and prayed that he was doing that.

Sporadic blitzes continued throughout the night and most people deemed it wiser to remain in the comparative safety of the Air Raid shelters for the night. I felt that I simply had to go home. I knew that the family would be frantically worried about me. I joined Peggy, my pianist friend and her husband and together we started to walk home.

The roads were like battlefields, a shambles of rubble and debris. Plate glass was strewn about and buildings were burning everywhere. The number and intensity of the fires was frightening. There was much shouting and activity as these were being dealt with frantically by fire-fighting units. Through all this the three of us picked our way gingerly making for home. An Air Raid Warden shouted to us to 'Get under cover!' but we disregarded his admonition and continued on our way. All the while I kept singing, 'There Are Angels Hovering Around'. Peggy retorted sourly, "Don't forget the Jerries are up there, too!" But White Wing's promise of protection was ringing in my ears and I felt secure in my trust that Angels were hovering between the Germans and us and that no harm would befall us.

When we eventually reached home it was only to find that the German Luftwaffe had been at their diabolical work even there and Whitchurch was ablaze from incendiaries. Neighbours had taken refuge in our house, and I found them with Alec and Mother nearly frantic with worry about my safety, for they could see the thick pall of smoke from the fires as Cardiff burned. I received a joyful, if tearful, welcome home.

We were just preparing for bed, thoroughly worn out, when there was a knock at the door. We opened it to find two of our sitters from the circle dejectedly clutching blankets and requesting accommodation for the night. It appeared that Whitchurch had been evacuated. They had a narrow escape when a land mine had been dropped quite close to their house. Its parachute had become entangled in the branch of a nearby tree and there it hung, suspended precariously a few feet from the ground where, had it fallen and made contact, it would have spread death and destruction. We all appreciated the protection we had received from Spirit.

Our theatre had closed because of an unexploded bomb embedded in the pavement outside. So, I was asked to play at the New Continental Restaurant where I remained for the next three and a half years. This restaurant closed at 6pm each night. Finishing early made it possible for us to give voice circles for Park Grove Spiritualist Church in aid of the Building Fund. We continued with these for some time, as well as with our Sunday circle. Some remarkable evidence was received confirming life after death as Spirit servicemen were reunited with their loved ones. The joy on the faces of those at our circles was our treasured reward.

Apart from the normal run of Spirit activities, such as rescue work, healing and helping newly arrived souls to make contact with their families and friends and so forth, the Guides frequently put themselves out to assist us in a material way. For instance, I remember there was an occasion when having washed all my net curtains I found, to my dismay, that they had just disintegrated in the water. I was upset because being war time I knew that it would be impossible to replace them.

That night we had a circle and Chang gave an unusual demonstration. The curtains of the cabinet were suddenly drawn apart to reveal Alec clearly visible sitting in his chair in deep trance. Beside him stood Chang. The Chinese Guide then proceeded to draw a vast amount of ectoplasm from the region of Alec's solar plexus, wrapping it around his arm as he did so. The filmy gossamer substance somehow reminded me of my net curtains, now sadly languishing at the bottom of the dustbin.

"Oh, Chang!" I said, "How can you show me all this lovely gossamer material when you know I haven't a curtain to any of my windows? And I know I won't be able to buy any."

"Little Lady," he replied, "you will have your curtains, do not worry."

The next morning I was walking through a large department store when I saw a man carrying a large package. When I saw that he was going towards the soft furnishings department I followed him and being curious I waited for the assistant to unpack the parcel. To my delight it contained a large roll of beautiful net curtaining. Being the first on the spot, I was able to purchase sufficient to drape all my windows. Within ten minutes the entire roll had been sold. I felt that Chang had guided me to that shop at exactly the right time in order to fulfil his promise. A trifling incident, maybe, but it confirmed again Spirit guidance in our everyday lives.

The circles improved every week; the forms grew stronger and clearer each time. It occurred to me that the powers in control had been preparing for these manifestations for some time, perhaps even while we had been sitting for voice. Now our Sunday circle was being used as a testing ground to perform experiments and assess the progress made.

Mary Hewitt came to Cardiff for a few days holiday from London and requested a sitting with Alec. As Mary had been instrumental in putting us on the path of Spiritualism in the first instance and realising how much an experience of materialisation would mean to her, Alec agreed. There were just the two of us and what a wonderful sitting she had. Her Guide, the French nun, Marie Thérèse, came through that night. She was so well materialised that one could see the very folds and drape of her robes. These seemed to glisten as they fell about her form. Clear for us to see was the large cross she wore at her breast. She looked particularly beautiful; and her voice was quiet and gentle. She spoke lovingly to Mary, who at that time was in especial need of comfort.

Many of our Spirit friends came that night to show themselves, including Rohan. He had requested us to sit on the settee, which stood a good distance from the cabinet. Toi-Toi, the little Chinese boy, came over and chatted happily with 'Maly', as he called Mary, whom he loved dearly. So engrossed was he with his chatter that he ignored repeated requests from the Guides to return to the cabinet. Whereupon, he was whisked unceremoniously back inside the cabinet in the manner of dealing with a naughty child.

The most memorable experience of that night was when a tall lithe figure stepped out of the cabinet and placed himself where we could see him directly under the red light. He appeared to have on a cloak of draped ectoplasm caught up at one shoulder. He turned to the cabinet and uttered a word. The cloak was removed from his shoulders and returned to the cabinet, to reveal an Indian Brave, standing stripped to the waist, wearing only a loin-cloth swathed around his lower torso. He stood there, tall, erect, with strong, firm limbs; his skin reddish-brown and his hair jet black. Slowly he raised his hands to his head and loosened his dark plaits, which fell down to his waist. A truly remarkable sight he was. Then he turned from side to side, slowly, so that we could get a good view of him. Then, looking at me, he murmured, "Louie-One" and was gone. By those words I knew him for my beloved Ewonga. Although we had spoken together many times it was the first time that I had ever seen him and I was moved by the experience.

Ewonga's work, we learned later, was to guard and protect Alec's body while he was in trance. Needless to say Mary was ecstatic at what she had seen and profusely expressed her gratitude for being permitted to witness wonders such as these.

The greatest event of the year, for us, was always our annual Christmas Tree Circle. The children of Park Grove Sunday School, always looked forward to this with a great deal of excited anticipation. The twenty or thirty of them who were invited, would file into the séance room and sit around the walls, forming a circle round the large Christmas tree, which always stood in the middle of the room, reaching right up to the ceiling. It was beautifully decorated, dressed with tinsel and streamers and literally covered with toys hanging from its branches from top to bottom. Toys of every description were in evidence, all of them contributed by friends, who very often put long hours of loving work into making and painting innumerable playthings to delight a child's heart. All of these, after the séance, were donated to the poor. They, therefore, served a double purpose by giving pleasure to the children of both worlds.

The circle would commence in the usual manner with a prayer and a hymn and the materialised Guides would come, bringing their Christmas greetings. David, a dear old gentleman, was

DAVID.

David ~ the Spirit who guided Spirit people through to their family in the Circle

Bradley's Guide, Grey Rock as drawn by Alec in 1955

always the first to do this and he would go around shaking each child by the hand. By cracking jokes and making funny remarks he would ease the tension and have all the children laughing gaily, just as they would at any ordinary children's party. Rohan would then come next. Then my son Bradley's Guide, Grey Rock, would bring his greetings to the sitters. All the Guides wished us the blessings of the season. The Sunday School children accepted all these manifestations without fear, chatting amiably to the Spirit friends.

One incident stands out particularly in my memory. The youngest child attending the circle was a small girl named Anna. She was only five years old and had a sweet singing voice. Her teacher had asked her to sing a Lyceum hymn as a solo. Obediently Anna commenced singing. After only a few bars another little voice joined in and it became a duet. Their teacher, explained to the children that this was Anna's solo and therefore no-one else should sing at the same time. All went quiet and Anna started again, but still the childish voice persisted in joining in. I could see a tiny Spirit child standing materialised right beside me, singing for all her worth. I thought how wonderful it was to hear two little children, one from each world, mingling their sweet voices. So we let them complete the hymn together.

The preliminaries over, the Spirit children would pounce on the tree, pulling the toys from the branches. They would create a bedlam of noise as crackers were pulled, balloons exploded, rattles crackled, clockwork trains and cars hooting and whining, to the accompaniment of drums, bells, mouth organs and toy trumpets.

When everybody was exhausted and the merriment began to die down, White Wing would come to close the children's circle. The following night we would hold the circle for adult sitters and the same things happened all over again. The adults became as children again, joining in the fun with gusto and sharing in the enjoyment of the little Spirit people.

It was at one of these Christmas Tree Circles that the Guide Ginger made himself known to us. At the height of all the activity little Sunny said, "There is a little man taking all the toys off the tree!" Being clairsentient, I could sense this little man standing beside me. I asked him his name and back came the answer in broad cockney, 'Ginger, Lidy'.

"Hello, Ginger," I said, "God bless you, dear. Tell me, how did you come to be in Spirit?" I asked. "Well, Lidy, it's like this 'ere," came the cockney voice again, "I was a barrer boy in London, see and I was knocked dahn by a bus." "Oh, what a shame!" I commiserated.

"Nah! Don't be sorry for me, Lidy," he quipped with cockney humour. "It was me own blinkin' fault, see. I wasn't lookin' where I was goin' and 'ere I bloomin' well am, among the angels."

We all had a good laugh at that and welcomed him to our

Ginger - a London barrow boy, whose humour often lifted the vibrations after the emotional reunions with loved ones from Spirit . Painted by Alec in 1960s

circle. Ginger always brought his cockney humour to amuse and ease the tension of the sitters when necessary. Sunny came to say that Ginger would work with the rest of the Spirit band in the circle. Ginger had a very misshapen nose. Spreading as it did, seemingly, all over his face, it was a nose that any prize-fighter could have been proud of. He always insisted that sitters explore its deformity by feeling it. I rather think that this was merely a means of providing evidence that his nose and Alec's nose were, by no means, one and the same.

When I felt the deformed nose for the first time, I was shocked and enquired, "However did you get that, Ginger?"

"Oh, that! Ha!" He gave a short laugh. "Someone threw a tomato at me, only they left it in the tin!" At this the sitters would be convulsed with laughter. This of course was a very good vibration to have at any circle.

The chair used by Alec Harris for his sittings is now in the care of Cardiff's Park Grove Spiritualist Church and has been restored since this photograph was taken 12 years ago

Chapter Eight

Some Healings and a Haunting

❖ *Animal returns* ❖ *A double haunting* ❖ *Alec's healing gift & Jim Connors* ❖ *The Police are convinced* ❖*Alec is transported from the room* ❖*Maurice Barbanell reports on Helen Hughes' sitting with Alec .*

Animals have a place in the world of Spirit. Many animal lovers will be gratified to hear that their beloved pets still live on after death. Some are even able to materialise to their owners in the séance room. I personally had experience of this phenomenon and relate the story in a later chapter. It is a well-known fact that animals are naturally psychic and are readily able to see Spirit forms in their presence. I was to discover this one day in 1942.

I had owned a beautiful black and white Persian cat, affectionately called Dick. I had acquired him five years before my marriage and he continued to dominate our household for ten more years after that. Dick showed human emotions of possessiveness and jealousy towards the object of his affections, in other words, me. These symptoms became very marked when our baby son was born. Dick had been my baby and he knew that I adored him. So he felt that he had been relegated to second place. However, when he discovered that baby Bradley did not threaten his domestic status, or in any way usurp my affections from himself, he decided to accept the baby as his own and the child and the cat became firm friends growing up together.

In 1942, when Dick was fifteen years old and a much revered member of our family, we experienced a particularly severe air raid, after which poor old Dick was found dead by the fireside. It left me quite heartbroken. So desolate was I that I vowed never to have any more pets. But I had to go back on my vow. In the same air raid my neighbour's mother's house had been razed to the ground. She had to move in with her daughter, who found that she could not accommodate her mother's cat as she herself kept a bird. So she asked me if I would look after the animal for a while until they could make other arrangements. I agreed. It was a beautiful big black cat called Blackie and after three weeks I became quite fond of him.

One Sunday, he was sleeping very peacefully on my lap when he suddenly awoke. He immediately stiffened, his fur standing on end. He was obviously afraid, yet prepared for battle. Mystified, I looked round to see what strange animal could have wandered into the house to cause this reaction and found that there was none in sight. Before I could soothe him, he jumped off my lap and fell upon some unseen thing on the floor and quite a scuffle ensued accompanied by the usual terrifying cat battle cries. I was so taken by surprise that I could only sit and gape. Then Blackie abandoned the fray and, heedless of my calls, sprang through the door and darted away, as if all the demons in Hell were after him. He vanished from sight and though we made enquiries everywhere, he was never seen again.

Some weeks later, Bradley brought home a stray terrier, a lovely little animal and asked if he might keep him. I agreed, but only until we could find his owner.

One afternoon, when I was sitting reading in the dining room, the dog barked and jumped up at the window ledge. I was puzzled as I could see nothing on the ledge nor in the garden outside to excite the dog. Yet he was greatly agitated and would not desist in spite of my commands. Nothing I could do would pacify him. Suddenly, I realised the implication. The window ledge had been dear old Dick's favourite place to sit and while away cat time and it was more than a probability that the dog had seen the Spirit form of the cat.

The next day, as I walked into the dining room, the dog jumped down from the divan where he had been sleeping and started to prowl around me, snapping at my ankles. He was quite vicious in his attacks. So, thinking that the dress I was wearing perhaps reminded him of some person to whom he was averse, I went to my room and changed it. This was to no avail, still the dog growled and snapped at my ankles. When I put my face down to him he would immediately lick it. So it appeared that it was something around my feet which troubled him. I was puzzled and disconcerted by his behaviour and I was pleased when his owners were found a few days later and this fractious little animal was removed.

Some time afterwards, a Spiritualist friend, who was clairvoyant said, "Your cat is still with you, did you know? And he resents any other animal in the house." At once the reason for Blackie's and the terrier's strange behaviour became apparent. Even in death it seemed Dick was still jealously possessive.

A few days later, Alec came home from work with a mischievous twinkle in his eyes and a large bulge under his overcoat. "What have you got there?" I asked, my curiosity getting the better of me. He unbuttoned the coat and out popped the head of an adorable month-old puppy. For a moment my old misgivings returned about having another pet. These were soon dispelled when Alec put the little animal down on the floor and he began to cavort about; his bandy little legs protruding from a plump white body daubed with black spots, his ears flopping delightfully. I could feel my resistance weakening and my heart went out to him. Alec, seeing my expression, hastily sought to clinch the matter. "We'll call him Spot, I think," he began, but was immediately contradicted by a child's voice from the doorway.

"No, we'll call him WOGS, like the dog in my favourite story." Our son, Bradley, had just come in from school and was staring, eyes agog, at the funny little creature on the floor. The child had always wanted a dog and was so thrilled with the puppy that we happily consented to the name he had selected. So Wogs stayed and became the centre of our activities. A baby could not have had more care.

It was the time of year when the snow lay thick upon the ground and it was extremely cold. We lined a box with a warm woolly blanket, put a hot water bottle in it for Wogs and placed it in front of the fire. Then, having tucked the puppy up carefully for the night, we retired to bed.

Because of the air raids we slept downstairs in the lounge.

Wogs decided that being made to sleep alone was not the kind of treatment that should be meted out to a newly acquired puppy. He scrambled out of the box, trotted into our room and started whimpering to be taken into the bed. Eventually, for the sake of peace, but first ascertaining that Alec was fast asleep, I placed my hand under the little animal's legs and lifted him into the bed, where he snuggled up into Alec's neck and fell into a warm and contented sleep. So began a lovely companionship with an almost human pet, which lasted for ten years, when Wogs departed for the Summerland of Spirit where his devotion to us continued, as he demonstrated when he materialised for all to see at one of our circles.

Wogs soon became a great favourite with us. He always loved to sit on my lap in front of the fire. But one evening a strange thing occurred. A scuffle seemed to be taking place right there on my lap, as if someone were trying to push Wogs off. It was an eerie experience and I was mystified. Alec and Mother were frankly disbelieving when I told them. Then a couple of nights later it happened again, this time in their presence. Then we realised that it was Dick, our dear old cat, jealous as usual and doing his utmost to push Wogs off my lap which he considered his prerogative, even in death. So I spoke to the dead cat saying: "Dick, darling, you will always be my lovely baby. I miss you, but I need Wogs. Do let him stay." Afterwards, whenever I nursed Wogs, I would speak to Dick first and give him love, too, visualising him lying on my lap as well as the puppy. This had the desired effect as all became peaceful. On one occasion, Wogs was even seen to be playing with an unseen presence in front of the fire. We all breathed a sigh of relief, knowing that the feud between the dead Dick and the living Wogs was over.

Whenever we had our voice circles Wogs refused to be left outside the séance room. So, buttoning him up inside my double-breasted coat, leaving only his head sticking out, I would take him with me to the circle. The proceedings always delighted him. He would bark his appreciation as the trumpets floated past him. The Spirit children would imitate him, calling out in unison, "Woof, Woof," through the trumpet.

Eventually, he grew too big to be kept in my overcoat. So we trained him to lie quietly outside the door of the séance room while the circle was in progress. He made no sound until he heard us singing the closing hymn 'Lord keep us safe this night', at which he would stand up, stretch and shake himself in preparation for the opening of the door. But when he heard us singing the final hymn 'God be with you till we meet again' he would bark loudly and nearly knock the door down in his efforts to get in to us. When eventually he came in he would go straight to Alec in the cabinet and make a tremendous fuss of him. There was a great love between my husband and the dog. One could tell from the animal's expression that he was able to see all the Spirit friends around the medium.

Wogs was a strong healthy dog and a fine swimmer. Nevertheless, when he was five years old, he contracted a virulent skin disease which covered his whole body from head to tail. Despite prolonged and dedicated treatment by a competent vet, it failed to respond to all medicaments. We were advised to have him mercifully put to sleep. I was loath to terminate the life of our dear friend. I would lie awake at night enduring much heart-searching, trying to decide what was best for Wogs. One Tuesday, the dog's condition seemed to have deteriorated and he was particularly unhappy. He would not let any of us go near him. When we had our circle that night the Austrian Doctor came out of the cabinet and spoke to me, "I hear your little dog is not well."

I told him how very worried I was about our pet. The Spirit Doctor turned from me and went towards the door, as if to open it. I was immediately concerned, knowing that Wogs' temperament was extremely tetchy that night because of his distress and pain. I wondered how he would react to the presence of a Spirit being beside him. As if reading my thoughts, the Spirit Doctor turned around and said, "Don't worry about the dog. We have attended to him." He then opened the door and we could see Wogs stretched out on the landing. The Doctor went out and bent over the animal. It was a long way for a materialised Spirit to be from the cabinet, but this did not seem to deter him.

It was a moonlit night and the pale beams of light streamed in

123

through a landing window touching the Spirit's robes with silver so that they seemed to shimmer and glisten as he worked on the dog. He remained thus for a couple of minutes bent over Wogs. He came back into the room and said, "Your little dog will be quite well." Then he calmly returned to the cabinet.

The next morning we found that all the suppurations had dried up. Within the week there was healthy skin covering the little body, new hairs were starting to grow and Wogs was a different dog. He was never troubled again with this distressing complaint.

Jim Connors, of Cardiff, was a very fine healer and had many cures to his credit. He brought a young friend of his to us one evening, Harold Harvey. He asked if our band of healers would try to help Harold, as his case was proving to be very difficult and was not responding to Connors' healing. Harold had a most distressing complaint of wet gangrene in his foot and leg and he was suffering excruciating pain. The doctors had advised immediate amputation of the leg; but at the same time, unknown to Harold, they had taken his wife aside and explained to her that this was a serious case and that he was gravely ill. They said he had a generalised septicaemia and that the prognosis was not good.

The Spirit Guides advised him not to go into hospital until they indicated that the time was right. He received immediate and constant healing from Spirit from that moment. When I came home from the theatre on the healing night, Bradley and I would give the poor lad extra healing sessions. This we had been advised to do by the Guides.

Then at one of our materialisation circles, at which Harold was present, the Austrian Spirit Doctor told us to seat Harold upon a stool placed in front of the cabinet and instructed our son Bradley to stand behind him. At this point a tall Red Indian Brave, who went by the name of Blow Heart and was attached to Bradley, stepped from the cabinet and stood in front of the ailing man. This impressive Spirit commenced to draw a large amount of ectoplasm, as if from a roll of filmy material, from Alec in trance and proceeded to swathe it around the gangrenous leg. Then to Harold's surprise, the Austrian Spirit Doctor advised him to enter hospital immediately.

Trusting in Spirit, he wasted no time in doing this and the very next day he was admitted for operation and the leg was amputated. It appeared that it had been intended to amputate the leg from above the knee, but when the patient was on the operating table the doctors were able to pin-point the extent and limit of the gangrene and it was decided that it would only be necessary to remove the portion of the leg from below the knee. Harold was hospitalized for three weeks, during which time he was impatiently awaiting his new artificial limb. So, anxious to be mobile again and up and about, he improvised a leg himself, making expert use of a barber's pole.

He was a light-hearted jovial lad, always the life and soul of the party wherever he was. He accepted his disability with praise-worthy cheerfulness. Despite his fortitude, 12 months later the dreaded trouble recurred, this time in the other leg. Once again Harold entered hospital for amputation. His cheerfulness carried him through his ordeal. He was grateful that the rest of his body was in perfect health. He was equipped with two artificial limbs and educated himself to cope with these admirably. It was incongruous that Harold was the manager of a boot store where he spent his life making sure that people with two healthy feet were properly shod. He became a well known figure in his neighbourhood and many came to him for help, or just for the excitement of hearing him relate his thrilling experiences in the materialisation séance room. His wife, Susan, had been a pillar of strength to him throughout his illness. We eventually included both of them in our private circle.

Although his troubles overtook him in 1941, he and Susan lived happily together for 26 more years, always keeping the necessary close contact with Spirit which kept him in perfect health. Eventually, he passed very suddenly into Spirit in 1967 as a result of a heart attack. Alec and I missed him greatly and felt privileged to have known such a man. One memorable night, Rohan said, as he stood materialised before Harold: "My son, you have been through a very difficult and painful experience. We are proud of you because you have faced your disability with courage and fortitude. You are a shining example to many around you and to many on our side, too."

In 1942 we were still giving voice circles at our Spiritualist church on a Friday. One night I felt the presence of a young soldier who was trying very hard to communicate, but having no success. I sensed his bitter disappointment at this failure. When the circle ended I was drawn to a woman who looked very strained. I felt she was on the verge of a breakdown. I approached her, asking if she would like to come to our circle on Sunday. At this point the presence of the young soldier came very close and I knew that he had come for her.

On the night the lady presented herself with plenty of time to spare. Because of her obvious need, I placed her in the front row. We always sat in two rows, close to the cabinet. Shortly after we began, a young lad stepped from the cabinet. He held out his arms to the woman saying, "Mum, it's Derry." She gave an anguished cry, jumped from her seat and went to the boy. He put his arms around her. The mother broke down and wept unrestrainedly in her dead son's arms, releasing much of her tensions over the past months.

The boy gently comforted his mother, saying he was always with her. Then he changed the subject and quite unexpectedly said: "Mum, I want you to be quite sure that this is really me. Look, I've still got it, see!" He took her hand and placed it on his chest. "Can you feel it, Mum?" he asked. He had had a deformed breast bone which his family had laughingly called his chicken bone. To give his mother positive proof of his identity, he materialised his deformity to convince her. There was not a dry eye among us as we witnessed this beautiful and touching reunion of a lonely, grieving mother with her dead son.

Afterwards the lady told me that her son had volunteered for service with the paratroopers. He had not lasted very long, being shot down over Africa. When she heard the news the shock was so great she could not sleep or eat and had no desire to go on living. Her doctor was very concerned, but could do nothing to help. After the circle she was a changed woman, taking part in all the church activities.

It is not only the living who are in need of help. There are some in Spirit who are in despair. Consider the poltergeist disturbances from noisy, fractious or mischievous Spirits, or the more common ghost hauntings. These are frequently the work of distressed souls who have a persistent problem on their minds and who are in need of help. It may be a murderer with a guilt complex, or perhaps one who was falsely declared as such and wants to rectify the error. It could be a suicide who is suffering remorse, or one incorrectly accused of taking his own life and wishes to remove the slur on his name and memory. It could be one who has carried over a grievance because of some treachery perpetrated against him prior to his passing. There are many reasons for hauntings which require understanding and sympathy from our world rather than the fear which is generally exhibited when we encounter these manifestations.

Often the deceased person worries over the welfare or safety of those he has left behind and he does everything in his power to attract the attention of someone in the physical world in the hope that help will be forthcoming. Once this has been achieved and his problem is resolved the hauntings cease and the ghost gives no further trouble.

Jim Connors came to us to enlist our help for a friend of his who was having unpleasant and quite frightening manifestations in the house where he and his wife lived with their three children. I asked why they did not move to another house. Jim explained that they had tried to find alternative accommodation, but had been unsuccessful as houses were in very short supply during the war. He pleaded with us to help them as he said the family was very disturbed by the frightening things that took place each night.

I discussed the 'laying of this ghost' with Alec and he readily agreed to give his services and render what help he could. The following night Jim called to take us over to his friend's house and on the way we collected Grahame Watkins and several members of our circle.

The house was one of a terrace of houses. The front sitting room had been converted into a shop. Jim's friend let us in. We followed him as he led the way down a long passage which gave access to their living quarters. At the end of this passage there was a heavy glass door which opened and closed by means of strong springs. The young man pushed the door open. It seemed to require quite an effort to do this. We were ushered into a comfortable living room and introduced to his wife, who nervously suggested that she and her husband should withdraw and leave us to deal with the ghost. She seemed anxious to be gone and hastily retreated.

While we prepared for the circle downstairs, Jim and Grahame went upstairs to inspect the children's bedroom and the other upper rooms. They found the little ones tucked up and fast asleep. They then proceeded to lock and seal all the doors with adhesive tape and a length of cotton across each. The windows were similarly treated. Should any of the seals be broken, this would indicate if any physical being had passed through any of these apertures while our séance was in progress. Satisfied that no one could get in or out without our knowledge, they came downstairs again. The six of us formed a circle, linking our hands together.

I begged Alec not to allow himself to go into trance. Being unsure of the nature of the troublesome Spirit I thought that would be wiser. I did not want him to come to any harm. We said a prayer for protection and help and then we waited for the ghost to manifest. Nothing happened. There was utter silence. The waiting seemed unbearable. Nerves were taut as the tension mounted. No one spoke. The mantle clock ticked away loudly and the silence became so intense as to be almost palpable.

Then someone sneezed. "Ohhh!" we shrieked in fright, startled by the sudden sharp sound exploding out of the night. Realising that it was only one of our own sitters feeling the chill of the room, we burst out laughing at our own stupidity. This, fortunately, broke the tension. More composed now, we settled ourselves and mentally invited the appearance of the ghost. We did not have long to wait.

The large glass door at our backs suddenly commenced to swing backwards and forwards on its springs at an alarming speed. The draught caused by its violent movement sent a chill wind round the room. I shivered with cold, or was it uneasiness? Then, I heard them. Slow, heavy footsteps on the stairs. At first I could not be sure whether they were coming down, or going up. As I listened intently, I decided that they must be ascending the stairs. I was right, for later we heard the children's bedroom door being opened and shut and the sash window similarly opened and closed.

Grahame and Jim wasted no time. They jumped up and rushed upstairs to investigate. But they found the door of the children's room was still locked, sealed with tape and the thread of cotton still intact. To their surprise, after breaking the seals, unlocking the door and entering the room, they saw that the children were still fast asleep. The seals on the sash window were untouched and the window itself still locked. Mystified, the two returned downstairs and reported their findings to us. It was decided that we should remain sitting in the circle to see if there were any further developments where we could perhaps make contact with the Spirit.

All at once there was a loud tapping on the kitchen door which startled us. "Wait," I said. "Someone is trying to speak to us." The taps now indicated that there was an intelligence behind them. They began to spell out, 'I did not commit suicide. It was an accident. I fell into the docks'.

We indicated that we had got the message and that we would try to help set the record straight if we possibly could. This seemed to satisfy the troubled Spirit and he went away. It is interesting to note that we made enquiries afterwards and uncovered the fact that a man, who had lived in that very house, had fallen into the docks and drowned. It had been recorded as suicide.

The tapping now changed in character and came from another part of the room. It spelled out, 'Danger for the children!' The message was repeated several times. On enquiring the nature of the danger, the Spirit replied, 'Fire'. The Spirit then identified itself as being the children's grandmother.

Grahame asked if the fire could have anything to do with the wiring of the house? To which the Spirit grandmother promptly replied, 'Yes'. Later, Grahame, who was now in the Fire Service, made a point of examining the electric wiring of the house. He found that it was very old and faulty, and in some places the wires were actually bare. It was a miracle that the house had not gone up in flames long before this warning. Grahame reported his findings to the Council and the dwelling was rewired throughout. Once this had been attended to, the grandmother's Spirit was satisfied that the children were no longer in danger. From that day all the frightening disturbances ceased and the house returned to normal once more.

Jim Connors, now joined our materialisation circle. We felt that if he were to have personal contact with the Guides it would assist him in his great work of healing the sick. Alec and I held him in high regard. After some months of attending our séances Jim one evening, sitting behind Bradley in the circle, suddenly leaned forward and murmured to him: "My lad, you must be very careful not to lift anything too heavy. I'm getting a warning which I think must be for you." Bradley thanked him and promised to heed the warning.

The following Tuesday, Jim, who was employed in the maintenance of the Cardiff Hospital, was carrying heavy ladders and trestles with another man, when his mate was called away for a time. As he left, he called to Jim to wait for his return before trying to carry the stuff any further. Jim cheerily agreed. But when his friend's return was delayed Jim became impatient. Being a very strong man he started to carry the equipment alone. He was just negotiating the bend of the stairs with some difficulty when he collapsed, having strained his heart. Being on the spot in the hospital he received immediate cardiac treatment and was thus prevented from an untimely passing into Spirit.

We sat as usual that night and Jim's Chinese Guide, Li Bo, stepped out of the cabinet. He came to me and addressed me seriously: "Lady, you must take your husband to the hospital to visit my medium. Your own Guides and I will be there. You must go within 24 hours, otherwise he will be on our side. We are relying on you to do this."

I promised faithfully that we would do as he asked. Alec took the following afternoon off from work. Unfortunately, we were not permitted to see Jim as he was on the danger list. Only his wife was allowed in to him. I was feeling desperate and I said a prayer for help. Shortly afterwards, the sister in charge came along and I pleaded with her. I stressed that it was urgent and necessary that we be permitted just to stand by Jim's bed. We promised not to talk to him. Seeing our obvious distress she relented and gave us permission, 'but only for a couple of minutes', she said.

As we went in, Jim was conscious and he looked relieved to see us. We did not speak, only smiled at him, as Alec stood on one side of the bed and I on the other. As we laid our hands on him, I could feel a great surge of healing power surround Jim. Then we quietly left after we had said another prayer.

Two days later, Alec and the Vice President of our Church, Mr Trenchard, another very good healer, went to visit Jim again. They were pleased to see a decided change in the man. After this second healing he was very much better. There was a marked improvement in his condition. The doctors, who knew of Jim's healing gift, were amazed at his quick recovery.

On looking back, Jim realised he had misinterpreted the warning he had received that night in our circle. Being a strong man and in perfect health himself, he had assumed that the message was for Bradley. Spirit had tried to protect him and prevent his heart attack.

Jim eventually came out of hospital and returned to our circle, where Li Bo came to talk to him about his health. "The Spirit Doctors have repaired your heart," said the tall, elderly, oriental man. There was a serious note to his voice, "but you will have to take great care in future." The Chinaman advised him that, although riding his bicycle would not do him any harm, he was never, under any circumstances, to ride it up hills.

I was concerned about this as there was a sizeable hill up to our house which Jim would have to negotiate if he continued to attend the circles. So I invited another gentleman to join the circle who had a car, who willingly agreed to give Jim a lift. This arrangement worked very well for a while, until all motor cars were commandeered for military purposes. Then I had the unhappy task of telling Jim that he would have to discontinue attending our circles for his own good. I told him I could not take the responsibility of his riding uphill to our house on his bicycle and I reminded him of Li Bo's warning. Naturally he called to see us from time to time hoping, I knew, to be invited to rejoin our circle, although he said it was just to have a chat. But in his own interests I felt it best to leave things the way they were.

Later, while we were in the middle of a séance, Albert Stewart, Helen Duncan's famous Guide, materialised. He spoke firmly to me, "You must look after this medium." He was referring to Alec. "He is doing far more than his body can stand. If you don't he will be coming over to our side before his time, just as another medium, whom you know so well, is leaving your world right at this very moment because he did not heed the advice of his Guide." We were puzzled. But the next morning his meaning was only too clear. We were greatly shocked to learn that dear lovable Jim had passed to Spirit at the precise moment Albert Stewart was telling us.

Throughout his life, Jim was happiest while alleviating suffering and his whole life had been devoted to the needs of humanity. He surely must have found his reward in the Spirit world, if he had not already done so on Earth. But it was sad that he passed over while still so young and at a time when the world so sorely needed men of Jim's calibre.

In 1944 we had a most unusual visitation from Spirit. A tall, extremely thin man materialised. He left the cabinet, walked to the end of the room where there was an extra chair and seated himself on it. The figure spoke to us, quickly and urgently, in a tongue of which we had no knowledge. I dearly wished that I could understand the words and phrases that fell from his lips.

Unexpectedly, a young Belgian man, sitting on a chair near the materialised Spirit, suddenly spoke up saying that he was a linguist and that he understood what was being said by the Spirit in the chair. Conversation flowed freely and easily between them. They switched into several different languages and still conversed with one another with ease. Alec was certainly no linguist. English was the only language he knew. This was a very evidential point in favour of the authenticity of his mediumship. No medium could get away with a situation such as this, unless of course he was a fluent linguist.

It appeared, from the conversation that took place, that the tall thin materialisation was an Austrian Jew who had been a university language teacher. He had been rounded up by the Germans, along with others of his race and interned in the much dreaded Belsen concentration camp in Germany, where he had been submitted to the most ghastly torture. The last diabolical session of Nazi sadism went far beyond his endurance. Mercifully he died while undergoing the ordeal.

Leaving his broken, emaciated body and tormented mind had been an overwhelming relief. Yet he still suffered bouts of mental torment when memory flooded his mind with pictures of the horrifying atrocities committed on defenceless men, women and children for no other reason than they had been born Jews. After talking for some time the man seemed relieved of some of his tension. He rose from the chair, quietly returned to the cabinet and vanished from sight.

Rohan emerged and explained that the Guides had purposefully brought the teacher to the circle in an attempt to erase the suffering that still lingered in his mind. We sent him on his way with our blessings and promised to keep him in our thoughts.

At this same circle was a man I did not much care for. As he came with a group, I did not question his being there. I knew the group held themselves responsible for all newcomers they introduced. As a precaution, I placed him at the back of the circle. A Hindu came for this man and pointing at him said, "I belong to you." "How can you belong to me?" this sitter asked sarcastically, but the Spirit was not disconcerted. "I became attached to you when you lived in my country," came the calm reply. The Spirit then commenced to speak to him in Hindi. This seemed to make a profound impression on the rather unpleasant sitter. He suddenly became quiet and thoughtful.

Afterwards, when the circle was over and we all met in the lounge for tea, he came up to me and said, "Mrs Harris, I am a police officer. We know about your activities. I thought I would come along and see what it is all about. Frankly, I am amazed at what I have witnessed here tonight. First, that Austrian communicator spoke five different languages!"

"You counted them?" I enquired, surprised. "I counted them, yes. There were five. Then this Hindu chap coming for me. No one knows that I spent many years in India," he said. "This fellow spoke the dialect of the place where I lived. Fantastic! Quite unbelievable! I just can't understand it." He shook his head, still puzzled.

"I'm glad you were impressed," I smiled. "Rather I should say that I am happy you believe it all to be true, and not a fake." "A fake," he exploded. "How could it be? What about all those Spirit forms who were recognised by people in the circle? No, this is the genuine thing all right." and he nodded vigorously.

I was relieved we had convinced the police. That was quite something. I felt sure our beloved Spirit friends had known of the officer's intentions and specially arranged manifestations to enlighten and convince him. Otherwise he might have proved to be difficult for our circle in the future.

Grahame Watkins was originally introduced to our circle by his wife Marjorie, a brilliant pianist. She and I became acquainted when she played the piano at the Continental Restaurant where I was the resident violinist. Because of her professional commitments, she was only able to join us on rare occasions. Grahame became one of our regular and trusted sitters.

His Guide was a Spanish dancer called Conchita which we affectionately shortened this to Chita. She was all woman. There was no hint of the medium's masculinity about her as Grahame testified after she sat on his knee and he had his arm about her. His shy remark after that incident was, "She's certainly a lady!" By the emphasis he laid on the word we knew he meant female. "But she's very much lighter than a physical lady," he added.

Conchita's proportions were dainty and extremely feminine. She always materialised wearing flowing, filmy robes. She carried a fine gossamer veil made of thin white ectoplasm. She seemed to have perfect control of the available psychic power. Not only did she hold her materialised form for a considerable time, but she simultaneously danced and spoke while being at some distance from the cabinet.

As Chita danced, moving her limbs gracefully and expertly, her garments would billow out so prettily. Sometimes she threw the veil around Grahame's neck and laughingly drew him towards the cabinet, talking to him all the while. Then, planting a gentle kiss on his cheek before leaving, she would say that she was always looking after him.

By way of confirmation of the foregoing, I give below extracts from an article written by the then editor of 'Two Worlds', Ernest Thompson, who witnessed this extraordinary and lifelike materialisation of a perfect female form through a male medium.

"At the first séance I had with Alec Harris 15 Spirits materialised that evening. They were tall and short, fat and thin, male and female. Some were visitors from other lands, one being an American Red Indian who stood quite seven feet tall. As evidence of the genuineness of these manifestations Rohan, the Spirit in charge of the proceedings, materialised and drawing the cabinet curtains to one side revealed the entranced medium sitting in his corner upon a chair, so that we could see them together. On two further occasions the materialised forms were visible simultaneously with that of the medium. As further evidence of the genuineness of these materialised forms Rohan permitted us to witness the entire process of materialisation.

"First of all, there appeared what seemed to be a white rod which thrust itself along the floor from under the cabinet curtains. It moved as if it were alive and stopped about a yard in front of the curtains. The end began to enlarge into a ball until there was a mass of moving, pulsating ectoplasm about the size of a large stone. It became elongated vertically until it was the height of a human being. Gradually, as if it were being sculptured, there appeared a face and then a head. Soon the form was completely human, clothed in ectoplasmic draperies.

"The materialised Spirit began to walk about the room and was able to speak to us. As the power waned we saw the Spirit dissolve and collapse into empty space! Then occurred the most wonderful and beautiful manifestation of the entire séance. A charming Spanish girl gracefully glided through the curtains and enthralled us with a dancing display. It was fascinating to watch her elegant movements. As she turned quickly on her toes the hem of her billowing white dress flicked my cheek. It felt as soft and sensitive as gossamer.

"Then she came to the main purpose of her visit, which was to prove human survival by demonstrating to us that she was indeed a female and not the medium masquerading in disguise. Slowly she parted her robes revealing, beyond all doubt, a nude feminine figure."

Quite the most extraordinary phenomenon that happened to Alec was when he was dematerialised and rematerialised in a place outside the séance room. It was a Saturday night in 1944 and we were giving a circle for our church. I always made a point of including among the sitters one of our own regulars and Grahame Watkins attended that night. It was an excellent circle from every aspect, but it had a most unusual culmination.

Toi-Toi materialised and a sitter enquired of this little Chinese Spirit boy, "Do you remember the night you took off Alec's trousers, Toi-Toi?" "Hush!" I chided him, but before I could utter another word, Alec's trousers came hurtling through the air and landed on the sitter. Amid the laughter, I found myself thinking, "Thank goodness! the circle is nearly over!" Then Christopher, a Spirit friend, requested us all to leave the room very quietly.

Knowing Alec did not like to be left alone to come out of trance after a circle, Grahame offered to stay behind with him. I said that I would also stay. But Christopher was emphatic. No, he insisted, we all had to go immediately. "Leave the medium's trousers by the cabinet," he added. As the sitters filed out, Grahame saw my concern and whispered, "Don't worry. I will sit just outside the door, at the top of the stairs here. When I hear the slightest movement in the room I'll slip in and see to Alec."

Somewhat relieved, I went downstairs to make the tea. The front door bell rang. I rushed to open the door as I knew how best to handle the black-out curtains draped over the doorway. As I did so, I could not stifle a little scream as I saw my husband, now out of trance, standing there before me, a bewildered expression on his face and now wearing his trousers.

Grahame, who heard my scream, rushed downstairs to investigate. His face registered shock on seeing Alec in the doorway. Grahame's expression of amazement was almost comical as he stammered, "But .. but .. he never .. I mean I never .. but how?"

He had not heard anything untoward from the séance room and was mystified as to how Alec got out. Alec was not much help there either. His only explanation was that he had suddenly found himself in the front garden. He had no recollection of getting there. There was no normal way for Alec to have left the room of his own accord. Grahame guarded the door. The only window was permanently closed, fixed by a wooden frame fitted for black-out purposes. In any case it had become warped by the sun and was immovable. On checking, it was found to be jammed tight and no sign that it had been tampered with. I was thankful that my husband was all right. Obviously he had been in good and competent hands. I had to concede that to the Spirit world nothing is impossible!

At a voice circle given for the Spiritualist church in 1945, at which there were 27 sitters, we were treated to another of Raf's predictions. Through the trumpet came the cheerful and racy tones of Raf's voice saying, "Cheer up, folks. Get the jolly old flags out for you're going to use them soon." There were exclamations of surprise and pleasure from all present, some asking hopefully, "Is the war really going to end, Raf?" He replied with conviction, "Yes. In three days you will have good news."

The sitters were jubilant, but I treated this statement with caution. I pointed out to the circle that the Spirits' interpretation of time was perhaps different from ours and that they should not lay too much emphasis on what he had said. "But Raf is always right!" they insisted. "Well, he may not be this time," I said. I was afraid if he were proved wrong Spirit messages in general might be discredited. The trumpet then placed itself close to my ear and Raf whispered, "I am right, you know, jolly sure of it. Mark my words, in three days there's going to be a lot of celebrating," and he chuckled delightedly.

Three days later, I was listening to the radio when the programme was interrupted and a voice announced that the ultimatum which had been put to Japan had been accepted by that country and hostilities were at an end. Exactly one week after Raf's prophesy our whole street was out celebrating peace on VJ day in August and there were flags and bunting, and much singing and dancing and rejoicing, just as Raf had predicted.

In August 1946 Mr Maurice Barbanell, the editor of 'Psychic News' and the well-known medium, Helen Hughes, were on a visit to Cardiff. They approached us for a circle and Alec was only too happy to oblige. A circle was arranged which included sitters from the Rhondda Valley. It turned out to be a really excellent circle as there was complete harmony in the group, a very necessary factor to achieve good results, particularly in a physical circle. Enormous power was derived from such out-standing sitters as Maurice Barbanell and Helen Hughes, not to mention the beautiful Welsh singing voices from the Rhondda which did much to increase the vibrations necessary for materialisation that evening.

Maurice Barbanell

So it came to pass that ten years after Helen herself had prophesied this very sitting, it actually took place. Here is Mr Barbanell's report of this circle which first appeared in print in August 1946.

"There is in South Wales one of our most remarkable materialisation mediums. At his séances Spirit forms not only show themselves in good red light, but hold sustained conversations, after having walked about 10 feet from the cabinet.

"At a sitting which I attended I saw 30 forms materialise during two and a half hours, the length of the sitting. Alec Harris does not use his gift professionally, deriving his income from his work for a government department. The sittings have to be held fairly late at night because his wife is engaged in an orchestra at a local theatre.

"Thus it was not until almost 10.30pm that 27 of us assembled in the séance room. As most of the sitters had come by coach from valleys about 25 miles away, few got to bed before four in the morning.

"The story behind the sitting is a fascinating one. About 10 years ago, the medium's wife had a private sitting with Helen Hughes. She was then told that, if she and her husband sat in their home for development, they would one day obtain full form materialisations.

"Moreover, it was stated that Helen herself would witness the phenomena. She did at this séance I attended.

"I was asked beforehand to make a thorough examination of the room, of the cabinet, which was merely some curtains across one corner, and of the medium, who wore only a thin pair of trousers made of black material and a black vest.

"The black was deliberate, because the forms always appear clothed in dazzlingly white ectoplasm, which I noticed as usual did not reflect the red light. I was so close to the cabinet that several of the forms had to walk over my feet. On several occasions I handled the flowing ectoplasmic draperies, which were soft and silky to the touch. I shook hands with two forms. Their hands were firm and normal.

"Helen Hughes received two outstanding proofs. One was the materialisation of Douglas Hogg, a Battle of Britain pilot who has proved his survival to his parents through her mediumship. He showed his features distinctly and asked her to stand up so that he could talk to her face to face. He gripped her by the hands, thanked her for all she had done and kissed her, almost with reverence, on the forehead. She had no difficulty in identifying him, because clairvoyantly she has seen him on many occasions.

"Douglas Hogg also gave a greeting to Charles Glover Botham, another medium through whom evidence of his survival had been given to his parents.

"The other Spirit form to show himself to Helen was her Red Indian Guide, a magnificent figure complete with headdress, who gave his name. The cast of his features was typical of his race.

"Another Red Indian Guide, completely different in appearance, manifested and spoke to the medium's 13 year old son who has been brought up to regard Spirit visitors as a normal part of his life.

"From the standpoint of evidence, the highlight of the sitting was the materialisation of a man known to several people present and particularly to Tom and Mabel Hibbs, leading figures in the South Wales District Council of the Spiritualists National Union.

"He came right out of the cabinet, walked about 10 feet to the corner of the room and showed himself to Mrs Hibbs. At first he did not give his name, though asked to do so, because he declared that he ought to be easily identified by his features and his voice. He was right. Mrs Hibbs soon recognised this man, who had passed on recently and was one of the officials of the district council.

"To appreciate the remarkable nature of the sitting, you must remember that it is very rare to get materialisations venturing beyond the cabinet because there is an invisible lifeline connecting them with the medium.

"Yet the dead official, as well as several others, walked to the corner of the room, sat in a chair and carried on a long discussion. Some of the forms, after maintaining these conversations, were heard to say that they must return to the cabinet for 'more rations'. They walked back and a few minutes later came out, moved across to the corner of the room, sat down and continued where they had left off.

"Several turned round and showed their backs, to prove they were solid figures. Once a form stooped to straighten a rug which had been rucked by somebody else.

"From the spectacular point of view, the most extraordinary incident was the materialisation of a girl. She disposed of any suggestion that the results could be explained away by trickery by revealing part of her feminine form in which she was nude down to her waist!

"Then one materialisation parted the curtains so that we could see the form and the medium at the same time. Frequently throughout the séance I heard some of the Guides conversing with the medium in the cabinet. Apparently there are intervals when he is almost conscious.

"It was an impressive demonstration of materialisation at its best. The medium and his wife devote their spare time to

Spiritualism and make a speciality of healing. Already they have several striking successes to their credit. But no sceptic could attend one of these materialisations séances and still remain a sceptic."

This article from the Editor of 'Psychic News' I remember made me feel very happy that he and Helen had found the circle so rewarding.

After the circle Mabel Hibbs approached me, saying I could not keep these circles private as Spiritualism needed mediumship such as Alec's to prove survival. She begged me to allow her to arrange groups to attend sittings in our home. I was hesitant about this as I knew that it would place an added strain upon Alec. Though I realised that this perhaps was a call to service which should not be disregarded. After much deliberation Alec and I finally decided to give circles to such groups as Mrs Hibbs vouched for on Saturday nights during Winter.

This meant that our Sunday circle had to be cancelled. We retained the Tuesday private sittings. Later, I was glad that we had made this decision when I witnessed the wonderful reunions between lost loved ones and their grieving families and friends. Such a wealth of evidence came through. Mrs Hibbs' groups came in coaches from churches scattered all over the country. The circles normally lasted about three hours, finishing at 2am. After the refreshments had been served it would be 3am before they left for home, tired but happy. Through their happiness Alec found great joy and a reward for his labours.

Always when the sitters came from the Welsh valleys the singing would be absolutely magnificent. The heavenly cadences, the glorious harmonies and lilting melodies would pour forth so effortlessly from musical throats with such fervour of tone and expression. As song after song reached a climax in a rousing crescendo one would be left ecstatically breathless, uplifted both emotionally and spiritually. The state of mind thus created always augured well for Spirit manifestation. Consequently these were always particularly good circles.

During these circles, our 13 year old son, Bradley, would render solos. It was a joy to hear his lovely young voice singing such songs as 'Angels Guard Thee' and 'If My Songs Were Winged' by Hahn. At these times Bradley's Red Indian Guide, Blow Heart, would materialise and come and stand beside him. Taking his hand he would say, "Boy grow more!" He was always very interested in Bradley's height. Until one day they were of an identical height, confirming one of Blow Heart's earliest prophesies when Bradley was a baby, namely "Boy grow tall, like Blow Heart." This surprised us for Alec and I were not tall, but Bradley grew to be over 6 feet tall.

In Brighton on holiday in 1950.
Louie and Alec with their son Bradley, apparently doing
what Blow Heart prophesied ~ "Boy grow tall!"

Preparing oneself for a circle is most important. Prior to a circle it is always advisable to quieten and uplift the mind, preferably by meditation if possible, or at least making an effort to rid oneself of material concerns and worries. One should rid the mind of any unpleasant thoughts concerning oneself or one's associates. Strong drink should not be taken near the time of a circle and only a light snack, or none at all. Vibrations from the associations of the working day can be removed to a large extent by bathing and completely changing one's clothes. But the greatest asset is the changing of heart and mind.

At the beginning of our circles Rohan always came first and quietly addressed the sitters. He explained that it was not easy for loved ones to build their materialised forms. The Guides, had much experience of building, therefore found it comparatively easy. Rohan stressed that the work of the Guides in the circle was to prove survival. He pointed out that they could not guarantee that any particular person would come to the circle from the Spirit side. He advised that sitters should not hold strong thoughts of a particular person with whom they wished to communicate. This caused conflicting vibrations which interfered with the power and impeded their manifestation.

I saw the wisdom of this advice on one particular occasion when a dear man from the Rhondda Valley arrived at our door and asked politely if he could arrange for a sitting for his group of twenty people. Unfortunately I could not give him an early date and he settled for a circle seven months ahead without complaint or argument.

When the night of the circle arrived, I arranged them in their seats in the sanctuary and Alec went into the cabinet. As he sat himself down in the chair behind the black curtain the Spirit Scientist came out of the cabinet and thanked the group for 'preparing themselves so well' for the sitting. We discovered later that they had sat every week in preparation for, what was to them, this very special occasion.

"You have come to meet us," observed the Scientist, looking very impressive draped in a white gown. "You did not expect us to come all the way to you, so our work is made easy tonight and you will get the reward of your giving."

We all felt uplifted. We had a wonderful circle that night. Afterwards Alec felt fine, whereas after some circles he would feel depleted and tired for days. It brought home to us the importance of preparing for a circle, which proved to be to the advantage of both sides.

When my mother turned 80 we had a little tea-party for her out in the garden as it was a lovely sunny day. It occurred on a Sunday and we had medium friends visiting us from London, also my dear friend Mary Hewitt, as well as several members of our circle and my sister May. Alec wanted to give Mum a birthday circle, so at 7pm we all went into the sanctuary in a happy mood. It proved to be a delightful and memorable sitting.

So many Guides came to wish Mother a happy birthday and then came my father. He was so well materialised, just as I always knew him. He held out his arms to Mother and called her to him. It was a thrilling moment when he took her into his arms and kissed her saying, 'Happy Birthday, Poll', he standing so tall and she so tiny beside him.

"I thought I would have been with you long before this, Tom," she whispered. Looking lovingly at her, he replied, "I would love to pick you up and take you back with me, Poll, but I cannot. You have to stay a while longer." Then he smiled and squeezed her. "I could never give you the home I wanted you to have, but wait until you see the one I have ready for you here." Then he kissed her tenderly again and slowly began to sink into the floor still holding her hands until even those released their grasp and all that was left was a whisp of ectoplasm which drifted back into the cabinet. We were all overjoyed for Mother, for her heart must have been bursting with emotion. Quite a few eyes were moist that night, especially my Mother's! Afterwards her face was radiant; so much love had passed between herself and her beloved husband and she knew that he was waiting for her.

Thereafter, she attended several of our private circles, but I always made her sit on the settee at the back of the rows of sitters, which was some distance from the cabinet, so that the Spirit scientists would not draw any power from her and so deplete her in any way, bearing in mind her age and frailty. Energy and even ectoplasm, is always drawn from sitters during a séance, particularly from those sitting in the front row. This is used in conjunction with the medium's powerful energies to produce the phenomena present. So a lot depends on the quality of the sitters in the front row for they contribute much to the circle.

Undeterred by where my mother was sitting, my dear father would come out of the cabinet and walk around to the settee, where he would seat himself alongside her and engage her in animated conversation. It was hard to believe, seeing them together like that, that he had left this world 28 years previously, so real did he seem.

Many times I had thought about the name we had given our

house, LOUAL, being a combination of Louie and Alec. I still had a feeling that it was not the right one. I had a vague feeling that it was unlucky as we had been going through a difficult period for some time and I told White Wing. He replied impassively that there was no such thing as *luck*. "How you say this," he asked, "when you found us in your home?" However, I told him that I did not care for the name and would he please try and find us another one. He nodded, amused and consented to do so.

Some nights later, when Alec and I were in bed, Alec gave a puzzled exclamation. When I enquired the reason, he said that he could see letters of fire across the room. "Wait," I said and quickly reached for the pad and pencil I always kept by my bedside. "Now spell them out, Al, and I'll write them down."

Slowly he spelt out..P-H-R-E-N-S-A-D-E. "Yes?" I said, "Go on." "That's it," he said, "that's the lot."

"Nine letters!" I cried, "but what do they mean?" Together we puzzled over it. At first we could make neither head nor tail of it concluding that it must be some foreign language. Then slowly, after much pronunciation of the word, it dawned on us that it was a phonetic spelling of 'FRIEND'S AID'. "The name for our house!" I cried, "That's what it is!"

Alec smiled. "Very appropriate," he said, "I like it."

So did I and we decided to rename the house forthwith, and 'PHRENSADE' it has always been, even when we moved as far away as South Africa.

Later, at a circle, White Wing confirmed that it was, indeed, the name he had chosen for the house and commented, "Faithful, many will ask the meaning of this name; and when you explain its origin it will serve to open the door to many who will, themselves, become seekers after the Truth."

And so it was. Many people did ask about the strange name of our house; and when I explained how we had come by it and told them about the Spirit World and the many friends and helpers we had there, their curiosity was aroused more often than not and they too began to enquire into the fascinating subject of Spiritualism.

Chapter Nine

Under Psychic Investigation

❖*Barrie's healing* ❖ *Dr Moore, a Spirit heart specialist* ❖*Ectoplasm*
❖*Various Reports of Test Sittings by Spiritualists and Conjurors.*

On a cold winter night in early December 1946 our Austrian Spirit Doctor came to give us information regarding a little patient who was in dire need of Spirit healing. Alec's healing powers, by this time, had developed to a remarkable degree and many cures were attributed to his intervention.

"The sad plight of a young boy will be brought to your notice," said the Spirit doctor, "and we want you to take on this case. If you succeed it will afford sound proof of the power of Spirit. This is a case where all else seems to have failed." I said that we would certainly make a note of this and would wait for the patient to be brought to us.

"Don't forget, Lady," he reminded me, "it's a boy, a very young boy." Several weeks passed and no ailing boy contacted us, but we still kept him in mind, trusting in Spirit knowledge.

Meanwhile, on 20th December 1946 my dear mother had a severe stroke from which she never recovered and she passed into Spirit on 5th January 1947. It was a terrible shock to our little family as we were all desperately fond of 'Mam' and I could not envisage home without her dear presence. The Minister who officiated at the funeral, George Harris, afterwards came and had a few words with us. And here we encountered a strange coincidence. He mentioned that he had a letter appealing for help from the parents of a young boy named Barrie who was suffering from epilepsy, resulting from a fall downstairs. The fits were most distressing as they persisted through day and night, his little limbs jerking convulsively all the time. The doctors had prescribed maximum doses of sedatives to make him sleep, but he could not manage more than two hours a night. His parents, John and Gwyneth, took it in turns to sit with him as he could never be left alone and the strain was telling on them.

"It's a very bad case," concluded the Minister. "The boy can't speak and has not recognised his parents for three years now." He produced the letter and handed it to me. "It's strange," he remarked, "but when I held this in my hands I heard Alec's name being called."

Could this be the young boy referred to by the Austrian doctor previously? On an impulse I decided to tell the Minister of the incident in our circle and how we had been waiting for this call for help from a young boy for several weeks. Without hesitation he gave me the address of the patient and asked if we would see the child and help him if we could.

It was fortunate that I was on a week's leave from the theatre and would be available to go with Alec after he came home from work. Mr Jenkins, a member of our circle, offered to take us there in his car. We accepted gratefully on account of the inclement weather. It was snowing heavily and we had to cross Caerphilly Mountain.

When we eventually reached the house and saw the state of the patient we were shocked. I had grave misgivings. Had the Spirit doctor not pressed us to take on the case I think I would have dissuaded Alec from attempting to treat it. In fact, I was wondering just how Adoula could give the child healing as his seemed such a hopeless case.

However, we seated ourselves around Barrie's little cot and prayed. Adoula controlled Alec immediately and there was silence in the room. The little boy lay quiet as Adoula placed his hands on his ankles. The child was looking up at him, strangely still.

Adoula broke the silence with a question, his voice gentle and deep, "Boy not cry since his fall?" "No, not at all," replied the parents, their faces weary and lined by worry.

"Boy must cry," he stated. And then he seemed to go into consultation with unseen and unheard presences. For several minutes he listened attentively, nodding now and again and murmuring something unintelligible to us. Then he said, "Mmm, yes, yes," and nodded once more. Then he turned to the parents.

"Adoula help now. Do not give boy any medicine to-night. Leave him to us." They agreed to abide by his wishes and thanked him and blessed him. Then we took our leave at about 9pm, once again having to brave the snow-covered slippery roads to return home.

After we had gone, Barrie's mother prepared him for the night and made him as comfortable as possible. He promptly fell asleep. A phone call next day from the boy's delighted mother informed us that the little boy had slept right through the night and continued to do so well into the afternoon of the following day. And from that day he never had a recurrence of the dreaded fits. But the road to recovery was long and slow and much treatment was required. Barrie's cure was not spectacular and immediate.

Previously, the child had been taken to a brain specialist in London who announced that the case was hopeless. He said that he had never come across such rapid deterioration of the brain after an accident of that kind. The parents were utterly dismayed.

Alec visited Barrie twice a week over a long period to pass on the Spirit healing. All through the long hard winter, through heavy snow and rain, Alec would walk two miles to the station, take a train journey and undertake a further walk at the other end. He treated the child and returned home late at night, weary but happy that he had been able to help Barrie.

It took a long time, for the improvement was slow. Eventually Barrie overcame his malady, but still could not talk nor recognise anyone. Then, one day, a very excited John, Barrie's father, called to tell us that a wonderful thing had happened to his son. He said that Barrie now had his own room and, the night before, when he had gone to tuck the little boy up in bed for the night the child opened his eyes and for the first time there was recognition in them. He held out his arms and said, "Daddy!" He pulled his father's head down towards his own as he had done of old. John was quite overcome, "He knew me!" he sobbed. "And he spoke!" Barrie grew up a fine healthy lad and was a great joy to his parents, thanks to Spirit.

About this time we also made the acquaintance of a certain Spirit Dr Moore. He said he had been a heart specialist during his Earth life and now that he was in the Spirit world he was anxious to continue helping humanity from his side. He would like to attach himself to Alec and work through him. We were only too delighted to accept his offer.

The first call for his services came when Grahame Watkins called on us late one night. He was very distressed and sought help for his 76 year old mother-in-law who was dying. He asked if the Guides could help make her passing any easier. His parents-in-law lived with him and his wife Marjorie.

Alec and I immediately accompanied Grahame back to his home. Adoula entranced Alec and proceeded to give the lady healing. It was at this stage that Dr Moore took over. He introduced himself and said that he could help the patient. After giving her some Spirit treatment, he announced with confidence that she would not die but continue to live on earth for some time to come. He turned to me and said, "In 12 months time Alec will be calling on this lady bringing with him a large bunch of red flowers and he will present them to her while she is sitting in the garden." From that day the little lady grew stronger and made a remarkable recovery. As time went by Dr Moore's remarks were pushed to the back of my mind by other more pressing matters.

But the following year I had reason to remember them. I had found that summer that I had a lot of red carnations in bloom in our garden. I picked a large bunch and asked Alec if he would take them to Marjorie's mother when he passed the house. He did so and it was only when he found the little lady sitting in the garden and presented her with the red bouquet that he recalled Dr Moore's words. She was fully recovered and lived an active life into her eighties. Dr Moore became a welcome and well loved helper in our circle. His services were very much appreciated by patients and ourselves alike.

Ectoplasm, though usually white when visible in the séance

room is not always so. It can vary from black, grey, white and even be brightly coloured.

I recall a time when Dick Evans came to our circle with a group from a Cardiff church. Half way through the séance a tall stately Spirit stepped from the cabinet wearing a magnificent coloured Egyptian headdress, the predominating colours being purple and gold. We were impressed with this Spirit's proud bearing as he moved over to stand before Dick. Then he spoke in a deep and accented voice: "I am sorry that I startled you when you visited my country. I must tell you that I belong to you and we can do good work together."

"Who are you?" enquired Dick, politely.

"I was a priest in the temple. My name is Nemphis." After the circle, Mr Evans confirmed that he had been frightened by this Spirit in the past. Then he told us the story.

He had gone some time previously to visit his son who was a Colonel stationed in Cairo. One night he awoke suddenly from a deep sleep and was startled to see an eerie light in one corner of the room. As he watched it a figure slowly became visible within the greenish glow and he saw quite clearly this Egyptian man, resplendent in his coloured headdress and robes, just as he had materialised that night in the circle. The figure was speaking and he could see the lips moving, but he could not hear what he was saying. This kind of experience was new to him and he found it decidedly unnerving. He remembered how the sweat was moist on his palms and brow and an uncontrollable fear clutched at his heart which caused him to dive, childlike, beneath the bedclothes where he remained for some time. When he finally surfaced again the Egyptian apparition had gone taking his light with him. But an uncanny feeling persisted that the figure was trying to get a message through to him.

The next day he had received a cable from his daughter, with whom he lived in Britain, calling him home because his son-in-law had passed away suddenly. It was then that he wondered if this had something to do with his ghostly visitor of the previous night. Dick said he was very pleased to make Nemphis' acquaintance in our home in less frightening circumstances and would be pleased to co-operate with his Egyptian Guide. He was on the point of retiring, he said and would, therefore have the time to devote to Spiritualism. So I invited him to join our circle, which he did, helping with the healing work quite effectively and did quite a bit of good work in that field.

Whenever Nemphis materialised he always wore his coloured headdress. A friend from South Africa was among the sitters one night and, being curious about this gorgeous headgear, he enquired why especially he wore the colours purple and gold. Nemphis replied with much dignity and perhaps a note of pride: "Because I have earned the right to wear them." But he did not elaborate further. Nemphis assisted us by doing good work in the field of absent healing and always his splash of coloured ectoplasm was a joy to behold.

Alec became the focal point of psychic investigators as word of his extraordinary powers spread. We were asked by the SNU (Spiritualists' National Union) if we would give some test circles. Alec willingly agreed, relieved that should any doubts about the authenticity of his mediumship exist they would, under test conditions, be immediately removed. It is important that a medium should be willing to undergo the most stringent tests if he is giving circles to the public. In a sense, every sitting that Alec gave was a test circle, because the room and cabinet were always thoroughly searched, before and after the séance and Alec, wearing only a pair of black trousers and a black vest made of sateen, was examined to the satisfaction of the sitters.

Harry Dawson, a then Past President of the SNU and a psychic investigator had this to say about Alec's test circles.

"Indeed the Spirit people are co-operative to genuine research. In a series of test sittings with Alec Harris, the Austrian scientist in charge of proceedings on the other side said to me, 'Providing you give us warning that you are going to do certain things, we have no objection to reasonable experimentation of any kind'.

"On one occasion Gladys Mallaburn, a well-known North of England medium, was present. From a child she had long experience with séances and had profound knowledge of these matters. It was interesting to note that upon invitation of the

Austrian scientist, she was admitted into the cabinet to watch the process. She witnessed the building up, from a heap of ectoplasm on the ground, of a rudimentary figure and then saw a Spirit hand working upon this plastic material, moulding the draperies and touching up the actual features and then there came out a form from the cabinet.

"At one memorable sitting with Alec Harris were with me Ernest Oaten, John Steward and Ernest Thompson. During the proceedings a little stocky figure proceeded to lift Ernest off the floor. I myself was so fascinated I went down on my knees in order to watch the play of the muscles in the calves of his legs. As a Physiotherapist I know something about muscles. At the same time the Austrian scientist in charge of the proceedings invited another member of the group to reach out and ascertain that the medium was still in his chair.

"There is another incident which has been frequently reported as a classic example of the cooperation between the Spirit operators and ourselves. Certain critics had suggested to me that it would be possible for the medium to come out of the cabinet and to pass himself off as a female figure. In a sitting the materialised form of a girl of approximately 16 years came over to me from the cabinet, stood in front of me and opened her Spirit robes. There was the naked form of this young girl. The materialised Spirit form of the Austrian scientist requested me, in view of my many years of experience as a Physiotherapist, to give the figure a complete examination and to assure myself that it was in fact the figure of a young female and not the medium. This I did; and it is important to emphasise that the panel of investigators was quite satisfied she could not have been an accomplice.

"I witnessed a remarkable phase of materialisation. This was under the most stringent conditions imposed by the examining panel of observers. The curtains of the medium's cabinet suddenly swung wide open and we observed the medium slumped in his chair in deep trance, indicated by certain signs known to the trained symptomatologist, one of whom was present. The ectoplasmic form of the Guide, an Austrian scientist in his earth life, was visible to all of us. As we watched we saw the ectoplasm begin to emerge slowly from the medium's mouth, nose and ears. It rolled down his body on to the floor where it coiled itself into a sizeable mass and from the centre of this mass it began to rise, just as if someone was pushing it upwards. It took the form of a little black boy. Here I should mention that the mass as it first emerged was black in colour with white streaks in it. The figure finally presented itself perfectly, above the waist line, the eyes, squat nose and teeth when it smiled were perfect. After a short space of time it began to dissolve before our eyes and slowly like a thick black snake it climbed back over the body of the medium and was absorbed through the same orifices of the body. There was a kind of phosphorescent light during the whole time, which rose and fell in intensity. This was indeed a most amazing night.

"Another example of the evidential return of a Spirit friend was recorded at one of Harris' séances at which certain members of the National Council were present; amongst them was Wilfred Ely, a Minister of the Union. During the séance, many figures appeared and one gave outstanding evidence to Mr Ely. The Spirit who appeared and walked up to Mr Ely gave him the Sioux Indian salute and spoke to him. Then he took Mr Ely's hand and placed it upon his nose. Mr Ely immediately recognised his brother who passed as a result of wounds received in the 1914-18 war, for his brother had received an injury earlier in life which had disfigured the nose. Mr Ely was profoundly moved and was full of joy and emotion. He then confided to his colleagues on the Council the striking information that his father was a full-blooded Sioux Indian. This was a remarkable piece of evidence, as Mr Ely had not disclosed the ethnic origin of his father.

"The more I learn of these matters, the more vital it seems that a greater knowledge of the subject should be acquired and then we shall not be too hasty in our judgement."

From the foregoing comments it is obvious that Alec's materialisation mediumship could not be faulted and the investigations were, in our minds, definitely worthwhile, if not absolutely essential.

I would like to quote from an article written by the Editor of 'Two Worlds' dated Friday, 3rd January 1947. This corroborates

Harry Dawson's comments and will dispel any ideas that sceptics may have that there might have been any collusion between ourselves and that investigator.

"To be approached by a ghost, clad in the eerie draperies of ectoplasm, seized bodily and lifted approximately twelve inches from the ground would indeed be a terrifying experience to anyone without some knowledge and previous contact with such supernormal phenomena. This, however, was my experience in a materialisation séance at which the medium was Alec Harris of Cardiff. We were told when this Spirit materialised, that it was one of his characteristics to test his strength by lifting furniture. In a response to a request that he should lift me, the Spirit asked me to rise and without hesitation proceeded to take me in his arms and lift me up, to the astonishment of all present. This wonderful séance was characterised by the very matter of fact way in which the materialised forms moved about the room in search of their earthly friends.

"One form which appeared wanted to speak to a lady sitting immediately behind me and asked me if I would vacate my chair so that he could kneel on it. Without further delay he seized me by the hand and almost dragged me to the other end of the room. The hand was quite firm and one would have suspected that it was earthly, so real was its grip.

"On three occasions the materialised forms were visible simultaneously with the medium, who was seen resting on his chair in the cabinet, in deep trance, as these forms drew the curtains to one side when making their exits.

"Rohan, one of the Spirit Guides in charge of the proceedings, after materialising, drew the curtain to one side requesting a sitter to draw a second curtain, so that there could be no doubt of the co-existence of himself and the medium. One of the sitters nearest the cabinet was Ernest Oaten, who has perhaps had more experiences in psychic phenomena than anyone else in this country, having devoted over 50 years to psychical research. He stated afterwards that he considered this demonstration of material phenomena to be genuine and quite as good as anything he had previously witnessed. On two occasions during the séance he had taken the liberty to gently touch the medium through the curtain to satisfy himself that he was still there.

Ernest Oaten

"The proceedings opened with a short address by Rohan who made one special request that when shaking hands with the Spirit friends, the sitters should refrain from gripping too tightly the ectoplasmic hands. He pointed out that this tended to weaken their efforts, thus taking longer to rebuild the forms. He then walked across the floor to Mr Harris's son to speak a few words to him. The next visitor was a young Spirit operator, a member of the Harris band of Spirit workers, who had not yet been permitted to materialise, but was allowed to speak in the Direct Voice. The rather humorous remarks were characterised chiefly by the incredible speed in which they were uttered.

"The next Spirit built up in such a novel manner that we were provided with absolute and concrete evidence of the supernormal nature of these manifestations. Our attention was suddenly drawn to what at first appeared to be a small mound of ectoplasm. It was not only in a rapid state of motion, but growing miraculously in size. By the time it assumed the proportions of a white billowing pillar of approximately three feet in height, a human face began to form, in a very artificial way at the top rounded portion of the pillar. The final formation into a full sized human figure was very rapid but easily discernible in the ample red light available. From almost nothing, a full form had grown before our eyes within the space of a minute and soon the figure was moving round just as the others had done searching with keen interest for his earthly friend. The next figure was that of someone who had taken his own life only a short while ago and the reunion with his friends was very dramatic.

"Our next visitor was a well-known Spirit co-operator in this circle. Her name is Marianna and her chief mission seems to be to prove, as additional evidence of Spirit return, the difference between her sex and that of the medium. She gently raised her ectoplasmic draperies revealing beyond all doubt her female sex and at the same time lifting her leg like a dancer. On being asked to dance she swung her dress so that it billowed like that of a ballerina. An important feature of this demonstration of Spirit power over matter was the distinct and completely three-dimensional nature of both draperies and human form underneath. The details of the next manifestation were quite elaborate; it was a Chinese Spirit in national costume and his ectoplasmic hair and very long moustache consisted of black ectoplasm. He announced his name as Yang Shay. Approaching one of the sitters he told him that he had been receiving Spirit healing from him. Mr Aikman, to whom these remarks were addressed, stated afterwards that he had been taking a course of Spiritual healing and that whereas for years he had suffered from duodenal ulcers he was now able to eat any food he fancied.

"This was followed by a unique interlude of music. Mr Harris's son, who has a pure and soprano voice, sang a duet with one of the Spirit visitors and from the perfection of the rendering it was evident that they had had considerable practice together.

"The most picturesque figure of the evening then made his appearance. He was a tall American Indian with a majestic figure and noble bearing. He wore a very large headdress of ectoplasmic feathers and he turned his head slowly for all to see the extent and details of its formation.

"A second Indian named White Wing then appeared and invited Ernest Oaten to examine him closely. Mr Oaten walked towards him. As he minutely studied his dress and feature, he described each detail so that all could compare their own visual perception of the figure with his own. Mr Oaten concluded by saying that he would recognise him again anywhere now he had seen him.

"The next Spirit visitor finding its earthly contact, sat in a chair nearby. Making himself comfortable, he talked at some length to one of the sitters. As additional evidence one sitter remarked upon the different shapes of the hands of the various figures. The hand he had just touched was noticeably long and thin. The next materialisation was that of an Egyptian and the special feature in this case was the coloured headdress. He was followed by a fussy old lady who called for Edith amongst the sitters and wandered in and out in search of her.

"After this demonstration Rohan returned for a brief moment and requested sitters not to encourage Spirit forms to wander around and away from the cabinet as this extra effort was draining the power considerably. Yet another figure came and having found a contact knelt before the sitter and whispered her message.

"Many more figures came. A Spirit Healing Guide demonstrated the power of healing in the breath and referred to the curative value of herbs and trees. Towards the close of the séance a Russian Spirit, named Jolkim, sang in a powerful and resonant deep bass voice. Another Spirit called Bert, gave a wonderful

Jolkim- Our Russian soldier Spirit Guide with a lovely bass singing voice. Drawn by Alec in 1959

performance of whistling. Finally the Scientist, whom we were told was the brains behind the demonstration, appeared to us and imparted a few words of spiritual advice, ending the proceedings on a high spiritual level.

"It is interesting to note that the medium, Alec Harris, has no great liking for his part in the work and was one of the hardest to convince of the nature of the phenomena that took place during his trances, in the earlier stages of his development. The room in which the séance was held was just an average sized bedroom, but although there were twenty sitters, we were all quite comfortable, having been placed in three rows, thus providing a most powerful battery of energy augmented by the vibrations of community singing.

"On behalf of sitters and readers alike, I extend our thanks to Mr and Mrs Harris for their outstanding and valuable work on behalf of Spiritualism."

In concluding this chapter I would like to tell of the conjurer who attended one of our séances. Albert Fletcher-Desborough, a professional stage illusionist, would have been able to judge, if anybody could, whether the materialisations he saw were produced by a magician's 'tricks'. He pronounced the materialisations authentic and called them 'unique'.

He was biased against the phenomena before coming to the circle. He was a self-declared sceptic, disbelieving all the stories he had heard. But, after witnessing several of his loved ones materialise, he was convinced. He wrote with conviction to the 'Liverpool Evening Express'.

"I examined the cabinet which Alec Harris used. Having been on the stage as an illusionist and magician, I knew exactly where to look for such things as panel and floor escapes, ceiling and wall slides. I was satisfied that nothing could make an exit or an entrance in any way. There was no chance for deception."

Of a short stout man who materialised from the cabinet and went straight to him, giving the name Bertie, he said: "It was my father. In his mumbling way of speaking, he gave my family pet name used by my parents. No one but the family knew it."

Then a young man came who hobbled and walked with difficulty. He grasped the conjurer's hand and said; "Bertie! I am your brother, Walter." The Spirit was recognised immediately by the conjurer, who explained that his brother had had his left ankle shot away in the Boer War. "No one there knew I had a brother," he said. So who learnt his name and that he hobbled when walking in life? There certainly could have been no deception in this case.

Then from the cabinet walked a stiff, upright young fellow. Like the others, the figure went towards the conjurer. Then he swerved, and throwing out his arms he embraced the conjurer's wife, saying in a very pathetic voice, "Mother, Mother, I'm your son Ronnie." This was their third son born under fire during the Sinn Fein rising in 1916, who had been captured in Singapore Harbour by the Japanese and beheaded. "He turned to me after embracing his mother," said the magician, "and put his head against mine. I recognised his voice."

No one among the sitters or the medium knew the intimate characteristics of those who materialised. The conjurer concluded his article with the question, "Why all these manifestations on my behalf?" and answered his own query tersely, "Because I was an unbeliever."

This report also appeared in 'Psychic News' 2nd March 1974.

I hope that it will dispel any thoughts that my husband was a first class illusionist.

He was not.

But he certainly was a first class physical medium.

Chapter Ten

Dream of South African Voyage

❖ *Spirit demonstrate control of Alec* ❖ *A suicide's family helped* ❖ *White Wing materialises out of the sanctuary* ❖ *Materialisation in Spirit light* ❖ *Dream of South African voyage* ❖ *Prof Haarhof's report of his sitting* ❖ *Dr MacDonald Bayne vouches for Alec's mediumship.*

In early 1947, during a Canadian type Winter, the snow lay thick upon the ground and it was bitterly cold. The sitters of our circle were concerned for Alec, who usually wore only a pair of thin black sateen pyjamas. "We do think it wrong, Louie," they said, "to let Alec sit without any warm clothes on in this bitter weather." "I'm sure," I said to Alec, "that the Guides won't mind you keeping your clothes on tonight. They must know how cold it is." So Alec did not change his attire, but stayed warmly dressed for the circle. He left his black pyjamas on the bed in the bedroom next door.

The séance duly opened with the customary prayer, and we launched ourselves in to the first song. Unexpectedly, a soft neat bundle came out of the cabinet, carried by unseen hands, and was placed at my feet. At the same time Alec's Spirit Guide, Christopher, remarked chidingly, "Louie, have we not promised to take care of the medium's physical body?"

"Why do you say this now, Christopher?" I asked. "Will you please step inside the cabinet and feel the medium," was his only reply. I did as requested, and was surprised to discover that Alec was quite warm, while we sitters were all numb with cold. Then it was that I was astounded to see that he was now wearing his thin black pyjamas, which had been left in the other room.

Afterwards it was discovered that the neat bundle, which had been placed at my feet at the beginning of the séance, contained Alec's warm clothes all nicely folded with his belt securing it. It was then I remembered White Wing's instructions that Alec must never wear in the circle any clothes that he had worn during the day because in that event the Guides would have to spend time clearing any vibrations which these may have absorbed. So, trusting Alec to their care I never again let the weather interfere with standing procedures.

Spirit have remarkable control of the functions of the medium's physical body. This may be illustrated by the following story. The Spirit scientists succeeded where the apothecary's skill had failed. One evening Alec was suffering from severe bronchitis with an accompanying rasping cough, which had not responded to any medicaments. He should have been in bed but he remained up as it was our circle night. As the sitters were coming long distances he did not have the heart to cancel the séance. Among those attending the circle were three doctors and three ministers, one being a lay preacher at a Pentecostal Church. This man, a widower who had now remarried, objected to his wife having anything to do with Spiritualism, a subject in which she was very interested. She, however, had persuaded him to attend this circle to see for himself. Alec entered the cabinet coughing distressingly and soon passed into trance, the Guides doing everything possible to build the power in difficult circumstances.

A female Spirit emerged and spoke to the lady in the front row. Having kissed her, she thanked her for looking after her husband and son. Then she called up the lay preacher who was sitting at the back and conversed with him for a time while he looked dumbfounded all the while. The Spirit of his late wife then put her hands on his shoulders and said: "Don't be too hard on the boy. Try to have more understanding and you will find he will be much better. Remember, I am always with you, helping." It was heart warming to know that here was a mother who was still concerned about her son, and who was grateful to the second wife, who had taken her place after her death to care for the little family she had left behind.

Shortly after the circle I received a letter from the present wife of this Pentecostal Minister, saying how grateful she was for the circle as it had convinced her husband of the authenticity of Spiritualism. It had put him in touch with his dead wife, whose materialisation he had accepted completely. As a result, harmonious conditions now prevailed in their home.

One of the doctors present, an important man in his field, approached me at the conclusion of the séance saying: "Mrs Harris, your husband should be in bed; he's a very sick man, you know." "The Guides will look after him," I said with a reassuring smile. And he nodded, "I can quite believe in that," he said. "You know, with all the amazing things to be witnessed here tonight, what proved to me that your husband is a genuine medium was the fact that he was confined in that small cabinet for over three hours and never coughed once. This is quite impossible in the bronchitic condition he is in at present."

It was as well for Alec that he was unaware of some of what took place during séances. Had I not had such trust in our Guides, some experiences would have been frightening. What wife would care to see her husband being slowly dematerialised before her eyes, and then made to disappear completely. This I had to do. When it happened to Alec I must confess to experiencing a momentary pang of anxiety, until I remembered our Guides who were in charge of such experiments. Then I relaxed and let them get on with it.

At the circle when this happened there were a lot of well-known people present, among them a minister, a journalist, and a doctor. Just as the circle was coming to an end the Scientist requested us to link hands. We did as he asked, and waited.

After a few moments, the cabinet curtains were lifted by Spirit hands and Alec could be seen sitting, in trance, in the chair. I noticed that his legs were no longer there. Before I could reason this out, the curtains were dropped again. When they were lifted a second time, to my dismay, the lower half of Alec's body was absent. Nothing was visible below his chest. I could see the seat of the chair quite plainly. Then the curtains were lowered and raised for a third time. As I peered inside the cabinet with bated breath I could see that the upper torso of Alec was still there. But as we watched, this too disappeared, leaving only an empty chair. After a couple of minutes I noticed that a thick white mist began to form over the chair. Then there was a decided thud, as of a body being dropped into the chair, and we could discern the slumped form of the medium through the haze of the mist, sitting in the chair as before; only now it was complete again, much to our relief.

This demonstration by the Spirit scientists indicated that they have perfect control of physical as well as Spirit matter. I wondered at the necessity of such a demonstration, and I asked the Scientist why Alec had been removed in this manner. He replied that it was necessary to withdraw the medium for a time as there were adverse conditions prevailing in the circle. Powerful emotions were present of disappointment and frustration on both sides. Firstly by the sitters who expected to contact their loved ones, and having failed to do so were acutely disappointed; and secondly by the loved ones in Spirit who were unable to manifest for various reasons and suffered a sense of frustration as a result. These emotional conditions were distressing the medium, he told us, and could be dispelled more quickly if he were removed altogether from the physical world and then returned to the cabinet cleared of any unpleasant vibrations.

"We did it this way," explained the Scientist, "that is to say, in three parts, to enable you to witness the exercise as it progressed. We also felt that it would furnish you with further proof of Spirit power." It certainly left us all with a great deal to think about.

The scientist in charge of our circle would often come out and sit in the chair beside me during a séance and discuss matters pertaining to materialisation. I was afforded an opportunity of studying his face closely and satisfying myself that he was totally unlike Alec in every detail; not only his face, but also his stature did not resemble the medium's. He told me one night, that the Guides were anxious to help Alec's sister, Connie, to materialise. Knowing Alec's devotion to the girl, they also wished that he should be sufficiently conscious, in other words in only a very light trance, so that he could see her himself.

I told him that I thought this would please Alec very much. The materialisation of Connie commenced. At first, when the curtains parted, only Alec could be seen in his chair, and a large amount of ectoplasm bundled into one corner of the cabinet. Every week they worked with Connie, who seemed to have great difficulty performing the feat required of her. As the weeks passed we could see the form becoming stronger and stronger. At last, one night she was there, as shy as ever. But she was unable to move or speak. She merely stood still, holding her materialised form.

At this stage the Scientist asked if I would go into the cabinet to help by giving extra power. I did this, and while the Scientist stood behind me, I placed my arms lightly one on either side of her. To my joy she then found that she could move. She commenced to walk slowly towards me as I backed towards the opening of the curtains. Later, she was able to do this without any assistance from me, but she was never able to speak.

True to their word, the Guides allowed Alec to come out of trance sufficiently for him to see his beloved sister. He would leave his chair and together they would stand just in front of the curtains in full view of the sitters, smiling at one another and holding hands, a very moving sight. From Alec's point of view this reunion with his sister, which afforded him his only clear recollection in the whole séance, was always the highlight of any circle.

In 1949, when the power in the séances seemed to be at its peak and Alec's mediumship was going from strength to strength, we were obliged to disband the circle, mainly because some of our sitters were transferred away from Cardiff. Our disappointment was acute for it meant that we would have to form a new band of sitters and although this was not serious with Alec's degree of development, it nevertheless was a set-back. We need not have had any qualms, however, as four sincere and dedicated people came, as if they had been purposefully directed to us. They were John and Sally Caygill, and Joe and Edna Turner, who all hailed from Newport, some 12 miles distance from Cardiff. This quartet soon became our firm and valued friends and happily for us agreed to be the basis of our newly formed circle, with Dick, my sister May, son Bradley, and myself bringing the total of sitters to eight. Twelve months later two more dear friends joined us, Mrs Thomas and Megan, mother and daughter.

Aunty Thomas, as she was affectionately known, had received great help herself from the healing circle. At the first circle she attended she was greatly comforted when her husband materialised, as well as her son, who had not known any Earth life as he had died 'in utero'.

The ten of us became the perfect circle. We were so in tune with one another that when we sat together in that upper room we were very closely linked with our beloved Spirit band and their work was made easier. Even so, there were nights when nothing manifested at all. Nevertheless, throughout the séance we would all feel uplifted to a higher plane of consciousness, and in that state became hypersensitive to the vibrations of the Spirit World. The Guides called it their experimental circle and maintained that it was here that they did their work in preparation for the coming public circle.

Alec became, for the first time, really interested in what took place as a result of his mediumship, for John and Joe were at pains to tell him what had occurred during the circle. We had not done this before possibly because he appeared to be quite disinterested. This left him in the dark about his own mediumship, and he always seemed a trifle bored by the whole procedure. Now he felt really involved and could appreciate the good work the Guides were undertaking, which was a much happier situation altogether.

As Alec's mediumship had developed, so had my dear brother, Ted's, over the corresponding years. He had come a long way in the Spiritualist Movement since that memorable day some years previously when I had, in my ignorance, chided him for becoming interested in what I then believed to be a subject best left alone. Dear Ted had been so patient with me at the time, and had sent me home with much to think about. He had gently opened the gate to an inviting Spiritual path upon which Alec and I soon found our feet firmly planted.

Ted Bradley by this time had become a medium of some repute in his native Wales, and he had his own Church in the Rhondda Valley which he ran with the help of a close friend who was also a fine medium. But he also devoted much of his time to conducting church services whenever and wherever he was so required in other neighbouring churches. Frequently he would be asked to officiate further afield in the Spiritualist Churches of Cardiff and Newport.

Being somewhat delicate from childhood, Ted did not enjoy robust health, and this suffered further deterioration as a result of his involvement in the First World War. However, he would not allow his physical frailties to inhibit his church work in any way, and his familiar figure was frequently seen pedalling his bicycle in all weathers to attend one or other of the many small churches in and around the Rhondda Valley, determined not to disappoint a congregation expecting to hear him address them.

Over the years, Ted sat in our circle many times when he was in our vicinity. He was unable to be one of our regular sitters, much as we would have liked this, as he lived more than twenty miles away and as we always sat so late at night it made such a commitment impossible for him.

Whenever he was present at our circle his Guide, Michael, or his Red Indian Guide would materialise for him, and they would have lengthy discussions together. It was also such a joy, to see our Dad conversing with his son, and I knew that my father in the Spirit World was very proud of Ted, and was pleased with the work he was doing for humanity. The Spiritualist Movement is built upon the unselfish services of mediums such as my brother who frequently travel long distances in all weathers, often at inconvenience and discomfort to themselves, to comfort and console the bereaved, and to spread the truth of survival after death.

To dearest Ted I shall be eternally grateful for opening my eyes to truth, and for pointing out the path which, though not always an easy one, has offered Spiritual and emotional rewards beyond my wildest dreams.

Suicide for those souls contemplating such a tragic step does not provide an avenue of escape from their seemingly intolerable problems. They do not leap into a carefree life of Joy. The abject remorse they experience on finding themselves cast prematurely into Spirit by what they have done to themselves and their sense of hopelessness on seeing the sorrow and distress their act has left in its wake, becomes more terrible to bear than the Earth problems from which they originally tried, so drastically, to escape. For truly there is no way in which they can set matters right.

I remember the case of Connie Jenkins, the beautiful eighteen year old daughter of neighbours who lived higher up our road. At such a tender age, Connie found for no known reason that the burden of Earth life was too much to bear. While her parents slept she crept downstairs to the kitchen, turned on the gas stove and placed her lovely head in the gas-filled oven. When her poor mother found her next morning she was frantic with grief. She and her daughter had been so close to one another, almost like sisters, and quite inseparable. Worse! She was an only child. Both parents were bewildered, and numb with shock.

Early one Sunday morning I heard hurried footsteps coming down our pathway. They stopped at our front door. There was a clatter as a letter was pushed through our letter box. Feeling that something was amiss I rushed downstairs and saw a very dejected woman creeping quietly away. I recognised our neighbour, Mrs Jenkins, so I called her back before she reached the gate. As I looked into her face I could see that she was in a dreadful state of stress. On enquiring if I could help, the floodgates of her misery were suddenly opened and she sobbed out the story of her daughter's suicide. "Why?" she kept repeating, "Why? Why?"

I took her inside, and when she was calmer I asked for details. When she had finished her story she confessed that there was more to her distress than losing her beloved daughter. What she feared was that Connie might go to eternal damnation as a result of her actions in taking her own life. She had been to church for help, but none was offered, and she was desperately worried about her child's future. What punishment was there in store for her?

I did what I could to comfort her, pointing out that God, in His infinite Love and Wisdom, could not possibly set Himself to punish one so bereft as Connie, and one so obviously in need of His Love.

"How can we think of God, our Heavenly Father, as being worse than an earthly father?" I asked her. "He will forgive because he understands all about us." Then, on an impulse, I said, "Why don't you and your husband attend our Tuesday night circle?" After a moment's thought, she accepted with thanks and shortly afterwards she left.

On Tuesday night I decided to seat them in the front row, and the circle commenced. I suddenly had an overwhelming urge to sing 'The Londonderry Air', better known as 'Danny Boy' and we all joined in, in beautiful harmony. At the conclusion of the song the curtains of the cabinet parted and a little elderly lady stepped forward. She held out her arms to Mrs Jenkins and said, "Oh, my girl!"

"It's mother!" exclaimed Mrs Jenkins. The Spirit moved over to her daughter, and putting her arms about her, murmured: "Don't worry dear, I am looking after Connie. She's all right, and one day she will be able to come to you but not just yet." Mrs Jenkins broke down and sobbed unashamedly with relief.

Many times later Connie herself came. But always she begged for forgiveness for the sorrow she had caused. This seemed to be her most urgent need, forgiveness!

After the circle, Mrs Jenkins remarked: "How strange that you should sing 'Danny Boy'. That was my mother's favourite song." Then she smiled as she remembered something. "Whenever there were street musicians mother would give them a shilling and ask them to play that song; she loved it so much." Her face clouded, and she sighed, "Yes, she passed away 12 months ago to-day."

I explained that obviously the song had helped her to come through. "Well" smiled Mrs Jenkins, now looking happier: "This experience has done so much to help us. I feel better about Connie now." As a result of that séance their whole outlook changed. They enthusiastically took up the work of Spirit, and eventually we invited them to join our circle.

It is no good contemplating suicide to join a loved one who has passed earlier. It may take a long time to meet up with them again in the world of Spirit and the feeling of loss will persist. Time on Earth is transient compared with that on the Astral Plane. It is better to wait for our allotted span to run out. And the waiting is made easier when we know that our departed ones are always near. In fact, they are only a thought away.

Writing of this brings to mind a letter we once received from a certain Doctor Irving in the South of England. His was a sad story. His wife had met a tragic end in a car crash and, being a very devoted couple, he had felt her loss keenly. He said that the bottom just fell out of his world. He neglected his work, lost interest in life, and was seriously contemplating suicide so that he could be with her again. A friend of his, being worried about his depressed state, gave up his place in a circle that had been arranged with us by his church, and persuaded this doctor to attend in his stead. His reaction to this séance was gratifying.

Quoting from his letter, he says:

"You put me in the third row. A Spirit came out and called me. When I went up I was stunned to see my dear wife. She put her arms around me and kissed me. She told me that she had never left me; and that I must not do what I had in mind as our separation would be much longer. She begged me to carry on with my life and just look forward to the time when we would be together again. Then she just dematerialised as I held her in my arms. It was a most wonderful experience! I came away determined to take up my life again. I thank God for Alec Harris, through whom it was made possible."

I hope and pray that should there be any who feel that life holds no further attraction for them these last two stories will convince them that suicide is not the answer.

Alec always disliked having to go into the cabinet and sitting apart from the rest of us.

"Why can't I sit with you?" he protested, one night. "Why must I always sit in that wretched cabinet?" I explained that was what the Guides had requested. "It's the way they want to work," I said. "Well I want to sit with the others," he grumbled. He seemed so put out and discontented with the present arrangement that I thought, "Why not? Let's try letting him sit with us in the circle tonight and see what happens."

So we all sat round in a complete circle, I with my back to the cabinet, while Alec sat by the wall, but close to the cabinet, eyes closed, in trance. We opened the circle as usual, and I found myself wondering what, under the present conditions, could possibly happen. Suddenly the cabinet curtains parted behind me, and I could see my little Guide, Fiji, standing beside me. I thought, 'it works just as well without Alec being inside the cabinet! I'm so glad for his sake'. Fiji was smiling and made as if to step into the circle of sitters when her little form just seemed to close up. It crumpled up and fell to the floor like an empty sack.

Quickly, an ectoplasmic arm, or rather a rod with a forked prong on the end of it, protruded from the cabinet and lifted the entranced Alec with his chair into the cabinet. I was so taken by surprise that I could only gape! When I recovered from the shock of seeing Alec removed from our midst, I realised that the Guides were displeased with the new arrangement which interfered with the conservation of the power. They had tried to oblige us by materialising little Fiji, but she could not hold the form as she was unable to draw on any concentration of ectoplasm. Without the enclosed area of the cabinet the energies were easily dissipated, so they had to put the medium back where they wanted him. It certainly was a spectacular though frightening way of doing it.

After Alec had done this disappearing trick I glanced down at the floor in the centre of the circle of sitters and saw, what I thought was Alec's handkerchief lying there. I bent and picked it up. As I did so I was horrified to hear a groan from Alec inside the cabinet. At the same time I realised that what I was holding was a piece of his ectoplasm, moist, and rather solid, and I hastily put it into the cabinet, where I knew it would be returned to Alec's body.

The experience left me shaken. The Scientist's voice then gave me a firm rebuke: "Let that be a lesson to you! You must never touch anything without first asking permission as this has a deleterious effect upon the medium." We bore that in mind after that and were always meticulously careful.

I was perturbed to see that the public circles were proving to be a drain on Alec's strength. He was looking decidedly weary. He was coping with these as well as a full time job by day. We discussed the possibility of giving up the public circles, retaining only the Tuesday private sittings. Whenever the subject of terminating the public circles came up something always seemed to happen to make us change our minds. This time it came in the form of an invitation from a lady to visit her at her house to meet a certain Miss B, a medium, who was on her first visit to our church to give a demonstration. She had expressed a wish to see me. When we met she said that she was puzzled by the fact that Helen Duncan's Guide, Albert Stewart, had come to her the previous night and asked her to take a message to the Harrises.

"Oh? And what is the message?" I asked, interested.

"He said that I was to tell you and your husband that you must not give up. That you must carry on with the work as it is important that you should do this. Do you understand the message, Mrs Harris?" she asked.

"Yes," I answered thoughtfully. "Yes, I do. Thank you, Miss B."

"Oh, yes and something else he said. He told me to tell you not to worry that Alec would be looked after."

I was amazed to think that Albert Stewart was that concerned about our circles. Of course, he had manifested several times, but still his interest was surprising. It proved to me that there is a good deal of cooperation between the bands of workers on the other side. Albert's message had the desired effect. We continued with the public circles.

At this stage Aunty Thomas and her daughter, Megan, began to sit regularly in our public circles. I was grateful for their assistance because our son Bradley after leaving Cardiff University, had to go to Aldershot to start his National Service training. This left me on my own to handle the circles so I was fortunate to have Megan to take Bradley's place. She also gave invaluable assistance to Adoula during the Healing circles. This happy arrangement continued for some years, while Aunty Thomas took upon herself the task of organising the refreshments afterwards.

At a public circle held shortly after receiving Albert's message there was present a sitter from London. She was extremely sceptical of all psychic phenomena but had agreed to accompany her sister who was in need of comfort having lost her husband.

Needless to say the husband materialised very strongly, placing himself directly under the red light so that his every feature could be seen and readily recognised. Then he spoke for a while in his own voice to the two ladies present, convincing them completely of his identity.

The sceptical sitter was impressed with what she had seen. When she returned to London, she discussed the séance in detail with a friend, Sir Robert Archibald. He listened politely to what she had to tell him, and summed it up as an attack of hallucinations on her part. When she stood her ground he suggested that he be permitted to investigate the circle himself and asked her to arrange for him to attend a sitting.

On receipt of her letter I agreed to her attending with her friend. Before the séance began she introduced us to Sir Robert who proved to be a most charming man. This lady said she was anxious that he should meet and talk with us before the séance so he could see for himself we were 'just ordinary people'.

I placed him to sit next to me in the sanctuary, and the proceedings began. A Spirit, wearing a turban, came for Sir Robert. He gave his name and they spoke together for a time, and Sir Robert said he remembered the man.

Two visitors from Durban, South Africa, were sitting in the second row, a Mr and Mrs Veary. A Spirit came for them, and stepping out of the cabinet walked round the back of the circle until he stood behind Mrs Veary. Placing his hands on her shoulders he addressed her in a broad Scottish accent. He said he was interested in her as he intended to use her as a medium for healing. She asked him his name but he replied, 'Later'.

He then walked to the front of the circle and spoke to Sir Robert. "Goodness gracious," he said in his soft brogue: "Fancy seeing you here! You know me don't you? Murdoch Mackenzie; we were in Edinburgh together, remember?"

"Of course, yes." Sir Robert was amazed to see and recognise the Spirit, and the two chatted amiably together of old times. Afterwards I asked Sir Robert if he really had recognised the Scotsman, and his reply was emphatic. "Of course! Murdoch

Mackenzie, fancy that," and he shook his head in reminiscence. "We were in Edinburgh together; I remember very well. Only," and he bit his lower lip as his brow puckered in puzzlement, "there's one thing that puzzles me. As far as I know, he is still alive and on Earth."

I pointed out that this was possible, and had happened before, when living people had materialised at the circle while in their sleep state, or perhaps while their physical bodies were at a very low ebb due to extreme illness when they were between life and death.

However, the sequel to this incident came when Sir Robert had to have a medical check-up before travelling on a journey to South Africa. He found that his own doctor was away and there was a locum in attendance instead, and strangely enough it was a man who had also been with him in Edinburgh.

Sir Robert decided to enquire after his old colleague. "You remember Murdoch Mackenzie who was with us when we were both in Edinburgh?" "Yes, certainly I do," smiled the doctor. "Good chap! I kept in touch with him for years."

"And then?" pursued Sir Robert, anxious to find out more about him. "Then," continued the doctor, "he went to Australia. He died two years ago, I believe." Sir Robert nodded, now understanding. The doctor then turned to Sir Robert's friend, who had accompanied him to the surgery, and asked her if she knew the gentleman they were discussing.

"I met him for the first time in Cardiff last week," she said. The doctor's eyebrows lifted in surprise, having just told her that the man had died two years previously. She realised that an explanation was called for. With some trepidation she related her experiences at the Harris circle. She need not have feared. Far from being reserved about the story, he too wanted to attend a similar séance. This was the case with many other medical men who showed marked interest in the phenomena; but our Guides had advised Alec to rest for a while as he was feeling the strain of so many sittings, and was plainly very tired.

This Spirit, Murdoch Mackenzie, became known as Dr Mac in

Durban, South Africa, where he worked through the healer, Vi Veary. And whenever she attended one of our circles Dr Mac would materialise and encourage her in the work she was doing. He proved to be a very advanced soul.

I recall an instance which made a great impact on me. There was an epidemic in Cardiff of glandular fever. I contracted this virulent germ and was feeling very ill indeed, suffering with painful swollen glands. Alec phoned our doctor who advised him to get me to bed, and said that he would call first thing in the morning. It was our circle night. It was the first one that I had not been able to attend, and I was feeling very disappointed. My bedroom was next door to the sanctuary, and as I lay in bed I could hear the sitters singing. My frustration was acute at not being able to be in there with them.

All of a sudden I heard a click, then a movement, and on looking up I saw the door open slowly. My beloved White Wing stood there. I could see that Megan, John and Joe were with him. He walked right into my room and stood beside my bed. The curtains at the window were not lined, and by the light of the full moon which filtered through them I could see this loved Spirit as clearly as the other three physical beings in the room. The texture of his skin, his robes, in fact, every detail was visible to me as I lay there. Then he spoke, "Faithful, White Wing come to help you." He took my hands in his. His Spirit hands were as firm as my own. He held them thus for a moment, transmitting to me the healing power. Then he placed his hands on my head, and from that point I remembered no more. I passed into a state of deep sleep. The four visitors to my sickroom then left and returned to the sanctuary where they continued with the circle.

This was a most remarkable feat on the part of White Wing for it is extremely rare for materialising entities to move so far into another room. To move to the far side of the sanctuary is difficult enough, with the stretch of the ectoplasmic cord connecting the Spirit with the medium. I must confess to being a little awed at the control our Spirit scientists had over the psychic power available.

I awakened at 7am next morning fit and well. The swollen glands had all returned to normal and I felt on top of the world.

Quickly, I phoned the doctor and told him that I was better, and that there was no need for him to call. He sounded very dubious as he asked, "Are you quite sure, Mrs Harris." "Yes, quite sure," I replied, "I'm absolutely cured." That incident will remain in my mind as one of my most memorable experiences.

White Wing announced one night during a séance that he wished to materialise in his own light, requesting that the red electric bulb be extinguished so that there would be complete darkness for his demonstration. We did as we were asked and waited for developments, not knowing what to expect.

Presently, near the cabinet, a pin-point of light could be seen. This slowly increased in size and power until, in its unearthly luminosity, we were able to discern a figure standing in front of the cabinet curtains. The Spirit then stepped forward and I saw that it was White Wing, resplendent in his magnificent feathered Indian headdress. His features, hands, and robes were all so much clearer than when seen by the light of the red electric globe. This intense blue-white Spirit light was very much an improvement on our red light. It afforded us an opportunity of seeing the Spirit in every detail of clothing and form, even to the colour of the eyes! At times the glow would fluctuate, fading, and then resuming its brilliance as the power waned and was restored.

In later years many other Spirits learned to materialise with their own light. I noticed that some were unable to speak while holding the full form materialisation as well as the light. It seemed to take a tremendous amount of power to produce this phenomenon and required a large supply of psychic energy. White Wing, however, being an advanced Guide with much experience, had no difficulty in showing us the very best aspect of this form of Spirit manifestation.

A moment of amusement was caused once when Alec, for some reason, came out of trance while the Scientist, materialised outside the cabinet, was speaking to the sitters. Alec popped his head out of the cabinet and enquired, "Have you finished yet?" The Scientist broke off his speech in the middle of a word and gave Alec a scathing look as if to say 'When you have finished I will continue!' Alec looked so surprised to see the Spirit form standing there. Somewhat shamefaced he mumbled, "I'm sorry, Sir," and quickly withdrew his head behind the curtains. A chuckle of mirth went round the sitters at the incongruity of the situation. This was an interesting incident because, as in the case of Connie's materialisation, Alec was conscious during the Spirit Scientist's manifestation and was able to talk to us, as well as to the materialised Spirit. It was a rare occurrence.

In 1951 Joe Turner had a strange dream. He dreamt that he, Alec and I together with our son, Bradley, were in a boat on our way to South Africa. When he told me I laughed at such an improbable situation. I knew that dreams could be inconsequential and often quite unrelated to fact. "Anyway," I said, "Why on earth would we be going to South Africa?" He merely shrugged and laughed it off, and no more was said about Joe's dream.

Carl ~ Joe's Guide

Some weeks afterwards Joe's Guide, Carl, materialised and he and Joe had an unusually long chat. I remarked, "What's all this about?" When Joe returned to his seat his face was serious. "Now I know that Carl knows everything that is happening in my life," he said. I waited for him to tell me in his good time, which he did. "I have not mentioned this before, Louie," he confided, "but my firm is closing down its Newport Works, and they want me to take over another of their branches."

"But that would mean you would have to leave the circle," I cried. "Which I am not prepared to do," he said emphatically, "so I have turned the offer down. Now I hope to get another job near Cardiff." I received this news with mixed feelings. I was sorry at

Joe's disappointment at having to forego the new post offered, yet glad that he was still with the circle. Joe, meanwhile, had tried hard to get the right job in the right place. He had two posts in the offing when Carl again materialised at a later circle and said: "Not either of these, my friend, but the third path is the one you must take."

It so happened that Joe saw an advertisement for what seemed a very good proposition. He applied for the job and was called for an interview, only to return disappointed. "I was offered the job," he said, "but it is out of the question. They want to send me to Nyasaland!" Carl came again at the next circle and said: "This is the third path which you must take, Joe. We want you to take it as a stepping stone to the place where we want you to be."

Joe deliberated on this, and eventually decided to take Carl's advice. In 1952 he left to take up this new appointment in Nyasaland. It was a sad day for our circle. To make matters worse John Caygill had a good post offered to him in the Isle of Man, so he and Sally regretfully pulled out. Four such good sitters leaving all at once meant the breakup of our circle. Grahame, too, owing to pressure of work which necessitated his being out of town frequently, had to discontinue sitting regularly and could only attend circles occasionally.

However, Aunty Thomas, Megan, Dick Evans, my sister May and I did our best to keep the circle going. Later, we invited Mr and Mrs Jenkins to join us; also Harold and Susie Harvey. We continued to give circles for groups from churches which came from all over the country. In spite of the change of sitters wonderful evidence was still received, and Alec's mediumship remained undaunted.

In 1952 our circle was visited by Theophilus Haarhof, Professor of Classics at the University of Witwatersrand in Johannesburg, South Africa. He had remarkable evidence when a materialised Spirit spoke to him in ancient Greek, a language about which Alec knew nothing.

Professor Haarhof in 'Psychic News' 13th December 1952, told its readers:

"University men are usually very shy to acknowledge psychic phenomena because in most cases they cannot produce scientific proof. I was no exception until some sixteen years ago when I was privileged to share a type of experience that enabled me to reliably correlate theory to fact. Recently, I had a new type of experience in which subjective factors were completely eliminated.

"It was at the house of Mr and Mrs Harris of Cardiff. I want to say at once that no praise is too great for the high motives, the integrity and the self-sacrificing service of Mrs Harris; and that the materialising powers of Mr Harris are astounding, unique, and entirely above suspicion. I make these statements after many years of investigation and many disappointments and experience of fraudulent mediums.

"Some ten years ago, in Johannesburg, I was brought into touch with a Greek philosopher of Ionia, who gave me convincing proof of his identity and entrusted a certain very difficult task to me. He does not wish his name to be mentioned at this stage, but I was given descriptions of him. The Harris circle knew nothing of all this. But at the sitting a week ago, this philosopher materialised. He walked out and took me firmly by the hand.

"He brought his face close to mine and I saw that it corresponded to the descriptions I had been given. He held up his white robe for me to feel. The texture was that of linen but not so smooth. It had a fibrous yet silky quality. He spoke to me in ancient Greek, which is certainly unknown to the medium. He said, 'Autos Elelutha', meaning 'I have come in person'.

"He is one who very seldom 'comes' and who had the reputation of being unsociable. But he came because, unknown to me, something happened of which I heard only the following day. Margaret Lloyd, through whom I had contact with him, passed on in the Johannesburg Hospital. He wanted to encourage me to go on with the work and to say that help would be given in other ways. Otherwise I should have concluded that the work had come to an end.

"A small point for scholars; he pronounced 'Autos' very clearly so that the first syllable rhymed with 'cow'. Those who try to tell us that ancient Greek was pronounced exactly like modern

Greek should note that he did not say 'Aftos'. Also, he did not pronounce the first syllable like the sound in 'raw'.

"Mr Harris changes his clothes and has nothing about his person. His chair and the corner where he sits were examined by me and found absolutely bare. The ectoplasm which issues in abundance from his body and which the etheric entities use to make themselves visible, streams like a mist and assumes all sorts of shapes, yet can be compacted into something absolutely solid while the power lasts.

"These manifestations take place in accordance with definite laws which have not yet been adequately studied by men of science. The ultimate aim is to teach men the reality of moral law and the blindness of those who in public or in private life do not base action on that law. The enormous importance of the thoughts we think becomes manifest. Physical law goes hand in hand with mental and Spiritual law.

"At the cost of much sacrifice on the part of the medium and his wife as well as of those who communicate, the reality of the other world is demonstrated objectively so that all the sitters hear and see the same things, in order that men may be at last convinced of the existence of those who have passed on, and of the importance of progressing morally by keeping in touch with the higher entities.

"If all did this, we could have peace in our time."

What better testimony could one have than this? Alec and I were very grateful to Professor Haarhof, who voluntarily vouched for Alec's mediumship. In later years many Spirits spoke in different tongues which were unknown to Alec, proving time and again that not only was the mediumship genuine but also of a very high order.

The high standard of Alec's mediumship was also vouched for by Dr MacDonald Bayne. He was well-known in Pretoria and Johannesburg for his work in the School of Universal Science, as well as for his authorship of several interesting books on subjects relating to Spiritual development. One of the books entitled, 'Beyond The Himalayas', is a very readable account of his journey to Tibet where he came into contact with the Masters.

While in Tibet Dr MacDonald Bayne witnessed the materialisation of discarnate beings and was very impressed with what he had seen, claiming that the manifestations were of a very high order. We were delighted to hear him pronounce, after meeting the Guides of our circle, that what had taken place in the Alec Harris séance reminded him of the materialisation séances he had attended in Tibet.

We first made contact with him in 1954 when he wrote to us from London, while over on a visit from South Africa, asking to be included in one of our materialisation circles. We were delighted to accommodate him and invited him to attend our private circle on the Tuesday night. On meeting him, we found him to be a charming and most interesting man.

Dr MacDonald Bayne

The circle that followed was indeed a wonderful one, filled with remarkable demonstrations of Spirit power, which so greatly impressed Dr MacDonald Bayne. He had hoped that his personal Guide would come, to give him some advice about a certain venture he was undertaking in London at the time. No sooner had he mentioned this than his father materialised and said, "There is no need to worry about that, my son, because very soon you will be here on our side with us."

A disconcerting prophesy maybe, but one that proved to be true, for within six months Dr MacDonald Bayne passed into Spirit, and I was surprised to learn that he had been in his seventies, because when we had met him he had looked no more than fifty years old.

Even though he was now in the Spirit World, he never lost touch with us. When we settled in South Africa he materialised regularly in our séances, and always made a point of appearing whenever any of his friends or students were present in the circle. He also came occasionally to the healing circles and said that he was helping, for which service we were always very grateful. Alec and I felt privileged to have made the acquaintance of this second 'Dr Mac' during his Earth life, and we were happy that our association continued once he took up his abode in the Spirit World..

Yohannie ~ another Guide.
Drawn by Alec in 1954

Chapter Eleven

Emigration to South Africa

❖A mistake brings great changes ❖We go to South Africa ❖ Bradley marries and they return with us to Wales. ❖ Gandhi materialises & speaks Hindi with his friend ❖We settle in South Africa.

The year 1955 was to bring great change in the lives of our little family; changes which seemed somehow to be manoeuvred by influences working outside our control. The thing which started a strange chain of events might be considered by some to be nothing more than mere coincidence. I don't think so, but whatever it was, it produced a ripple effect which had far reaching consequences. It came about in this way.

Joe Turner had left Nyasaland by this time and was living in Durban, where he was Manager of a large motor firm. His earlier dream about his going to South Africa had come true; but as far as the three of us were concerned the dream had been wrong as we remained in Cardiff.

The influence, or coincidence, began its work when one night, at the theatre, I wrote two letters, one to Joe and the other to Vi and Ivor Veary in Durban. Being suddenly called upon to play in the orchestra front stage five minutes before expected, I left the sealed letters to be addressed when I got back after the interval. When I returned to the band room I completed the task but, inadvertently, got the addresses mixed up, and Joe's letter went to the Vearys, and the Vearys' to Joe. Naturally, along came letters from both parties endeavouring to sort out the mistake, Vi asking who was Joe, and Joe enquiring about the identity of Vi and Ivor. I wrote hastily to explain, and in retrieving their respective letters Joe and the Vearys met and became friends. Through them Joe became acquainted with Sam and Selma Peimer, two well known personalities in Durban, who were eventually to be instrumental in drastically changing the course of our lives.

In January 1955, Alec and I were in London on a week's holiday, and I had arranged a sitting with Daisy Carter, an excellent medium. It was important that we were complete strangers to her, as any evidence she might give me would be all the more conclusive. Her clairvoyance proved to be remarkable, and I was given much credible evidence in her messages. At the end of the sitting she said: "You are going on a long sea voyage to a foreign country."

"Impossible," I protested, "unless you mean Jersey; that's across the sea."

She laughed delightedly at this: "Oh dear, no. This is very much further than Jersey. You are going to receive an offer of some kind. There's a North American Indian Chieftain standing here beside me who says that you must take this offer as it is all in the plan of things."

I said that I would make a note of this and await developments. With that I thanked her and departed. Alec was waiting outside for me. When I passed this message on to him he laughed and said, "Oh, Louie girl. You will waste your time listening to a lot of nonsense." But I had a strange feeling that this was no chance remark, and decided to wait and see.

Six weeks later, on 1st March, we received a letter from Joe saying that Mr. Sam Peimer was most anxious to meet us, and had suggested that he write asking us to spend a three month long holiday in South Africa as guests of the Peimers. The invitation was extended to the three of us. Joe had told Mr Peimer about our work and he was extremely interested and wished to see the materialisation phenomena himself.

Alec had not been well as numerous circles were depleting him, and I felt that the sea voyage would be of great benefit to him. But he demurred: "It's impossible, Lou. I can't leave my work for three months." Joe, Bradley and I used all our powers of persuasion and eventually we won through. Alec finally gave in, and we sailed for South Africa in the 'Athlone Castle' on 28th June 1955. I thought back to that day in London, five months previously, when I had been given the prophesy of an overseas voyage. "Remarkable," I thought, "how Spirit precognition is never wrong."

The voyage was delightful and I could see Alec's health improving almost daily. I felt glad we had accepted Mr Peimer's kind hospitality. On board we had happy times and some lovely musical concerts. Bradley sang, and I played the violin, and through these we made many friends. I was sorry when it all had to end. However, the prospect of seeing South Africa was exciting, and we were looking forward to meeting the Peimers. Unfortunately, we had a cable on board to say that Sam Peimer had taken gravely ill and was in hospital and that his wife would meet us instead.

Our arrival was dead on schedule, and in glorious South African weather. As our ship slid alongside the docks and into her berth a thick bank of snow-white clouds dropped from a sapphire sky spreading the proverbial tablecloth on Table Mountain. It was awe-inspiring and lovely, while under its purple shadow Cape Town sprawled lazily in the brilliant winter sunshine. The beautiful panorama left me almost speechless, as I gazed upon tall buildings and elegant homes, the old and the new blending gracefully, linked by wide tree-lined streets. In the distance I could see large expanses of white sandy beaches lapped by the azure-blue waters of the Atlantic Ocean. Everywhere the eye roved it was met by unbelievable beauty.

My reverie was interrupted when a low contralto voice enquired, "Excuse me, but are you Mrs Harris from Cardiff?" I turned, and saw a tall, elegant, dark-haired woman. "Yes," I replied, "that's right, I am." She held out her hand. "May I introduce myself? I am Selma Peimer." The low-pitched voice had a marked accent, for Mrs Peimer was of Dutch descent.

No sooner had Alec, Bradley and I completed the introductions than we were surrounded by a number of people, all of whom had very kindly come to welcome us to their lovely country. Among them, to our delight, we saw the Reverend George May, who had sat with us in Cardiff, and with him were a number of members of the Spiritualist Church of Cape Town. To our surprise Professor

Theophilus Haarhof of the University of Witwatersrand came forward smiling, with outstretched hand. Such a warm welcome immediately made us feel at home in our new surroundings.

We spent three memorable days driving round the historic peninsular, sightseeing in Cape Town and its environs, and always, without exception, the scenic views were breathtakingly magnificent.

Our tour of Cape Town completed, we boarded a plane and flew to Durban, home of the Peimers, a city on South Africa's east coast and further north than Cape Town, where the climate was vastly different from the one we had just left. Being subtropical its shores washed by the currents of the Indian Ocean, temperatures prevailing there were very much higher and the atmosphere humid. As was to be expected in such climatic conditions the vegetation was lush and verdant; palms, tropical trees, shrubs, fruits and flowers abounded in profusion.

On the immediate outskirts of the town and in the residential areas, giant red and yellow flamboyant trees spread their feathery branches on either side of wide streets and avenues affording the much sought after cool shade. East and West seemed to thrive side by side here. We were shown many ornate oriental mosques and temples, which served the large Indian community, as well as churches for the followers of Western religions. Innumerable oriental shops offered for sale gorgeous coloured silks, beaten brass, silver ware and intricate jewellery. There were up-to-date department stores, couturiers and the like of the Western business world; while the streets were thronged with a motley cosmopolitan crowd of Whites, Indians and Africans, some in Western clothes, others in national or tribal costumes. We were fascinated by this unusual city and I knew that we would explore it further.

We had been met at the airport by our dear friend Joe Turner, who had been instrumental in negotiating our visit to the Peimers. He had brought along his mother, and a number of other kind people to welcome us. What a joyful reunion we had with Joe. Mrs Peimer's daughter, Dedoney, was also there to meet us. She was a strikingly beautiful girl, auburn-haired and lovely, and she captivated us all with her quiet gentle ways and sweet disposition.

We left the airport in Mrs Peimer's chauffeur-driven car. After taking us on a tour of Durban, it then left the hubbub of the city behind and took to the highway, driving into the hilly suburbs outside the town, where I noticed that the temperature dropped to a more comfortable level. It was another unforgettable drive. We travelled through beautiful countryside spattered with elegant homes surrounded by well-kept gardens, where literally everything appeared to be in bloom. There was on all sides a profusion of brilliant colours from unusual tropical plants and shrubs. After some fifteen minutes, we arrived in Westville, where the car turned off the highway taking a side road, and entered a winding shady driveway. After travelling through well-kept grounds it came to a halt under the porch of a large stone and timber mansion.

Wood Hall, Westville, Durban, home of the Peimers

"Well, here we are," said Mrs Peimer. "This is Wood Hall, our home and yours, while you are our guests." Before we could register our surprise at the magnificence of the residence, servants were taking our luggage inside and Mrs Peimer was leading us into the large hall from which a wide staircase wound its way to the upper floor. It all seemed very grand and sumptuously furnished and to us a little overpowering. Soon we had settled ourselves in and were enjoying our new surroundings.

After some refreshment, we all went to see Sam Peimer at the hospital. He proved to be a most charming gentleman though obviously gravely ill. He was very pleased to meet us and seemed to take an instant liking to us I as we did to him. "What a pity," I thought, "that our first meeting had to be in circumstances such as these."

Sam Peimer

We visited Sam every day for two weeks, but it was obvious that his condition was deteriorating and that he was slowly leaving this world. On one visit he beseeched us to settle permanently in South Africa. He had a deep affection for his country, and he felt people like ourselves were needed to enlighten his countrymen about life after death. His plea was so urgent that we promised to consider the possibility. He seemed content with that.

Each day, Bradley would sing for Sam, which soothed and pleased the ailing gentleman. Very quickly he came to regard our boy as his own. One day, near the end, he whispered to Bradley: "You are the son I always wanted." We were very moved.

Then drawing me near to him he whispered that he had planned a wonderful trip to the Game Reserves and Rhodesia, where he had arranged for us to visit Salisbury, Bulawayo and the Vumba Mountains. "But do not worry, dear lady," he said, "if I," and he paused, and we all knew what was in his mind, "if I cannot take you Selma will surely do so." He sighed heavily, "I will not disappoint you."

Sam never came with us on that trip for the end was very near. The day before he died he again asked us to settle in South Africa. The following day was a sad day indeed, for that was when he left us and passed peacefully into Spirit. It was then July 1955.

On the evening of the day that Sam was buried we gave our first materialisation circle at Wood Hall. It was such a pleasure to see our dear Spirit friends again. Though we were now some six thousand miles from our own séance room the distance made no difference to their materialising through Alec in the Peimer residence. The sitters were Mrs Peimer, Dedoney, Bradley, Alec and me, and also a few close friends of the Peimer family.

To our great joy, after the circle had been in progress for a short time, who should step out of the cabinet but Sam. He looked just as he had before, only not ill and frail. All present were able to identify him. He walked up to his wife and proceeded to discuss with her matters of a very private nature about which Alec and I knew nothing, but which she understood perfectly. By his remarks Sam indicated that he still had concern for the affairs of his family. In life, his was a dominant, strong personality, and this remained unaltered in all the years he manifested to us in the séance room. Only after his passing did we discover how many people he had helped while on earth. He was a good man, and we grew to love him very much. He is a fine soul: I say 'is' for Sam is and lives, as we all do, now and always.

I feel that Sam, particularly, must have been very happy when Bradley and his daughter Doney, as Dedoney was known, announced that they were in love and wished to get married. This pronouncement came as a complete surprise to both Alec and me. "How blind can one be?" I thought. "It was all happening under our very noses."

Bradley wanted to take Doney back to Cardiff with him when we all returned, but I had misgivings about how Mrs Peimer would react to this suggestion, because Doney was physically incapacitated. She had contracted an infection when she was nine years old which had affected her legs. Although she was an agile girl and could swim as well as any, the muscles of her legs had become so weakened that she was unable to stand or walk unaided. It was a great tragedy that this lovely girl had been thus condemned to a life in a wheel chair. Her father, Sam, had taken her to consult many of the world's leading doctors, but to no avail. They were all unable to help her. Bradley believed that if she were in our home she would receive the help she needed from our beloved Guides. Still, I had misgivings about removing her from Wood Hall where she had many servants at her disposal, and the necessary funds to cater for her needs. Our home in Cardiff was in a different category altogether.

However, the young couple were adamant, and Doney was confident that she could cope away from home. She even seemed anxious to perhaps prove her independence. So the alliance was agreed upon, and the marriage was solemnised one September day in 1955, after which we all set sail for Cardiff, and home. We were feeling very proud and happy at acquiring a daughter so unexpectedly, and the young people were blissfully happy in one another's company. It gave us both much joy to see them together. So Sam's wish had been fulfilled: if we had acquired Doney as a daughter, Sam now had Bradley for a son.

Once we got back home we continued with our private circles, but decided to abandon all public sittings for a time in Alec's interests. The Healing circles proceeded along the same lines, and Doney received a lot of help. She now found that she could walk with Bradley up and down the garden by just holding one finger of his hand, and we had great hopes of a complete cure for her in the not too distant future.

In 1956 my sister, May, left Wales to live with her daughter in Southampton. I missed her dreadfully and felt quite lost without her. It was while I was in this sorry state of mind that I received the very welcome invitation to spend three weeks with John and Sally in the Isle of Man. I accepted with alacrity for both of us. My sister kindly agreed to come and look after Bradley and Doney while we were away. Our only concern was for Dick Evans who was ill and in need of our help. Fortunately, by the time we left his condition had improved and he seemed much better. Alec and I departed for our little holiday with lighter hearts.

It was April, and a delightful time of the year to be in the Isle of Man. Our reunion with Sally and John was a happy one. During our sojourn we made a most interesting contact. John informed us that a certain medical man of international repute, and one with extraordinary powers of his own, had expressed a wish to meet us. He wanted to witness Spirit materialisation through Alec's mediumship, of which he had heard excellent reports. "His name is Dr Sir Alexander Cannon," said John. "He is a great friend of mine and very erudite indeed as far as occult matters are concerned. In fact, he is the author of several most fascinating books. I'd like you both to meet him, and perhaps you will give him a sitting? I'll take you along there tomorrow if you like."

John duly took us to Sir Alexander's mansion and introduced us. We had a most interesting discussion on esoteric and occult subjects, of which the doctor had profound knowledge. Sir Alexander said he had long wanted to sit with Alec, and the meeting concluded with an arrangement for a circle to be held in John's house a few nights later.

It proved to be a very good circle. The highlight of the evening was the materialisation of Mahatma Gandhi who came especially for Sir Alexander. The little Indian holy man was exactly as he had been on earth. He was painfully thin, almost emaciated, through many long fasts. Gandhi wore his customary loin cloth and the well remembered steel-rimmed spectacles.

He conversed at length with Sir Alexander in Hindustani, a language familiar to the doctor, but certainly not to Alec. Our eminent sitter was 'very impressed' with the manifestation, particularly at the accuracy of detail in the materialised form, and the timbre of his voice. Sir Alexander knew Mahatma Gandhi extremely well. Gandhi's conversing in his vernacular tongue was even more convincing evidence as far as he was concerned.

But the doctor was to have further indisputable evidence. Two Tibetan Monks materialised. They conversed with him in a little known Tibetan tongue. Sir Alexander averred that he was one of the few white people in the world who could understand this ancient Tibetan language. He was highly satisfied with what he had seen and heard that night.

One evening, when John, Sally and I were having a voice sitting with Alec, just the three of us, we were surprised to hear Dick Evans voice calling: "Lou! Where am I? Help me!" There was no mistaking the note of agitation and bewilderment in his voice. Remembering that poor Dick had been ill when we left, I feared that he had had a serious relapse. So I quickly tried to reassure him: "The Guides are there with you, Dick, and Nemphis. They will help you." There was a moment's pause, then Dick's voice came through again, calmer now: "It's all right now. They are here with me." Then there was silence. Although we were relieved that our beloved friends were taking care of Dick's astral self, we were nevertheless worried that all was not well with him back in Cardiff.

Early next morning, we phoned Bradley in Cardiff and enquired after our friend, only to learn that he was seriously ill after a relapse the previous day, and had gone into a coma. Further enquiries revealed that he had passed over at precisely the time when he had called for help in our circle. Such a dear, kind and faithful friend was sadly missed by all of us. Never, at any time, had Dick let anything prevent him from attending a circle. It was natural that we should get around to reminiscing about past experiences with our old friend, and we recalled with amusement the time when Dick had strongly defended Spiritualism in the papers.

A London Sunday Newspaper was investigating the subject of Spiritualism. Some disbeliever had written in that newspaper that the whole concept of life after death, and the return to earth of Spirits was just a lot of rubbish. He had stated categorically that no one ever came back from the dead; in other words, once you were dead you stayed dead.

Dick was incensed by the bleak picture portrayed by this writer. Mediumship in general had been openly discredited, and he felt that Alec's work had been denigrated. He promptly took up his pen and wrote to the newspaper, vehemently defending Spiritualism which he avowed had proved that life definitely continued after death. He proceeded to give an account of his many experiences in the Alec Harris séance room.

His letter in the Sunday edition painted so realistic a picture of literally hundreds of occasions when he had shaken hands with Spirit entities who appeared as if in the flesh, and of how he had had intelligent conversations with them, that it immediately brought two reporters to his door at breakfast time the next morning. They wished to investigate this remarkable circle on behalf of their paper, and asked if they might be included in a sitting.

Poor Dick was now in a quandary. On joining our circle, he had given an undertaking not to broadcast what took place in our séances, for fear of unpleasant repercussions from possible belligerent disbelievers, or over-enthusiastic investigators. "Now you've put me in a fix," he said. "This will probably get me thrown out of the circle. That's the last thing I want."

When they showed no sign of retreating, he decided that he had better bring them down to me. After meeting them, I consulted with Alec, who after consideration and a searching appraisal of the gentlemen, gave his approval to these two strangers being included among the sitters at the circle the next evening. I told them it would be our private circle, and urged them to refrain from taking any alcohol. I received a firm promise that they would comply with this request. I silently prayed that it would be a satisfactory circle. One can never guarantee how a circle will turn out. We are entirely in the hands of those on the other side.

Fortunately it was a good séance. My mother came fully materialised and was recognised by the two reporters who had seen her photograph before going into the sanctuary. When Kitty, our saucy little child Spirit, showed herself with her two plaits hanging down either side of her face, one of the gentlemen remarked: "You're a pretty little girl. How old are you?" To which she pertly replied, "It's very rude to ask a lady her age." which raised a laugh all round.

Alec, Dick and I breathed a sigh of relief when a good report

Kitty, drawn by Alec in 1950

of our circle appeared in the next Sunday's edition of the paper. Dick, however, vowed that he would be more careful in future how he defended Spiritualism. My heart ached as I remembered that Dick was no longer with us.

Only seven months later, we were to experience another shock. My dear sister, May, also passed into Spirit after going into a decline following an operation. To our dismay she died on 15th November 1956.

But, three months before her passing she was able to rejoice with us when Doney gave birth to a son on 1st August 1956, as had been prophesied by the Guides previously. Doney now felt fulfilled in achieving motherhood, and was a very proud girl indeed.

Our grandson was christened Anthony Samuel Alexander by the Reverend George May at a service held at the Spiritualist Church in Park Grove. It was an impressive service. The Rev May, holding the tiny bundle in his arms, said that the boy's Spirit name was 'Harmony' and that he would spread this

Rev George May

quality wherever his path led him in life. It was a truly lovely message.

We held our circle as usual on the following Tuesday night, but earlier than usual, because by this time I had left the Prince of Wales Theatre after 15 happy years. I now had engagements with the BBC and did other freelance work. We sat at a more satisfactory time and Doney was able to be present. She was anxious not to leave the baby alone while she attended the circle, so brought him along. Our séances were held in the dining room which had a large bay window. The cot was placed in this recess and we commenced the séance.

Through all the singing and talking the baby slept, the Guides obviously keeping him asleep. Then Sam Peimer materialised, and going to the cot he gently lifted the baby and held him in his arms, and spoke so lovingly of his grandson. It really was an extraordinary sight to see the Spirit grandfather nursing his earthly grandson. It brought it home to us how near our loved ones are to us at all times.

A letter arrived from Selma Peimer in Durban saying that she would be visiting us shortly, and bringing with her Doney's sister Jeannette and her husband, who lived in Australia, as they were all anxious to see the new baby. In due course they arrived, and we spent a happy time together, Selma being very proud of her new grandson. She did not wish to leave him behind, and proceeded to use all her powers of persuasion to influence Bradley and Doney to return to South Africa, if not with her, then at some later date.

The children, however, were reluctant to leave us behind, so Selma suggested that Alec and I should emigrate and make South Africa our new home. The idea of leaving Cardiff for good did not appeal to either of us and we declined the suggestion. Doney seemed restless and ill at ease. She explained to us that she had fears that trouble would erupt in the Suez Canal zone. She was unhappy that the family could be broken up, and begged us all to stay together. We too felt that the parting would be an unbearable wrench.

After much deliberation we finally succumbed to the children's pleas and agreed to follow them to South Africa at a later date, after having wound up our affairs in Cardiff. So it was that we bade them a tearful farewell on 17th December 1956 as they boarded a plane bound for Durban and we repeated our promise that we would join them sometime in March after selling up our belongings.

I promptly gave notice to the BBC and Alec asked for his release from the Ministry of Works in Cardiff, and the machinery for the move was thus set in motion. Having made this momentous decision, I found myself a couple of weeks later feeling very despondent. When we retired that night I was unable to sleep. Though Alec soon fell into a deep sleep, I tossed and turned, tormented by indecision. I knew what was troubling me. I did not want to leave Cardiff, my home, and all our very dear friends, not to mention our Spiritual work.

In sudden panic I woke Alec and said: "Al, don't let's do it! Let us stay here where we belong. Ask for your job back and I'll do the same." "Mm?" Alec grunted, and I repeated my request. "OK that'll suit me fine," he murmured drowsily, only half awake. He turned over, and his breathing, accompanied by heavy snoring, indicated that he was once more fast asleep.

I lay beside him deep in thought and filled with a longing to continue with all our old associations. "I won't GO!" I said aloud. And then I heard it! Someone had called my name. "Louie!" A strong male voice. It repeated, "Louie!"

I turned, and saw the Spirit form of Sam Peimer standing beside the bed. I could not be mistaken. In the pale silvery moonlight which filtered into the room through the unlined curtains at the window I could make him out clearly; every detail of his face, and his eyes which looked at me with deep concern. "Louie," he said, "you must go to my country, you promised!" His voice was urgent.

"Oh, Sam!" I pleaded. "It's asking a lot to dig up our roots and go to a strange country to start life again at our age! I worry, not knowing how things will turn out for us." When the Spirit did not answer, I continued, "You must understand, Sam, it is not an easy decision to make."

"You must go!" he urged, "and I promise that you will be looked after."

I began to feel that perhaps there was some hidden purpose in our move to South Africa. So, reluctantly, I replied, "All right, Sam, we'll go," and I sighed in spite of myself. With that he murmured, "God Bless you!" and promptly dematerialised, leaving me with a sinking feeling in the pit of my stomach for now I felt committed. "The die is cast," I thought. "Now what?"

I realised that Alec had passed from the deep sleep state into trance, as he had done on numerous occasions before, thereby making it possible for Sam to materialise. So when I had assured myself that the Spirit had definitely gone, I deemed it safe to wake Alec and tell him what had taken place. We discussed the position and decided that we had better revert to our original plans. In the morning we set about winding up things in earnest.

We stayed with dear Auntie Thomas and Megan for our last two weeks in Cardiff. They had very kindly agreed to look after our adored Persian cat, Bobbie, who was very dear to us both. We would gladly have taken him abroad with us but we feared that he would not adapt easily to a strange country, nor to such a hot climate. We regarded Bobbie as being very special. When Wogs, our dog, had passed away, Bobbie had taken it upon himself to fill his place by being both cat and dog to us, doing all the funny little tricks that Wogs used to do to please us, and generally endearing himself to us in so many ways. He sensed that we grieved for Wogs, as he did himself, for they were great companions. I wondered just how I was going to leave him for ever. But I consoled myself that he knew Auntie Thomas' home well as we had always taken him there when we visited her; and I hoped that he would soon forget us and love them as much.

I was just as broken when Wogs died; but the little dog had done a remarkable thing. He had materialised at the end of one of our circles and was seen sitting contentedly on Alec's knee in the cabinet. At other times when he came he would give his sharp characteristic bark of greeting that we knew so well, so that we felt that Wogs was never far away. The Guides had said that he would always stay near us to guard us. What a happy thought that he will be there to meet us when we enter the Spirit World.

On 9th March 1957 we left our beloved country for good, both of us with aching hearts, sailing, this time, in the 'Jagersfontein' bound, permanently, for South African shores. There was a terrific welcome awaiting us when we arrived in Durban, and our misgivings paled as we were reunited with our little family once more. We were driven to Wood Hall, where we were once again the guests of Mrs Peimer.

While Selma Peimer was in Cardiff she met my niece Phyllis, now married to Trevor Cowley. Selma had spoken so convincingly of the wonderful opportunities awaiting young people in South Africa, on the spur of the moment they had decided they would come with us. We were overjoyed at their decision and felt that we were no longer going away alone. They too stayed at Wood Hall and were able to participate in our circles once again.

About four weeks after our arrival in Durban, I suddenly had a depressed feeling about our cat, Bobbie. I told Alec that I was sure that there was something very wrong with him. I kept seeing his dear little face rise up before me, and I became very anxious about his well being. No amount of soothing on Alec's part made me feel any better. The next Tuesday when we had our circle Phyllis touched my arm saying, "Lou, I can see a Persian cat walking around the room." Phyllis herself was very psychic. Just then, the Scientist emerged from the cabinet carrying something under his robe. He came right up to me, and as he turned I saw a bushy tail protruding from under the arm of his robe. A sudden fear clutched at my heart and I asked, "Is that a cat you have there, Sir?" He did not answer but returned with the bundle to the cabinet.

Six days later, we had a letter from Auntie Thomas saying that dear Bobbie had passed away. In spite of all the loving care that had been given him, he had apparently pined for us and died of a broken heart on the very Tuesday that the Scientist had brought him to the circle.

When I asked that Spirit at the next circle if it was indeed my cat, Bobbie, he had brought with him, he replied: "Who else? He wanted to come to his mother." I suffered terrible pangs of guilt at having forsaken him for he was just like a baby to me, giving me so much love. But once he went into Spirit I always felt him close to me.

There were many instances of animal materialisation in our séances. My niece's cat, who had been poisoned, was once placed on her lap and she was able to stroke its soft fur. While a doctor's wife's pet Siamese cat, Ming, materialised, giving the characteristic hoarse Siamese cry, and then proceeded to brush itself against her legs and clawed at her shoe. After the séance the claw marks were still visible on the suede material of the shoe.

Our dog Wogs materialised to us in South Africa. He came wagging his tail, barked, and licked my hand. At which a Spirit voice from somewhere above the cabinet warned, "Do not touch the dog!" To which I replied, "I did not touch him, he touched me." Then I saw that the little body became transparent and the animal slowly dematerialised. The other sitters in the room were fascinated by this unusual manifestation.

We were renewing acquaintances with many friends in South Africa who had sat with us in Cardiff. One gentleman who we were particularly happy to meet up with again was Hyman Klein. He had been one of the pioneers of Spiritualism in South Africa. He had met his materialised Guide, Shalom, at one of our Cardiff circles. He had then been able to express his thanks to this Spirit who was the inspiration behind the learned and very enlightening lectures which Hyman gave in all parts of South Africa.

We were also delighted to see Mrs Vidie Carlton Jones again. She was a well-known figure in South Africa as her husband, Guy Carlton Jones, had been the chairman of a large mining group. When he died Vidie had been distraught. Going through Guy's books one day in his vast library, she came across a volume on Spiritualism. She was fascinated by its contents and began to investigate the subject herself. After sitting with some of the best South African mediums, she travelled to Britain and had sittings with many well known mediums there until she heard of the materialisation medium Alec Harris and travelled to Cardiff to ask for a sitting.

We included Vidie in our next circle. She had convincing evidence when her husband, whom she always called Peter, materialised and they conversed at length. She was overjoyed at seeing him again, hearing his voice which she had thought to be silent for ever. Thereafter, she became a confirmed and dedicated Spiritualist, and proved to be a very good friend to us in the years that followed that meeting. We came to appreciate that underneath her forthright manner and disconcerting outspoken directness of speech lay a heart of pure gold. For the rest of her life she worked tirelessly for Spirit, and assisted the movement and mediums wherever necessary in a practical way. For us it was a most propitious meeting. We were overjoyed at being reunited with our friend in South Africa. When we were in Johannesburg, holding circles in Joe's house, Vidie was always included.

Professor Haarhof of the Witwatersrand University asked if we would meet some friends of his, a Mr and Mrs Aronsohn, who had suffered a heartbreaking tragedy when their 21 year-old son, Michael, had died very suddenly while they were on holiday on the Continent. Both parents found the loss of their young son almost unbearable, and Professor Haarhof begged us to help them, and if possible give them a sitting. He said that he had told them of his outstanding experiences in our circles, and they were anxious to contact Michael again. It would help for them to know that the boy lived and had not gone from them for ever. When we eventually met them, Alec and I immediately liked them and we became firm friends. A circle was arranged and to their great joy Michael materialised and spoke lovingly to them, giving them the comfort they so sorely needed. Michael often came after that whenever his parents were among the sitters of a circle.

Nora and John Rumble were another couple who had sat with us in Cardiff, and who were doing much good work bringing healing and understanding of Spirit to people in their part of the world. They lived in Pretoria, about thirty miles from Johannesburg, a historic old city and the administrative capital of South Africa. When the Rumbles heard that we were in Johannesburg for a few weeks they promptly invited us to visit them, which we did, accompanied by Joe, and we celebrated a wonderfully happy reunion with these old friends.

There were many reminiscences about past experiences in the séance room. John reminded us of when, having met their respective Guides, the cabinet curtains were drawn aside by the Spirit people to reveal that Alec had completely dematerialised, and the cabinet was empty! John, being a hard headed business man, said he could not accept that Alec had disappeared. He felt that he might have been secreted somewhere in the folds of the curtains of the cabinet. On hearing this remark, the Guide called John to the cabinet and invited him to inspect it for himself, which he promptly did. Somewhat bewildered by his ineffectual search he exclaimed, "You can't hide a rabbit in there, never mind Alec."

Still mystified he turned from the cabinet and started to return to his seat, when all of a sudden a soft object came hurtling through the air from the direction of the cabinet and struck him on the back. We discovered that the cushion from the back of Alec's chair had been flung at John by Spirit hands in playful protest at his disbelief of the Scientist's capabilities, which raised a good laugh all round, but most especially from John himself. It was an incident that he never forgot.

Just talking about our experiences in Cardiff brought on a wave of nostalgia, and we confided to John and Nora that, in spite of the comfort in which we lived in Wood Hall, we both felt unsettled, and thought that perhaps we had done the wrong thing in leaving Cardiff and coming to South Africa.

Our friends asked us what we intended to do in the future, and we confessed that we were undecided, but felt that we should return to our home country. I pointed out that we could not continue to live indefinitely as Selma Peimer's guests, although it seemed that is what she would have liked. Alternatively, we could look for a home of our own and endeavour to find some form of employment to keep ourselves. We could not make up our minds what to do. The only thing that was really holding us back was that we were reluctant to go away and leave the children behind. We told the Rumbles we felt depressed when we thought of our lovely home with its comfortable furnishings now sold, and the security we had left behind in our native Wales. It would be hard to start over again.

John and Nora showed tremendous understanding. They offered us the use of their lovely home in Durban North which they kept solely for their holidays at the coast. "Go there, and be happy," they said, "and carry on the work of Spirit as you were meant to do." We were quite overcome by such generosity. The Rumbles brushed aside our protests and persuaded us to give it a trial, 'for a time, anyway', they said.

Our few weeks in Johannesburg stretched to five. Eventually we left for Durban again, and took up our abode in the Rumble's home in Durban North. It was a beautiful place, an absolute haven, affording us the peace and serenity so necessary for creating a sanctuary and recommencing our Spirit work in earnest.

The house faced the sea over which it had a magnificent panoramic view, and we spent many restful hours gazing out on to well-kept lawns dotted with flowering shrubs and shade trees, with numerous flower beds ablaze with brilliant subtropical plants and flowers. All were thrown into vivid relief by a backdrop of an unbelievably blue Indian Ocean. We were more content than we had been for some time and our circles commenced and fell into their usual pattern.

The Rumbles, by their kindness and understanding, had done much to influence us to remain in South Africa, and it was a relief to have come to a definite decision about our future. But now, a new and pressing problem confronted us. How would we keep ourselves in the years that lay ahead?

Chapter Twelve

Becoming Semi-Professional

❖Alec becomes semi-professional ❖The Spaceman and his flying saucer ❖Holidays in Britain 1958 & '59 ❖ 1959 Spirits hold up the cabinet for 2½ hours ❖Christmas circles ❖ Scepticism disrupts circle harmony.

The realisation that we could not go on indefinitely enjoying this idyllic existence without working brought us up with a jolt. It became obvious that we would have to find some means of acquiring regular financial support. Alec's employment in Cardiff, together with mine at the theatre, had provided us with all our needs. We had lived in comparative comfort, but we had not saved for a rainy day and we had to admit that our financial climate was beginning to look decidedly overcast as we contemplated the years ahead. We were not unduly downcast as Alec was a good businessman and clever with his hands, and I felt that I would be able to find employment with my violin. But we were not getting any younger, and we now felt that if we were employed all day we would have to abandon our materialisation circles at night. The hot climate of Durban left us depleted when doing practically nothing at all and we knew that we could never manage to carry on full-time employment and have late night séances as we always had done in Wales. We felt these would have to be discontinued.

We had almost come to a decision about this when a prominent Spiritualist heard of our plans and he came in haste to dissuade us. "South Africa has never had a medium such as Alec Harris," he said. "He is needed here, and he must not deprive genuine seekers of his valuable services. It would be a tragic waste to give up the circles," he pleaded.

"But we have got to live," I pointed out. He responded: "But why should you abandon the circles altogether? You can run séances on a professional basis."

The idea was most unwelcome. The gentleman persisted, saying that we would be doing a great disservice to a lot of people, not only to those in Spirit who still had much work to do through Alec, but also to countless bereaved souls who were in need of comfort from Alec's mediumship. We thought deeply, weighing the pros and cons of embarking on such a grave undertaking. There was much heart-searching and heated discussion as Alec was very averse to becoming a professional medium. It was well known that all professional mediums left themselves wide open to dangerous practices perpetrated by unscrupulous disbelievers, and that he would no longer feel secure. This would have a disastrous effect on his mediumship. I agreed with Alec, but at the same time felt that we had committed ourselves to the work of Spirit over the years and now was not the time to give up. I cannot express the turmoil that beset our minds as we contemplated the whole unhappy situation.

There was much persuasion from all quarters of the Spiritualist movement. Eventually we accepted the idea as inevitable, and commenced to give a few professional circles for Durban people in the lovely little sanctuary we had created in the Rumble's holiday home. We had decided that we would limit the number of professional public circles we would give, enough to provide for our sustenance and incidental expenses and no more. We had no desire to make a lucrative business out of Spirit mediumship, for then I felt sure the power would be taken away from us. We naturally consulted with our beloved Guides and received their blessing on this new arrangement. We would never have gone ahead without their consent.

The news of our activities soon spread far afield, and many people came from Johannesburg just to attend our circles. Willie and Gipsy Aronsohn brought groups of friends for special circles of their own. We had developed a close bond of friendship with this couple since our first meeting, and over the intervening years we had come to value their friendship and were grateful for their many kindnesses to us. It was always a pleasure to have them at our circles.

Hyman Klein came regularly. At one of the circles which Hyman attended a strange thing happened. A tall Spirit materialised wearing a mask which covered his whole face leaving only his eyes visible. This figure approached Hyman and taking him by the hand led him to the cabinet. Then in a serious voice he said: "I want to tell you that flying saucers do exist, although your world is sceptical of any reports of such. But I say to you that they will one day be an established fact, and will arrive on your planet before man destroys himself; but the time is not yet ripe."

With that he turned and disappeared into the darkness of the cabinet, only to return a few seconds later carrying a large model of a flying saucer which stood several feet in height, in fact it was taller than he was himself. "This," he announced, "is the type of machine men from space will use when they come. This is only a model. But this is what it will look like; this is what they will travel in when they come, these people from Space." We all inspected this strange contraption and were fascinated by it.

The Spirit spoke again to Hyman, "I will be with you on Thursday evening when you attend the Flying Saucer Meeting." Hyman thanked him, wondering how on earth he had known that it was his intention to attend this meeting, which was to be addressed by an investigator and author of several books on this controversial subject. Certainly none of us present at the circle knew anything of the impending lecture. What is more, we had not had an opportunity prior to the sitting of having any conversation with Hyman, apart from the usual greetings, as he had flown in from Johannesburg and had only arrived just in time for the circle.

Naturally there was much discussion over tea after the séance. It was then that we usually analysed and exchanged opinions on anything unusual which had taken place. As the cabinet was very small and only able to contain the medium sitting in his chair, we were mystified how there had been enough room to include a fully materialised man plus that enormous model of a flying saucer which stood taller than the man himself. And what had happened to it once the Spirit returned to the cabinet? It is truly amazing the things that can be done with ectoplasm for that is what it was, an ectoplasmic model which had dematerialised as quickly as it had been materialised.

Then there was the case of the girl in Spirit who, although she had been successful in coming through a trance clairvoyant medium with messages for her parents, was unable to convince them of her presence. In desperation she had sought Alec's mediumship and asked a sitter to pass on what he had seen to her parents in an effort to convince them. The sitter concerned was Noel Griffin, President of The Spiritualist Union of South Africa. The girl, beautifully materialised in detail, stepped up to him. Though softly spoken, she was obviously determined to get her message through, "Please help me!" she pleaded.

"If I can, certainly I will," replied Mr Griffin.

"I am Betty. You know my mother and father, but you have never met me. Please, will you tell them that I came to you to-night? Will you tell them that you saw me clearly and that I told you that I am their daughter, and that I was killed in a car crash? You see, I go to their circle all the time and impress upon their medium that I am really there. I give them messages telling them that I am alive and well; but they won't accept it because the medium knows all about me. They are doubtful of her clairvoyance, and they are so unhappy; they grieve for me." The girl's voice choked back her sobs.

Mr Griffin remained silent while she collected herself and gained control once more. "Tonight, when they were holding their own circle, I told them that I would find another medium and show myself and prove that I am alive. That is why I am here. Please tell them that you saw and spoke to their daughter, Betty, and that I do contact them in their own circle. Tell them they must not doubt. They must believe me." Again she was overcome by emotion. "Please, will you help me? Please!" As Mr Griffin was uttering a promise, she disappeared.

True to his word, when Mr Griffin got home, even though the hour was late, he phoned Betty's parents, and told them of their daughter's materialisation at the Harris circle, and of the conversation he had with her. The poor couple were overjoyed. At last, they said, they had the proof they needed. Immediately they set about building their own sanctuary and began to sit for voice as Betty herself had requested them to do. Months later they attended one of our circles in Johannesburg and they were thrilled to be able to see and speak to Betty.

In the October of that year we had an invitation to visit Johannesburg again which we gladly accepted because, although we liked Durban very much, we were finding the almost tropical climate difficult to tolerate. We realised that the Guides were working under unsatisfactory conditions. The heat and humidity were not conducive to easy materialisation. We had found that a dry, cold climate always provided the best materialisations. The manifestations had been really excellent during the cold winters in Cardiff.

While we were in Johannesburg we were inundated with requests for circles. Regrettably we had to refuse many who were anxious to sit, pointing out that we had really come for a holiday and to have a little respite from the enervating heat of Durban. However, we did give quite a few circles, and at one of the voice séances a Spirit whispered distinctly in my ear: "Stay here!" I thought about this, and wondered if that was what the Guides wanted us to do, go to Johannesburg.

I discussed it with Alec, and we decided that, perhaps, we should move to Johannesburg and remain there permanently. Being some 6,000 feet above sea level, on a vast plateau, the climate there was dry; very cold and crisp in winter, and comfortable in the summer months. We felt that such a move would benefit the circle and certainly afford a more comfortable existence for us away from all the heat and humidity. Not long after we had reached this decision, we left for the high veld to look for a home.

Our friends in the Transvaal were delighted that we would be near at hand, and they assisted us in house hunting. Eventually, we found a house that suited our needs, in Bramley, a pretty suburb some six miles outside the bustling city of Johannesburg. The house was a double storey, English-type dwelling with quaint dormer windows. From the large airy lounge downstairs, complete with a traditional English fireplace, French windows led on to a large veranda, which, in turn, looked out on to a charming garden.

At the back were a good number of fruit trees which, apart from supplying us with copious amounts of peaches, apricots and plums, in season, also made the house very secluded.

No home was complete without pets so very soon we collected around us a Ridgeback hound called Jock, who became our faithful protector; Micky, a large tabby cat; and Judy, a Staffordshire Bull Terrier. When she strayed one day and never returned, she was replaced by an adorable thoroughbred miniature Dachshund, called Trudy, a gift from Doney and Bradley. Trudy became almost as a child in our home and was the joy of Alec's life.

But our prize possession was a very regal Sealpoint male Siamese cat who came from a long line of champions and who, by his bearing, never let any one forget this. We named him Toi-Toi after our little Chinese Guide. As a kitten Toi had selected Alec for his master, not the other way round as is usual. When we first saw the litter of kittens Toi took one look at Alec and it was love at first sight. He promptly left his little cat family and took Alec unto himself remaining with him all afternoon. Our friends decided to present us with this kitten who remained with us for 14 years.

Toi-Toi appointed himself as a permanent sitter at all our healing circles where he would sit on the floor at Alec's feet gazing expectantly up into his face waiting for Adoula to take control. By his expression of recognition it was obvious the cat knew exactly when the Spirit entranced the medium, after which the animal would settle himself down to enjoy the circle with feline equanimity.

We again called our house 'Phrensade', the name that had been selected for us in Cardiff by our Spirit friends. We spent ten happy years in this home where we continued to pass on the Spirit friends' aid to the bereaved, the lonely, and the suffering. So the Spirit work continued under better conditions.

Alec was agreeable to giving a certain number of public circles on a professional basis, but insisted that he would sit for only as many paid séances as necessary to provide the money needed to pay for our immediate living expenses and no more. Other circles were to be free. We sat for these circles for six months of the year, during the winter. The rest of the year was devoted to private sittings for friends or for needy sitters. The healing circles were carried on through the entire year, and were always free.

Mondays and Thursdays were set aside for the healing work. Some patients attended in private in the afternoon, those who were very ill and had to have special or lengthy treatments, or those who were unhappy about being treated in public. The large open healing circle took place in the evening. Always at these healing circles our dear friend Joe Turner assisted us, giving invaluable service for many years. He was a most diligent helper, never allowing anything to prevent his attendance. Alec's work was long and arduous on these healing days, hardly ever coming out of trance to eat, drink or rest. Afterwards his face would light up with pleasure whenever his efforts at passing on the Spirit healing were blessed with a cure. This was the only aspect of his mediumship in which he found true pleasure. To heal the sick he would drive his body to the limits of endurance, placing it at the disposal of Spirit helpers and doctors for long hours in trance in his efforts to alleviate suffering.

Our private developing circle, called the 'experimental circle' by the Guides, was always held on Tuesday nights, the same sitters always forming the basis for development and experimental work. The public circles were held on Saturdays; and Vidie Carlton Jones took it upon herself to make the necessary arrangements, always vetting prospective sitters closely. She rigorously guarded Alec's well being and safety, and for this we were both very grateful.

There were not many occasions when sitters were able to gain access to our circle without first submitting themselves to Vidie's close scrutiny, but there were times when the decision was left to my discretion. One Saturday morning, a gentleman came to our front door and after introducing himself came straight to the point with the plea: "Will you please help a fellow countryman? My wife is desperately in need of help." Alec was with me at the time and we immediately invited him in. As soon as we were all seated in the lounge, he told us his tragic story.

It transpired that he hailed from North Wales and was a medical specialist, a surgeon practising in Johannesburg. It was December

1957 and nearing Christmas. Their only child, David, a lovely fair haired boy of 11 years, had been taken by a crocodile and drawn beneath the waters of False Bay near St Lucia in Zululand while they were on holiday. The horror of this ghastly tragedy had so affected his wife that she was in a terrible state of mind, and he feared for her. Could we please help, he asked. He said that he had heard from reliable sources that we could prove that life continued after death by materialising the dead. Such proof might help his wife to rehabilitate herself and give her purpose in living again, for she had lost interest in life itself. We learned that it was even more tragic as it appeared that she could not have any more children due to complications in giving birth to this first child. Sadly he remarked that their lives seemed bleak indeed. I urged him to bring his wife around to see us and we would help her all we could, and he left us with a promise to do so.

The following afternoon, Sunday, this doctor came again accompanied by his wife. I could see her state of shock; she seemed numb and listless, and my heart went out to her. Being a mother myself, I could appreciate just what she must be suffering. I suggested that she should come to the healing circle the next evening, which she agreed to do, but without much enthusiasm. At the appointed time on the Monday evening they both arrived and took their places among the other patients in the sanctuary.

Adoula, entrancing Alec, gave this lady healing, which was then performed in a yellow light. Quite suddenly Adoula requested that the yellow globe be removed and the red lights switched on. Surprised at such a request I gave instructions for this to be done. Alec, still entranced by Adoula, then went into the cabinet, and immediately a young boy's soprano voice could be heard from the cabinet singing a traditional Christmas Carol 'The Holly And The Ivy' and the doctor's wife's attention became riveted on the cabinet. The singing stopped and my niece, Phyllis, then led the lady to the cabinet where the curtains parted of their own accord to reveal a child draped in ectoplasm standing in front of Alec. Then the boy spoke, "You see, Mum," he said, "I am still singing."

Both mother and child became so overcome with emotion that

they both dissolved into tears, and the little boy dematerialised before her eyes. But she had been convinced that it was her son who had spoken to her, for she had recognised the child's voice as he sang the song which as a choir boy he had been singing in the school's Christmas Carol Service, when he had been a soloist, only four days before he had been killed. I could see that she was now ready to receive her son's Spirit form, so I invited both mother and father to attend the next Tuesday night's private materialisation séance.

At the circle in question, after the Guides initially opened the proceedings, the first materialisation was Peter Carlton Jones, who came bringing with him a young Spirit child, his arm about its shoulders. Peter explained that the boy was David and that he was looking after the child as he had been present when David had passed over. False Bay and St Lucia, he said, had been favourite fishing haunts of his during his life time, and he knew that part of the country well. He happened to be in the vicinity at the time when the accident had taken place. Because the boy had been much distressed he had taken charge of him, and would stay with him until he was able to cope with the change that had overtaken him. The mother seemed much relieved that someone was caring for her son and thanked Peter for his help.

Adoula continued to give this lady healing in the hope that she might have another child, and in fact assured her that she would. Mutual friendship sprang up between us, and we invited both the doctor and his wife to join our Tuesday private circle as permanent sitters, which they did, and received some very remarkable evidence.

Alec still had a hankering for Cardiff and his native Wales. So Vidie, who was going on one of her regular trips to Britain, which she did every two years, persuaded us to accompany her, maintaining that it was essential to keep Alec happy and healthy if he was to carry on satisfactorily with the work he was doing. We did not need much persuading! And in June of 1958 the three of us left Johannesburg for the UK where we intended to have a wonderful three months' holiday.

We had left Wales so hurriedly in March 1957 that we had

omitted to bid many of our good friends farewell, so we decided that when we got home we would make amends by having one great big party in a hall and invite everyone that we knew. It proved to be a wonderfully happy reunion. Vidie came down from London to Cardiff especially for the occasion and showed films of the Wild Game Reserves in South Africa, while we showed others of our family, our home and friends in the new land of our adoption. Everybody was extremely interested in these films which depicted such glorious African scenery. Before the party ended we all linked hands and sang 'We'll Keep a Welcome in the Vales' and 'When You Come Home Again to Wales'. This brought tears smarting to my eyes, tears of joy, yet tears of regret that we would soon have to part again. Marjorie and Grahame also gave parties in our honour, inviting only our nearest and dearest family and friends. We could not have been made more welcome, for truly the red carpet had metaphorically been rolled out, and we were given VIP treatment wherever we went.

Unfortunately the weather was bad that Summer, drearily overcast and with rain most days, so that I must confess to a sneaking relief when, on a cold wet day in September, we left for the warmth and sunshine of South Africa once again.

On arrival back home in Bramley, Dr and Mrs R, David's parents, called to see us with the news that Adoula's healing had been successful and she had conceived another baby, but had a miscarriage at twelve weeks. She was feeling very dispirited and downcast over the loss of this new child. I persuaded her to continue with the healing from Adoula, and assured her that she would have another child. She consented to do this, for now her belief in Spirit healing was firmly established, and we all prayed that her dearest wish would be granted.

In 1959 we again accompanied Vidie to Britain; but this time the weather was absolutely glorious, every day seemed like a South African summer day, showing Wales at its very best.

We were persuaded to give several circles for friends in Cardiff, which we were only too happy to do. Then Vidie asked if we would give a special séance for some of her friends in London who were most anxious to sit with Alec, having heard so much about his mediumship from her. We replied that we would be delighted. A date and time were arranged, and we arrived in London and stayed with Vidie in her town flat.

We encountered problems as soon as we endeavoured to hang the curtains across the corner of the room to form a cabinet, because in her lease it was stipulated that 'no nails were to be driven into the walls for any purpose'. Vidie suggested that we use drawing pins to fasten one side to a large wooden bookcase standing near the corner, whilst the other end could be stuck onto the wall with a stick-on hook. Alec put the suggestion into effect, which seemed to be satisfactory. Apart from a small chair placed behind the curtains, there were no other preparations necessary, and Vidie's friends began to arrive at the appointed time.

I seated them as I thought best and the circle commenced. Connie, Alec's sister, was the first Spirit to materialise, and she and Alec came forward and stood together in front of the cabinet for all to see, and there were gasps of amazement from the sitters. But, to my horror, as Alec and the Spirit of Connie made to re-enter the cabinet, the hook dislodged itself from the wall and the curtains fell to the floor. It was a remarkable sight to see the way in which Connie immediately took care of Alec. She gently placed him, still in trance, in the chair behind the, now fallen, curtains and stayed by his side, while a young man among the sitters jumped up from his seat and, lifting the curtains, held them aloft to form a cabinet once again. Being tall, he offered to hold them in this manner for the duration of the séance, rather than close the sitting down. "No, dear," I protested, "that would be too difficult. You won't be able to hold your arm up for two and a half hours!"

"Auntie Louie!" suddenly Sunny's childish voice piped up, "Don't worry, we will hold the curtains up for you." This is what these little Spirit children did, never letting them drop once throughout the duration of the two and a half hour séance. As I closed the circle, and Alec gave his characteristic little cough, which always indicated that his trance was becoming light, the curtains suddenly fell to the floor as the Spirit children relinquished their hold on them. It was an outstanding demonstration of Spirit power.

Dr and Mrs R had also been over to Britain on holiday during the summer of 1959, and Vidie had arranged for them to have a sitting with Jack Bullard, a fine voice and clairvoyant medium, who lived in Welwyn Garden City outside London. Mrs R was told that she was with child and should return home to South Africa immediately. Adoula also came and said that she must take great care of herself this time, have plenty of rest, and have healing 'through my instrument' as he put it, meaning Alec, as soon as she got home. The doctor and his wife curtailed their trip and returned to South Africa at once prepared to carry out all Spirit instructions to the letter.

When they visited us some time afterwards, they told us nothing of what had transpired at the Bullard circle, but merely asked if Mrs R might attend the healing circle every week. She looked quite fit and well and we were puzzled at the request, but consented to giving the healing when told that it was on Adoula's advice.

However, once in the sanctuary, Adoula announced that she was to have another son. He said he was glad that they had obeyed instructions, and insisted that she must have special healing at this critical period. She did, and her pregnancy went to full-term. Adoula described the baby as being a fair-haired blue-eyed boy, and 'just like David' he said. He even went so far as to name the exact date of the baby's birth, which was two weeks earlier than the expected and correct date according to her medical history.

The pregnancy was straightforward and to everyone's amazement a beautiful blue-eyed fair-haired boy was indeed born in April 1960 on the date Adoula had given, and there was great rejoicing in our circle. It is interesting to note that during the actual labour a Spirit Doctor was present who was clearly seen by Mrs R. Later, when Dr and Mrs R were attending a séance, this Spirit Doctor materialised, and Dr R went up to him and shook him warmly by the hand and thanked him for looking after his wife, to which the Spirit replied, "Well, having started it, we had to see it through."

Ginger came with his congratulations. He received a light chaffing from the doctor for he had predicted that the baby would arrive two days later. When asked about the error in his calculations, he replied; "Eh, Doc! 'ave a 'eart! 'Ow was I to know that 'e was comin' by jet!" Ginger's cockney humour would keep us in fits of laughter, which was his very special work. His job was to raise the vibrations of the circle, and laughter was a very good way of doing it. He would stand in front of us, a mere dwarf telling funny stories, and bantering with his quick repartee, his remarks always bearing the stamp of East End London cockney humour.

"Larf!" he would say. "Tha's right, go on larf! Wotcha dunno is that while I'm makin' yer larf these blokes inside the cabinet are pinchin' yer power!" Which remark always brought roars of mirth.

Ginger had an accident to his nose while on earth as a London barrow boy. It was a rather oversized nose, and having been broken, was quite a disfigurement. He always seemed to take a delight in making sitters feel this malformed feature. One sitter kindly remarked during a séance, having just examined Ginger's nose, that she thought it was a 'Roman' nose. "Yers, that's right, Lidy," joked the little Spirit man, "that's just wot it is .. roamin' all over me fice!" which convulsed the sitters once more. Whenever Ginger was present it was always one long laugh.

Ginger and Vidie were great friends and there was always a lot of good humoured banter between them at séances. One night Ginger emerged from the cabinet evincing an air of importance. "I'm the Boss 'ere tonight," he announced, strutting about. "No loved ones are comin', see! Nah, only us Guides."

"Now, Ginger," said Vidie, "I know my Peter is there; you tell him I want to speak to him." "Lidy," he said mischievously: " 'e ain't got no eyes for you tonight. Nah! You oughta see 'im! 'E's got a luverly hangel on 'is knee!" Vidie enjoyed the joke better than any of us.

There were about six widows in the circle that night, also a doctor. The ladies all pleaded with Ginger to help them to get in touch with their husbands by helping their husbands to come through and materialise for them. Ginger turned to the doctor, " 'Ere, Doc!" he said, "Wot do yer call them doctors wot attend to women?"

"You mean a gynaecologist?" enquired the medico. "Tha's right," laughed Ginger, "that's wot I am over 'ere. I bring lovin' 'usbands into the world!" And so in this manner he helped to build up the power by means of laughter, and the Guides would use the power so generated to help Spirit people to materialise. Ginger's work was important, although on the surface it may have appeared to be pointless.

When Christmas came around each year we held our Christmas circles. One year we were asked to give a circle at a place approximately a hundred miles away from Johannesburg. We agreed to the request provided those attending the séance brought the toys to decorate the tree, which after the Spirit children had their fun playing with them, would be distributed among underprivileged children, bringing to them all the love which the Spirits had instilled into the toys during the circle.

There were present fifty sitters, doctors, lawyers, and many well known people of the district, and a great number of lovely toys were provided. The little Spirit children of all ages had a wonderful time playing with them excitedly around the tree. I had stipulated that no toy guns were to be among the toys as the bangs caused by these could distress the medium.

At some stage during the proceedings I could feel someone fiddling under my chair, and when I enquired, "What are you doing under there?" The red light of a torch flashed on to reveal Ginger in the process of extracting a toy gun from under my seat. Where it had come from I have no idea for it was not there when we prepared the room. But there it was, and Ginger ran around having enormous fun firing the gun and shining the red torch alternately. In the dull red beam of light from the torch we could see six or seven little Spirit children around the tree, all busily and noisily blowing bugles, beating drums, playing mouth organs, winding up or pushing along whining mechanical toy trucks and cars, or pulling crackers and throwing streamers. Besides the unknown Spirit children, quite a few loved ones also materialised or spoke through the trumpet or cone.

Suddenly a small voice piped up right beside me. "I want to speak to my Mummy and Daddy," it said. "Darling," I replied, "you know where they are, you can see them plainly, can't you?" A moment's pause followed, then the child whispered, "Yes." "Well then, dear," I said, "you go over and speak to them. It will make them very happy."

I saw the trumpet float over to the other side of the room and come to rest in front of a man and woman. We could then hear the same little voice pleading; "Please Daddy you must not cry any more. I am all right now." There was an audible intake of breath from the man; it could have been a sob. "Oh please, Daddy, don't cry," went on the little child, "I am here beside you." The child had now materialised beside his parents. "Feel my head and face Daddy; it is quite better now."

The man put out his hand and felt the tiny head, and then the face. He said something to the child which was inaudible to the rest of us in a voice choked with emotion, and I knew that he was quietly crying. "Don't cry any more Daddy. I want you to be happy," pleaded the little one again, and then the child was gone. It was a heart-rending incident always to be remembered.

Afterwards I heard from this man the tragic story. He had gone into his car one morning before work, unaware that the little fellow had followed him to the garage. He had reversed out of the garage, running the vehicle over the child who could not be seen from his position in the driving seat, and his little son was crushed to death. Terrible injuries had been inflicted on the little boy's head and face, and the horror of these, and the fact that he had caused them, had remained to torment the poor father night and day until he was but a shadow of his former self through his unbearable guilt and grief.

As he spoke to me he actually smiled and said that he felt better than he had done since the accident. Speaking to his little son had been the most wonderful thing that had ever happened to him and he felt that this would help him to face up to life again. The incident was all the more convincing because we knew nothing of this tragedy.

I could go on recounting story after story of loved ones being joyfully reunited with their dear ones whom they firmly believed had been removed from them forever by death. Sadly for some, there is not even a hope of a life after death. These people believe that to die is to cease to be. Because of their conviction negating the continuity of their existence after death when they do pass over it will take them a long time to be convinced by the Spirit helpers that they are in fact very much alive, albeit in another dimension, and consequently they will be denying themselves the many joys and pleasures awaiting them in this new World into which they have passed.

In their disbelief they will find themselves much bewildered. They will have some difficulty with their new conditions and an arduous adjustment period. However, the Spirit helpers persevere with their efforts to enlighten and assist, and eventually they win through. Their success is always assured, although not always accomplished by Alec or me when they came as sitters to a materialisation séance. If only they understood their adverse thoughts severely interfered with the phenomena which the Spirit friends were endeavouring to produce for their benefit. As a result, the séances were not always at their best.

One night in particular we experienced unreasonable difficulties with a sceptic. All the sitters were in harmony with the exception of one man who was sitting right next to me. As usual Rohan, gentle, calm, and fully materialised, came out from the cabinet and stood before him speaking words of welcome. To my amazement this sceptical sitter said that he could not see the Spirit figure, though everyone else confirmed that they could discern Rohan very clearly. Neither could this man hear anything that was said to him. I was nonplussed and awaited the next materialisation.

It was not long before the curtains parted and the magnificent figure of a Red Indian stood before us. Slowly, he walked towards the sceptical one and demonstrated his physique. There were exclamations of pleasure and excitement from the sitters, but none from the doubting Thomas who insisted that he was unable to see anything at all. There were gasps of surprise from those present and much protesting. With a show of arrogance, this gentleman indicated that he wished to examine closely the space in front of the cabinet. He proceeded to do so, while we all sat in bewildered silence not knowing quite what to do.

The Red Indian stood his ground while the man deliberately avoided any contact with him as he peered around astigmatically, making passes with his hands above, in front of, and to each side of the silent Spirit figure standing stolidly, and quite patiently, before him. Then he turned to us and said; "I still can't see anything. I don't think there is anything there at all!"

I was absolutely dumbfounded and asked: "Is there perhaps something wrong with your sight? You're not blind are you?" He did not deign to reply, and our attention was diverted at this point, for at that moment a female Spirit form emerged from the cabinet carrying a baby in her arms. She spoke to her sister who was sitting behind me, saying, "Annie, I am looking after your baby for you." And she bent forward close to us so that we could all see as Annie stepped forward to fondle her little one. Both Spirits were perfectly clear, the woman and the child. I reached out my hand to touch the baby and it put its fingers around one of mine.

I turned to the difficult man and said triumphantly: "Look! Here is a little one brought by this lady's sister who has been recognised and accepted. Can you not see that the baby has hold of one of my fingers? Look!" I implored, anxious for him to be convinced. He looked at the baby casually, and then in a flat voice remarked, "Too real to be true." I was completely deflated. "What a pity," I thought. "What a pity." and I was near to tears.

At that point the Scientist stepped out and said that this sitter's scepticism was unacceptable to the Guides as it disrupted the harmony and interfered with their work. He gave us a simple simile: "If a cog were to be taken from a clock, that clock would not go. So it is with us when there is imbalance among sitters." He advised us to close, which we promptly did.

White Wing knew that I was not happy giving public circles. Though I had confidence in our band of Spirit workers, there was always present a fear that Alec might come to harm. I did not want to have him hurt in any way through his mediumship. I was well aware that too many mediums in the past had suffered injury through thoughtless, sometimes deliberately vicious tactics on the part of sceptical sitters to disprove the authenticity of a séance of which they themselves were in doubt.

White Wing, aware of my fears, always materialised early in the circle. He would stand towering above us, his feathered headdress almost level with the top of the cabinet; a tall magnificent figure draped in white ectoplasmic robes. Slowly, he would turn from side to side, then completely around, so that all could see that he was fully formed in every details. Then he would put out his arms to me saying, "Come, Faithful!"

As I stood in front of him I barely reached up to his chest, so tall was he. I could so clearly discern his Red Indian features as I gazed up into his face, the high cheek bones in a lean face, clean-cut jaw, and prominent aquiline nose, altogether a strong face. Then he would turn me around to face the sitters. As I stood there with my back to him, he would raise both his arms high so that the folds of his robe would hang from his arms like two huge white wings. Then he would enfold me, so that only my head could be seen against his chest above the folds and drapes of his white robe, his own dark magnificent head above mine, surmounted by the impressive Indian Chieftain's headdress with feathers trailing down his back to the floor.

I cannot put into words my feelings at these times. I felt inexpressibly close to this Guide of mine, and trusted in him implicitly as he said in his deep and resonant voice, "Faithful, White Wing here to help you." Through the years he remained a pillar of strength to me, always imparting sound advice. He always urged us to reach for the highest, to strive to develop our spiritual rather than our psychic gifts.

To illustrate the meaning of this entreaty, I remember how he uttered these memorable words: "White Wing say the 'phenomena' of what you call Spiritualism is the 'Door': the 'philosophy' is the 'Hall': but we want you to come into the 'Dining Room' and partake of the 'Food' the Great White Spirit has prepared for you. So many people are content to remain at the 'Door'. The Master Jesus attracted multitudes by performing miracles, but when they were gathered around Him He preached to them of Spirit. So we come to demonstrate phenomena, but we expect you to go forward, to search, to learn more of the Great White Spirit."

Chapter Thirteen

Healing ~ The True Vocation

❖Healing - Alec's true vocation   ❖ The 'Healing Light'   ❖Reports of various healings ❖Report by Dr B Laubscher ❖ The materialisation of the 'living' ❖ Dr. MacDonald Bayne materialises ❖ More foreign languages

All work for Spirit, in any of its aspects, was a happy task and always undertaken by Alec with a willing heart; but his real joy in life was the alleviation of the suffering of the living resulting from the many frailties of the flesh, rather than the materialisation of the deceased. The sick always aroused his deep compassion and he had an urge to lay his hands upon them, and channel the God-given Spirit healing in their direction so that they could be made whole again. Many were the cures which resulted through his intervention.

For six months of the year we gave public materialisation circles. By this we just managed to keep abreast of our living expenses, which was all we required of life so that we could continue to devote ourselves to the service of both Man and Spirit. However, the healing circles were carried on throughout the year and were a joy to us, for we were able to witness quite miraculous cures brought about by the Spirit healers with Adoula, his Healing Guide, always in charge of the proceedings. This healing aspect of Spiritualism was Alec's true vocation. It was to this that he would have liked to have devoted himself full-time, but without private means at our disposal this was not possible. Nevertheless, he counted himself lucky that he was not tethered to a full-time job so that he was available for use by Spirit as and when required. All healing circles were entirely free of charge and were available to anyone and everyone in need of help at all times, regardless of colour or creed, just for the asking. No one was ever refused treatment, however hopeless the case might have appeared on the surface, for we knew that miracles could, and did, happen through the intervention of the dedicated Spirit healers on the other side.

Alec liked seeing the results of the healing sessions. The cures delighted him as much as the patients. While sitting for materialisation he saw nothing, heard nothing, and felt completely in the dark about what transpired, relying on second-hand snippets of information passed on to him after the circle. This was an unrewarding occupation from his point of view. If the vibrations in the circles were not completely harmonious, he could suffer depressing after effects, and could feel depleted and tired. I could understand his reluctance to sit for such circles. During the war I had asked White Wing if it would not be possible for us to serve Spirit equally well by doing just the healing work. I explained that Alec was anxious to give up materialisation. "He's really only interested in healing," I said.

But White Wing seemed adamant. "Materialisation," he said, "is also a form of healing. Do you not understand that when sorrowing people see their lost loved ones before them, can touch them, and speak to them, and know beyond doubt there is no finality in death, that knowledge heals their grieving minds? As you must know the mind governs the body. I say to you, this is the hidden cause behind much sickness. There are so few like Alec in your world, and we must carry on with the work."

So Alec reluctantly agreed to continue with the materialisation circles, feeling perhaps a little better about it than previously. He had not fully appreciated the benefits the physical circles afforded to those poor souls who were sick of heart and mind.

I would like to mention here the strange phenomenon known as the 'Healing Light' which had the most extraordinary power to heal almost all physical ailments. While we were in Cardiff in earlier days the Spirit Scientists were experimenting with this 'Healing Light', a term they used themselves, and perfected it to a marked degree so that it could be used in all our healing circles, whether visible or invisible to our eyes.

At the very beginning of a circle the Guide, whom we called

the 'Healing Scientist' would emerge from the cabinet fully materialised, draped in his gossamer fine ectoplasmic white robe. Almost immediately a strange light, an unearthly blue-white luminosity, appeared in the region of his solar plexus, glowing with a pulsating energy, increasing and decreasing gently in strength. At the peak of its brilliance the whole body of the Spirit was illuminated by a sort of inner radiance. In fact, one evening when the Spirit Scientist was bending over me his robes parted and it seemed to me that the light was situated deep inside his body making the whole figure luminous. It was a breathtaking sight. I cannot find words to describe the beauty of this shining vision, or the effect of contact with the 'Healing Light'.

"This is the light that heals," explained the Scientist. "When a medium gives healing this is the power that flows to the sick. Although you cannot see it in the healing circle, it is always there and brings great relief."

Often he would single out one sitter from the others telling him to cup his hands. He would then draw ectoplasm from the medium and place it in each of the cupped hands whereupon it would immediately start to glow with this strange blue-white light. If it had a marked degree of brilliance the Scientist would inform that person that he was undoubtedly a healer and should use his power to help others.

I have seen this Scientist holding out both his hands which each contained a 'Healing Light', and at the same time another such light glowed in the region of his forehead, and yet another deep inside his body. The whole presented a very Spiritual vision which was exceedingly moving.

At a circle in South Africa there were present Major and Mrs Chisham. It transpired that the Major had been 'stone deaf' for 20 years. His wife explained that she had brought him with her to the séance as he was very anxious to witness Spirit materialisation and would be content only to see the Spirits even if he was unable to hear them.

During the circle the Healing Scientist made his appearance, and pointing to Mrs Chisham said: "Bring your husband here to me. We may be able to help him tonight." Major Chisham left his chair and stood in front of the Scientist. The Spirit raised his arm and seemed to draw ectoplasm from out of the air. Shaking it slightly so that it billowed out, he proceeded to lay it over Major Chisham's head, then placing the ends of it in each of that gentleman's ears it glowed with the same unearthly blue-white light. It had a phosphorescent quality. The two figures stood motionless for a few minutes, illuminated by the glowing ectoplasm pulsating gently. Then this strange substance was withdrawn, and it disappeared as mysteriously as it had materialised. Major Chisham then returned to his seat and the circle continued.

The next morning my phone rang and an excited Mrs Chisham on the other end of the line exclaimed: "Oh, Mrs Harris, I can't believe that this has really happened. My husband can hear perfectly, even the faintest whisper." Her voice shook with emotion. "After all these years! It's a miracle! Really a miracle!" As I replaced the phone I once again said a mental 'thank you' to our wonderful Spirit Healers.

Mr and Mrs Kleynhans of Roodepoort and their daughter, Kay had sat for years in their own home circle and were conversant with the subject of Spiritualism. They came to one of our materialisation séances one evening and Kay brought along two of her sons. The younger, Tony, had suffered from persistent wet eczema on both his hands and always had to wear gloves. Every remedy possible had been tried by skin specialists without any success. Although this was a materialisation circle, the Healing Scientist came out to demonstrate the healing power.

Kay summoned up enough courage to ask, "Please, will you help my son?" The Scientist asked the lad to come up to him. Standing behind the boy, he turned him to face us. Suddenly, the 'Healing Light' began to glow. It could be seen shining right through the lad's body. The next day all traces of the eczema had completely disappeared from his hands, and even years later, there was no recurrence of the distressing complaint. Kay and two other sons were healed later by our Spirit friends through Alec, and I have a charming letter from the Kleynhans expressing their gratitude to my husband for his help.

I have another letter from the grandmother of little Guy

Wheelwright. Guy was gravely ill with measles in 1965. He suffered complications and suddenly went into a coma. He was rushed to the Children's Hospital in Johannesburg where encephalomyelitis was quickly diagnosed. The doctors said that his was a particularly bad case of inflammation of the brain, and that his recovery was doubtful. They added, however, that in the unlikely event of his body overcoming the dreaded disease he would suffer permanent brain damage and would be, what is termed, a mere vegetable.

Many years after Guy's complete recovery, his grandmother wrote as follows:

"After the doctor's verdict I contacted you and Alec. On the evening that Alec was to give him his first treatment Guy took a turn for the worse. He was dying when we brought you and Alec to the hospital. Adoula worked on our little boy, who was only 2 years old. The next morning there was a miraculous improvement. You and Alec came twice a week to the hospital to give the child healing. During all this time Adoula always prophesied what changes would take place in his condition, and he was always correct. After remaining in a coma for six weeks, Guy woke up while his parents and grandfather were visiting him in the ward. He was sufficiently conscious to recognise them. His condition steadily improved every day, to the amazement of the doctors and staff of the hospital. Within a week he was discharged. He was called the miracle child of the hospital. Today he is 14 years old and a champion long-distance runner for his school. There is absolutely nothing wrong with his brain or body coordination." What a wonderful testimony to Spirit Healing.

Dick Dawson, of Coulsdon, Surrey, who in 1976 was the public relations officer of the National Federation of Spiritual Healers, found that after due consideration and a great deal of experience of Spirit manifestation and healing he had to come to the decision that the continuity of life after death was a positive fact.

At an interview at London Weekend Television Studios he told a 'Psychic News' Reporter in 1976; "There were certain physical phenomena which made a great impression on me. I came to the point of decision some years later where I had to say 'yes' to the irrefutable evidence I was given. The most startling, which made up my mind completely, was attending the famous physical circle run by medium Alec Harris of Cardiff. He was probably the greatest materialisation medium of all time. At his séances I saw a dozen full-figure materialisations.

"During a séance he was curtained off in the cabinet. One by one these materialised figures emerged. The extraordinary thing was they disappeared in a flash towards the floor. It was startling and dramatic. I could see no possibility of fraud. He was tested thoroughly by leading researchers and journalists of the day. There was never any hint of fraud." ('Psychic News' 30th October 1976)

After recounting his experiences in some detail he discussed his involvement with Spirit healing, being a well known healer himself. He closed the interview with the words, "However, it is pleasantly surprising to note the number of doctors who make public their sympathetic view about Spirit healing." This is a fact that we have also encountered.

Dr B. Laubscher, a trained Psychiatrist with a great deal of practical psychic experience, in his book '*In Quest of the Unseen*' recounts his experience and that of a colleague, Dr Williams, while attending one of Alec's materialisation séances. "One of the amazing psychic manifestations which has to be experienced to be fully appreciated, is that of materialisation of a discarnate being by means of ectoplasm. The following experience with Alec Harris, one of South Africa's greatest materialising mediums, must be accepted as authentic in every respect, as there is no other possible explanation except contact with Spirit people from another dimension."

Then follows an account of the many materialisations he saw, felt, and spoke to, after he had satisfied himself, by a thorough examination, that the cabinet 'was completely bare of everything except a chair'. He met a good many of the Guides attached to our circle, and the Scientist went out of his way to demonstrate some remarkable phenomena, knowing that the medical men were showing a genuine and sincere interest in the subject. Demonstrations were given to show how the ectoplasm could be manipulated to produce literally anything required, from a pair of spectacles, to perfume, water, or metal. The Red Indian Guide of a friend, Teddie Foster, seemed to arouse Dr Laubscher's particular interest. In his book he writes:

"The Red Indian Spirit was of striking personality, with a decidedly aquiline nose. He was much taller than Mr Harris and appeared to be a man in his thirties, whilst Mr Harris was 68 years old. The Spirit was known as Black Feather, and there was the black feather clearly visible sticking out of his headdress. Down the sides of his neck hung two distinct black plaits of long hair. He came up to Dr Williams and myself and asked us as medical men to examine him. He turned his face in every direction within the illumination of the red light so that we could study his strong chiselled features, most unlike that of Mr Harris. Then Dr Williams and I counted his pulse rate, felt his heart beat and his ribs and actually passed our hands around his powerful naked chest. His abdominal muscles were taut and we could feel the hollow under his ribs as his chest billowed outwards. Having done physical culture and muscle control as a young man I was aware that such control of the abdominal muscles could not possibly have been exhibited by Mr Harris, a man of 68 years.

"The Red Indian seemed an entirely different personality and informed me that all this was for my benefit. He displayed his majestic bearing and his warrior build, as well as his desire to prove to myself and my colleague that ectoplasm could be condensed until it was flesh and bone. This solid being with a clearly defined personality came to give Dr Williams and myself a demonstration of how ectoplasm could perform miracles by means of laws manipulated by thought. He stood there before us, and then melted away into the world which our physical senses could not penetrate."

Black Feather always came when Teddie Foster was present at a circle. Her first encounter with this Guide was when she first attended a séance with Alec at which her late husband had come to her, calling her by her pet name. He talked of private matters, and discussed the welfare of the children.

Both Dr Laubscher and Dr Williams are advocates of and firm believers in Spirit healing, as are many other medical men of our acquaintance who are convinced that this healing power transmitted through a medium is an established fact. They witnessed remarkable and inexplicable cures through Spirit intervention, some being instantaneous, others requiring longer treatment, and sometimes quite miraculous bodily repair of the medically incurable.

I remember a night when a blind gentleman stood before the materialised Healing Scientist who applied the 'Healing Light' to his afflicted eyes. When the light faded the gentleman glanced up at the Spirit before him, and then unbelievingly around the room at the other sitters. "I can see!" he said in amazement. Then excitedly, "I can SEE!" and he did not have to be led back to his seat.

Then there was the case of Robert Parker of Surrey, England who lost his sight and as a result had to retire from a very good job where he held a high position. A friend of his who had witnessed what took place in our healing circles suggested that he enlist Alec's help when it was found that his condition was beyond orthodox medical repair. Mr Parker scorned the idea. "What can a man like that do?" he had said, doubtfully. "When all the finest eye specialists in Britain have been unable to cure me. They, with their wealth of knowledge and consummate skill, have not been able to do anything. How could this medium possibly help me? No," he said firmly, "it would be a waste of time."

Eventually his friend overcame his reluctance and he was persuaded to visit our sanctuary. He attended every two weeks for several months, at the end of which period his sight was so improved that he could discern distant objects fairly well. Then one night, when he was attending a séance, the Healing Scientist called him up and quite casually asked, "What is the time, Robert?" Mr Parker glanced down at his wrist and found that he could see the figures on the face of his watch quite clearly and promptly gave the correct time. We had another convert, and yet another cure credited to our wonderful band of Spirit friends.

Our dear friend Vidie Carlton Jones found herself in need of help. She suffered a thrombosis in her left eye, and as a result the sight in that eye was so impaired that the vision was nil. Her eye specialist said that there was absolutely no hope of recovery and feared that the sight in the other eye might become affected. She immediately had healing from Adoula and other Spirit doctors through Alec. When she visited her eye specialist again he was surprised to find the sight in the thrombotic eye had been completely restored and she could see perfectly. Puzzled, as medically this could not happen, he asked her what had occurred.

"Well" said Vidie, reluctantly, "I'll tell you. I know you won't believe me, but I have very good friends in the Other World." The doctor thought about this statement for a moment. Then he nodded. "You certainly have!" he replied, without a trace of the wry smile that Vidie had expected. So once again the truth of Spirit Healing had been demonstrated to the medical profession and had not been dismissed as mere superstition.

Man is a Spirit while still in the flesh. All Spirits who materialise at séances need not necessarily be those of discarnate beings. The living have also come to our circle very occasionally while in their astral bodies during the sleep state, or perhaps while suffering severe illness when they are literally hanging between Life and Death and when their astral bodies are more easily able to detach themselves from their physical vehicles than at any other time. I will give an instance of such materialisation of the living through Alec's physical mediumship.

My niece, Phyllis, was estranged from her brother over some personal matter where their differences of opinion conflicted, and he had gone to live in America. They were not on speaking terms and had not communicated thereafter. One night a young man stepped from the cabinet and called to me, "Auntie Lou." I went up to him and as I came close to him I realised with shock that it was Johnny, my sister May's youngest son and Phyllis' brother.

"Oh, Johnny," I cried, "I did not know that you had passed over." And then turning to Phyllis I called, "Phyl, it's Johnny!" Phyllis let out a cry and jumped from her seat to join us outside the cabinet, hardly believing that the figure shrouded in ectoplasm was her own brother. Her voice broke as she murmured, "Oh, Johnny I did not know. When? When did this happen?"

The Spirit raised his hand to calm her. "It's all right, Phyl," he said. "I am only asleep. Mam brought me." Obviously his mother, who had already passed on, was no doubt concerned that her two children were still estranged, so she had endeavoured to bring them together to effect a reconciliation. Phyllis and her brother conversed quietly together, Phyl obviously emotionally overcome. Then Johnny bade her goodbye and dematerialised, and was never seen again in the circle.

But the mother had managed to achieve her object. Phyllis promptly wrote to enquire about her brother in America, telling of the incident at the séance, saying what a shock it had given her. She was surprised by a return letter from her brother which expressed puzzlement as he had no knowledge or recollection of ever having been in a séance room, even in a dream. Unconscious astral projection happens to all of us, although few can remember out of the body experiences which occur when we are detached from our physical bodies during the hours of sleep. Needless to say, Phyllis and Johnny became reconciled and kept in touch with each other thereafter. What a comforting thought to know that we can meet our departed or absent loved ones while we sleep.

Dr MacDonald Bayne, of whom I have already written in connection with our Cardiff circles (*p178*), started a school in Pretoria, South Africa, for the study of Universal Science which attracted quite a number of dedicated pupils. After the doctor's death in February 1955 his group were anxious to renew contact with their mentor, now in Spirit. One of the group, a lady who resided in Pretoria, approached me to obtain a materialisation sitting with Alec. We included her and her husband in a circle which took place in January 1958. This séance proved to be an outstanding experience for them. Not only did the doctor materialise and speak to his ex-pupil, greeting her with his cheery "Hello, you there!" delivered in his familiar Scottish accent, but when he kissed her she noticed that he still wore a moustache, and he was readily recognised by both of his old friends. He said that he had come to keep a promise he had made the husband in 1945 when he had given his word that he would come back after his death and prove that he could materialise to them in a form apparently as solid as that of his previous physical flesh.

Standing well materialised before his friends in our Sanctuary in Bramley, Dr MacDonald Bayne stretched forth his arms and said: "Take my hands and feel them. They are just the same as yours. I have now fulfilled my promise to you." The couple marvelled that the Spirit doctor had remembered that promise made 13 long years before. It was the first time that the doctor had materialised in our Sanctuary and I was as delighted as his friends were to see him again.

The Spirit then made reference to the incident over three years previously in Cardiff, which I have written about in Chapter 10, when his father had come and told him that his passing was near at hand. To his ex-pupil's teasing remark that "he had been very clever to write his books and then not return to South Africa to face the questions that his pupils had ready for him," he replied; "I had intended to return but my father appeared to me and told me I had to come over on to this side soon, as there was work for me to do. Even then I did not believe him," he smiled. "But here I am!" It was most evidential having his Spirit's confirmation of what had transpired at our Cardiff séance over three years previously.

At the end of a happy reunion he bade his friends goodbye using a well remembered phrase; 'So long for now', which further delighted his friends. Excited about what she had seen, this lady later brought a party of ten of Dr MacDonald Bayne's students to a séance. Once again the Spirit doctor materialised and smiling he said to me, "I see you have my crowd here tonight!" He went to them and taking their hands, he greeted each one by name, saying how lovely it was to see them all again, and having no difficulty in identifying his former pupils.

A guide named Auronama materialised for one of the gentleman sitters. He came with his hands outstretched, holding in the palms a lovely greenish-blue light, which one sitter remarked that it reminded her of glow worms. "This is the 'Healing Light' which we give to you for your healing," said Auronama. "You have worked for a long time for this, and now you will get results in your developing healing circle." The glow from the unearthly light in his hands illuminated his beautiful face. Then he raised his arm above his head and gave all the sitters his blessing. Just before he disappeared he gave the students who would be familiar with it the 'hailing sign' of Astara, and he was gone.

Many of the student group received visitors from the other side that night. Ida's guide, a tall figure with a long black plait of hair hanging down his back and wearing on his head a small round black cap, announced himself as 'Seelong'. He said that he brought power to her, and advised her to persevere with her healing efforts. While another Spirit, Robert, who was on friendly terms with one of the sitters, proved that Spirits do not forget previous earthly standards of courtesy when he chivalrously offered 'to see the lady safely back to her seat'. Jolkim also delighted the group by singing, 'I Love You Truly' with my niece, Phyllis and me making a trio.

Then a Spirit of slender physique materialised and started to grow stouter, and stouter, before announcing himself as the grand-father of a lady in the group. She promptly recognised him and greeted him delightedly. When he spoke to her it was in her mother tongue, Afrikaans. The medium had no knowledge of this language, a fact which greatly impressed the sitters.

A Spirit then materialised looking just like his daughter. The similarity was most striking, and apparent to all present. He took his daughter in his arms and embraced her murmuring, "My dearest child (he mentioned her name), I told you I would come to you." The daughter laid her head on her Spirit father's shoulder and they hugged and loved one another; it was a beautiful sight to witness this loving reunion.

Among the many who appeared to be lining up behind the cabinet curtains that night waiting to materialise was Ginger. Apparently he had made several unsuccessful attempts for Sunny, one of our child Guides, came out and said: "Aunty Lou, Ginger would like to materialise but the scientists will not let him, and he says," continued the childish voice, "that if they won't let him come, next time there will be a hell of a row!" This unseemly remark was so unexpected that it caused shrieks of laughter to erupt around the circle; and with that Sunny said that the meeting had better close, and I was inclined to agree with him.

Altogether, this had been most satisfactory circle for the group of MacDonald Bayne students and naturally they were all anxious to come again, which they did, many times thereafter.

At a subsequent circle attended by the same group of students the father who had such a loving reunion with his daughter materialised again, and this time he made a point of showing his hands to his son-in-law, who was very sceptical indeed about the phenomenon of materialisation. The Spirit father had done a lot of woodwork in his Earth life and this had caused hard calluses to form on his hands which were still present when he came in Spirit form to the séance. By showing these to his son-in-law it enabled him to accept, almost but not quite, that the Spirit was the person he professed to be. The Spirit's granddaughter, however, readily recognised him and required no other proof than that of her eyes. This same granddaughter at another séance had a very evidential materialisation when a Spirit came for her by the name of Marrietzie and reminded her of their schoolgirl friendship at the Loreto Convent. They were able to exchange a few reminiscences before the Spirit retired to the cabinet again.

However, to revert to the son-in-law who was still not one hundred per cent happy about the reality of his wife's father's materialisation, in spite of inspecting the callused hands, he decided to put a further test to the Spirit. As his wife's family came from the village of Lengweisen near Zurich, Switzerland, they spoke Schweizer-Deutch. The gentleman was conversant with the language and felt sure that nobody else in the circle could speak it, or would be able to understand if he conversed in this manner with his father-in-law. But he had to wait a further ten months for the next circle to prove his point.

In February 1959 he was again in our Sanctuary eagerly waiting for an opportunity to put the test into practice, and he earnestly hoped that the Spirit purporting to be his father-in-law would come again. He was not to be disappointed for it did. It stepped from the cabinet, tall and well materialised, and after first speaking to and embracing his daughter, he approached his sceptical son-in-law and shook him warmly by the hand. It was not long before both men, the mortal and the Spirit, had their arms about one another's shoulders. The conversation was conducted in English, then suddenly the son-in-law switched to the Swiss-

German dialect. Without hesitation the Spirit responded in similar fashion, and they chatted amiably about certain family matters about which only he, his wife and her father could possibly have had any knowledge. This was more than sufficient evidence to convince him that the dead live on unchanged, and can return materialised to speak to us and show their love and affection.

One lady sitter had the interesting experience of meeting her Spirit grandmother, whom she had never seen, as the lady had passed over before the sitter was born. The Spirit showed herself as a middle-aged stout woman who looked very much like the lady's own mother, who was also in the Spirit World. The Spirit informed her that she was 'Grandma Clancy' and when the sitter enquired if her mother was with her the Spirit replied, "Your mother is here, but the scientists and chemists are having difficulty in persuading her to step from the cabinet."

I explained after this materialisation that many Spirit people do build up into a materialised form behind the cabinet curtains, but find that the process of lowering their finer vibrations to correspond to the coarser ones of this physical plane, and endeavouring to co-ordinate both their materialised body and voice, needs considerable practice if a satisfactory manifestation is to be achieved. At the last moment some of them become too nervous to step from the cabinet to face the gaze of so many strangers. It seems to them that as they move away from the Scientists helping them to build and hold their forms, it is as if they are stepping down from a two-storey balcony as they emerge from the cabinet. One can understand their hesitancy, and it is our job to encourage them as much as we can to give them confidence.

Grandma Clancy told her granddaughter that her cousin, Mary, in a nearby town had injured her knee. "It is worse than you think it is," she pronounced. "You must go over to her and lay your hands on the knee, and the Spirit doctors and healers will work through you to help her pain." As Grandma Clancy had passed over more than a hundred years previously, the lady wanted to know how the Spirit had known her, never having met her. To this the Spirit lady replied: "Oh, I often watch you," and then with a hurried, "I must go now," she disappeared.

My husband was no linguist, and on this night alone the Spirits spoke in several tongues. One foreign Spirit materialised for a sitter who, as a girl, had been educated at a certain Convent in Switzerland. One of the nuns had been particularly fond of her, and when she spoke to her it was in French, the language spoken in the Convent, and which the ex-pupil understood, but which the medium certainly did not.

All the Spirit manifestations were extremely evidential that night up to the very last appearance which was that of a Spirit called Tom, who had died from pneumonia in Cape Town in 1919. As he stepped from the cabinet to greet his sister she promptly recognised him and remarked, "Tall and good-looking as ever." He turned and smiled as one of the group said to him: "Oh, Tom, you were the most handsome man I knew." He even remembered to send his 'warmest wishes' to Mary, an old friend of whom he had been very fond in the early days of his youth.

The day after the séance Tom's sister and her husband drove over to see Mary to tell her about the sitting, and of Grandma Clancy's advice regarding her knee. Mary's eyes shone when she heard of Tom's message which made her very happy. "If only I had been there," she sighed wistfully.

* * *

I believe I have given enough material to indicate without any doubt that the materialisation of discarnate Spirits is a proven fact and not just a figment of the imagination. This remarkable phenomenon has been witnessed and vouched for by numerous sitters from all parts of the world and from all walks of life, artisans, businessmen, investigators, professors, medical men and scientists - people of integrity whose findings can be relied upon.

One can see and analyse the wealth of evidence presented, the variety of bodily forms that materialised, the different physiques, heights, features, colourings, characteristics, the numerous foreign languages spoken, and above all the differences in sex and ages of literally hundreds of Spirit entities who manifested in our

Sanctuary. These have ranged from a day old infant to young and beautiful dancing girls and a withered emaciated nonagenarian.

Something supernormal had taken place and the something supernormal at work can only be explained as being visible proof of the continuity of life after death. The discarnate inhabitants of the other world are able at will to re-enter the physical plane and become visible to us by clothing themselves in a remarkable substance called ectoplasm exuded by unique members of the human race known as physical materialisation mediums. Such a one was Alexander Harris, and he was one of the most powerful physical mediums of his time.

Louie and Alec with their grandson, Anthony, 1965

Chapter Fourteen

A Judas in Our Midst

❖ Spirit warning of danger ❖A séance is disrupted ❖ Holiday in Britain 1962 ❖ We move to Durban 1971 ❖ Doney passes to Spirit 1973 ❖Alec passes to Spirit 1974 ❖Alec returns 24 hours later to comfort Louie & then through many mediums to prove he lives on

In July 1961 we had a Spirit warning that Alec was likely to be in danger. It came during the penultimate circle prior to our departure for Durban. Alec and I were to have a couple of months much needed and well earned holiday with our son and his family who resided in that city.

Being a Tuesday we had assembled in the sanctuary for our weekly private sitting. The séance commenced with the usual prayer followed by a hymn. Then a most unusual manifestation happened, something quite foreign to the normal phenomena which usually occurred. Alec, in trance, stepped out of the cabinet and stood before us with ectoplasm streaming copiously from his solar plexus, mouth and nose. It literally poured from his body, forming a large pool of this gossamer substance on the floor in front of him. After a few minutes it started to build into a Spirit figure. The process was arrested, and the outlines of the form were indistinct and shapeless, only half built.

It began to move, resembling an animated piece of cloth. Without warning it rose swiftly into the air. With trailing wisps of ectoplasm it floated eerily around the room above our heads. The semi-built form was attached to and manipulated by a long psychic rod which protruded from the lower extremity of Alec's chest. At the end of it were two finger-like protrusions which grasped and activated the ectoplasmic structure. After a few excursions around the room the apparition and its trailing ectoplasm returned to Alec's body to be reabsorbed. There was consternation and much discussion among us over this.

Alec now turned to re-enter the cabinet. Still in trance, he walked in a slow dazed manner. As the curtains parted and he stepped inside, the Scientist, without a second's delay, stepped out, in his own materialised figure. They passed one another in the entrance to the cabinet. It was as if the Guide had been standing behind the curtains awaiting his cue to appear. He bustled towards us, stocky of build, with an authoritative manner and an incisive tone of speech. Our excited comments ceased abruptly as the old Scientist spoke.

"I see you are all surprised by the demonstration of the floating form which you have just witnessed. That is what a lot of people believe Spirit materialisation is really like, and what they expect to see at your séances, a ghostly apparition, shall we say. Because we come in a body as solid as their own, they do not believe the evidence of their eyes. They cannot! And therein lies the danger."

His voice grew serious. "I come to warn you that you are continually jeopardising the medium's safety by allowing such people into your circles. The confirmed disbeliever always constitutes a danger. More care must be taken to weed them out beforehand. This medium is valuable to us in our efforts to prove survival. There are so few in your world that we can use in this way. I implore you to select your sitters most carefully."

He turned to me: "Remember, lady, before you undertook the task of physical mediumship we stressed that we could protect the medium only 'three parts of the way'. The other part was your responsibility. See that you take all steps to ensure that he is protected at all your future séances." I assured him that I always did, to the very best of my ability. He nodded curtly, and left us. His warning greatly alarmed me. This Guide rarely appeared, and when he did it was always to impart important instructions.

There was only one more sitting planned before we left on holiday. I was so perturbed about the Spirit warning regarding Alec's safety that I asked Vidie to cancel this circle. "There will be no more materialisation circles!" I said emphatically. "Alec is very dear to me, and I simply will not risk his health in any way."

"Please do not disappoint these people," begged Vidie. "They have waited patiently for such a long time for this circle. Anyway I have vetted them all very carefully. They have all sat before and are good sitters, I know."

Much against my better judgement, I agreed that the circle should take place as arranged the following Saturday. "After all," I thought, "Vidie is right. All the people coming can be trusted."

But I had not bargained for treachery. Despite Vidie's rigid precautions, an evil element entered our band of trusted sitters. A Judas came among us, one deemed to be above suspicion. He was the secretary of the Spiritualist church in a nearby town, and I would have staked my life on his integrity. Because of his position of trust his deed was all the more despicable.

At the very last minute this man, who had booked two seats, approached Vidie and asked if he and his friend might transfer their seats to two gentlemen friends for whom he could vouch, as they now found that they were unable to attend themselves. The idea of collusion never entered Vidie's head. Thinking that the substituted sitters would be from the same church, she agreed to the exchange. Never for one moment did she realise what dreadful plans they had to break Alec's wonderful mediumship!

The two substitute sitters later turned out to be journalists from a small magazine. It was their intention to expose what they firmly believed was a gigantic hoax to hoodwink gullible sitters. In so doing the pair hoped, no doubt, to come up with an exciting story which would please their editor. They duly presented themselves at our door on the appointed night. Unfortunately, Vidie was indisposed that evening and was unable to attend the circle.

The two substitutes arrived about an hour before the others. Alec answered their knock and let them in. They asked if they might inspect the sanctuary. It being a reasonable request he readily agreed and led them to the room. They made a thorough inspection and professed satisfaction. Then they asked if they might be left alone for a while to meditate in the sanctuary. Though surprised at this unusual request, Alec nevertheless agreed and left them.

Unaware of this intrusion into the sanctuary, I came downstairs and was on my way to the lounge to greet the other sitters when I encountered these two men walking out of the séance room. The sight of them caused me to stop in my tracks. Over their heads I could see a dark cloud. I strongly felt the presence of evil which greatly disturbed me. Without seeing me they made their way to the lounge to join the others who were arriving.

When placing the sitters immediately before the séance began, I remembered the evil cloud and deemed it wise to seat the strange couple on either side of my niece's husband, Trevor Cowley, in the second row, where I felt they could do no harm. However, there was an opening through the centre of the front row which afforded access to the cabinet should back-row sitters be called up by Spirit friends.

I said a special prayer for protection as I opened the circle. Bearing in mind the Scientist's warning I felt a heavy responsibility for Alec's safety. I was worried that the exchange of the two sitters had been permitted. The prayer completed, we sang a hymn and some bright songs, and waited. When nothing happened, we sang again. There followed a longer period of waiting. Still nothing happened. The Spirit entities seemed disinclined to materialise. I began to feel that something was decidedly wrong.

At last there was a movement of the cabinet curtain. The slim, bearded figure of Rohan appeared, standing uncertainly in the aperture in front of the cabinet. This calm, strong Guide always opened our circles with greetings, explanations and advice. It was his practice to come straight out and speak to each sitter in turn, taking his or her hands in his own slender ones. With his deep, soft voice he would welcome each one warmly. But this night things seemed different. Rohan remained for a long time within the opening of the cabinet curtains, standing very still. He surveyed the two semi-circular rows of sitters before him searching the faces intently. Fear clutched at my heart for I knew instinctively that something was amiss. But I trusted Rohan.

After a pause he came hesitantly forward and commenced his welcoming gesture of taking the hands of each sitter in the front row. Somehow, Rohan seemed wary, not as relaxed as usual. When he came to me and held my hands, he looked deeply into my eyes. Seeing I was troubled he gently squeezed my hands in reassurance. I felt that all the Guides were present and would help should there be any trouble. Despite that, my anxiety persisted.

Rohan released my hands and returned to the cabinet. He took hold of the black curtains which hung down to conceal Alec. He parted them, then held one side high above his head to reveal Alec in trance. Seated in his chair, he was clearly visible to all. Rohan, still holding the curtain, backed away to stand by the window some distance from Alec. It was obvious that there were two separate entities before the sitters, the physical body of the medium, and the Spirit form of Rohan.

"Now, can you see the medium clearly?" asked Rohan. "Here am I, standing quite apart from him. Are you sure you can see us both?"

There were excited cries of 'Yes' and 'Wonderful!' from the sitters. Rohan let the curtain fall back, and came forward to take the hands of those seated in the back row. He always made sure that everyone was similarly greeted, and that they saw and touched him. Major Chisham, who was healed earlier of his deafness, was one of the sitters in the second row at this circle. It was most gratifying to hear him conversing easily with Rohan and hearing every word that was said to him.

Eventually, it was the turn of one of the substitute sitters to be greeted thus. As Rohan was about to take his hands in welcome, the man sprang forward and grabbed him! Throwing his arms around the Spirit figure, he held on to him tightly, shouting: "I've got you!" The sitter was obviously convinced that he had captured the draped medium in the act of duplicity, masquerading as a Spirit form.

As Rohan's Spirit form quickly dematerialised there was a loud groan from Alec in the cabinet. Then came a cry of pain as the ectoplasm swiftly returned to his body with the impact of a sledgehammer.

The treacherous sitter fell dazed to the floor as the 'solid' body he had held so tightly minutes before disappeared. I threw myself upon him, desperately flailing him with my hands, sobbing: "Oh, don't. You'll kill my husband! You fool, you'll kill him!"

The man looked up at me, his eyes wide, terrified. The realisation had dawned upon him that it had not been the medium he had grasped, but a fully materialised Spirit form.

Meanwhile the second imposter, taking advantage of the commotion that ensued, rushed to the window and pulled aside the closed curtains, having previously tampered with them during the bogus meditation session earlier. This revealed his confederates outside the window. They had a battery of cameras focussed on the séance room, and on the cabinet in particular.

Lenses immediately started clicking furiously as flash bulbs exploded. Had the light from one of these touched my beloved Alec as he sat in deep trance it would have killed him instantly. I glanced frantically in the direction of the cabinet, and realised with profound relief that our Guides were doing all in their power to protect their medium. They had swathed the curtains around Alec, completely enveloping him so that he was immune to the blinding flashes of light being so ruthlessly directed at him. I was utterly bewildered and sick with dread for Alec, knowing what he must have suffered by the sudden impact of the returning ectoplasm. It all happened so quickly that everybody was stunned.

The two journalists were the first to recover. They made a dash for the door in a bid to escape, but my niece Phyllis and her husband, Trevor, followed close on their heels in hot pursuit. One chose the kitchen exit, where Trevor managed to rescue him from the clutches of the dog who had added its services in intercepting the fleeing man. The other ran wildly down the passage and was cornered by a very irate Phyllis and several of the male sitters in the lounge. This, to his chagrin, he found securely locked. Escape was impossible. All arrogance deserted him, and he cringed apologetically.

"You tried to kill my uncle," Phyllis raged. "Why? Did you think he was a fake?" When the man did not answer, Phyllis went on angrily, "Well, now you know he isn't." In disgust she told him to leave and take his friend with him. Two very frightened men, sobered by what they had seen, ran off into the night to join their confederates in a waiting car parked some distance down the street.

When Alec came out of trance he was patently very ill. He had a severe pain in his solar plexus which persisted for some weeks. He was promptly put to bed and a doctor called. He continued to treat Alec every week for many months. Rohan, too, suffered adverse effects and needed, we were told by the Scientist, a period of recuperation.

There was a sequel to this unhappy encounter. A short time after the failed 'exposure' Alec and I were sitting in front of the fire in conversation with a doctor friend when Alec stopped speaking in mid sentence and was entranced. His eyes closed, his face became relaxed, and a soft baritone voice announced, 'Rohan'. The doctor and I bade this dear friend 'good evening' and 'welcome'.

"I have come to tell you," the gentle voice continued, "that greater care must be taken of the medium in future. If there should be a repetition of the accident which took place a few weeks ago we will not be able to protect the medium as we then did. It was fortunate that it was I who was materialised at the time, for I knew what to do, and was able to take the full shock of the encounter. By the time it reached the medium it was less severe. But I doubt that I shall be able to do this again," he warned. "So take care." I thanked him and promised that it would never occur again if it was humanly possible to avoid such a catastrophe.

I then raised a point which had been worrying me. "Rohan, what about all those photographs they took and are going to publish?"

"Do not worry about that," the calm voice reassured me. "We have made certain that all the films will be blank." So it turned out to be. The magazine had promised its readers in a previous issue that it would give full photo coverage to the 'exposure' of Alec's mediumship. Neither pictures nor any article ever appeared. Obviously there were no photographs to print.

When Vidie heard how the exchange of seats had been engineered she was very upset and reacted in her typical outspoken manner. She wrote a letter to the gentleman who had originally secured the two seats with the words, "Herewith your 30 pieces of silver!" The Biblical inference was appropriate and humiliating to the perpetrator of such shameful treachery.

I noticed a great change in Alec after the exposure attempt. His health was not as robust as before. Something seemed to have gone out of him. He had slowed down considerably. Alec had always been such an energetic person, constantly looking for things to do about the home. Now everything seemed to be an effort for him.

Vidie thought a trip to Britain might help Alec, and restore his zest for living. In May 1962 we once again accompanied her to the United Kingdom. On arrival, we spent a few days with her in London, and she kindly lent us her car to visit friends in Staffordshire and Cardiff. Alec did not look at all well and I was worried about him. I decided that as soon as we reached Cardiff he should see our doctor and have a check-up.

We drove on until we arrived at Auntie Thomas' house where we were to stay. She and Megan came rushing to give us a joyous welcome. It was lovely seeing them again and we were all a bit moist eyed at our reunion.

The following afternoon we visited Peggy, our dear pianist friend of yore, and spent happy hours chatting of the old days. After we left her, and were on our way to visit Alec's brother, I noticed that Alec's driving was very erratic. He seemed to be having difficulty keeping the car on a straight course. When I enquired if he was feeling all right, he replied that he was quite well. Alec managed to negotiate the vehicle through the busy streets of Cardiff without mishap, and we were driving slowly along a quiet road in the residential area where his brother resided when the car suddenly swerved violently and landed on the pavement, where it came to a halt. Alec was slumped in his seat looking very strange.

"I can't feel anything down my right side," he gasped. "My right leg and arm are numb." In addition his speech was slightly slurred.

Fortunately my brother-in-law was anticipating our arrival and waiting by his gate. He saw the mishap take place just down the road and quickly ran to give us assistance. Moving Alec across into the passenger seat, he got behind the wheel and drove us to his house, where he massaged Alec's limbs to revive his circulation, but without success. He then drove us back to Auntie Thomas' house. Alec refused to allow us to call a doctor as he did not wish to disturb the household as it was by then midnight. "I will be better by morning," he insisted. So we put him to bed. I stayed awake all night, holding his hands and praying.

The doctor came early in the morning and told me he would get my husband to hospital at once. As we were in Cardiff where members of our old healing circle lived, I felt that Alec would be better at home receiving Spirit healing from them. The doctor reluctantly agreed, provided Alec was watched very carefully. He was insistent that if there should be any change for the worse in his condition, he should be taken to hospital without delay.

Alec was kept under sedation for five days. When the doctor made another examination he was very surprised at the improvement in my husband's condition. Alec continued to make good progress and we remained in Cardiff for a further four weeks. Then Vidie came down to drive us back to London as Alec would be unable to handle a car himself for some time. We stayed on in Britain and completed our holiday, but always travelling by train now to visit our friends. We finally returned to South Africa by sea.

The sea air and plenty of rest on our return trip did Alec a lot of good. He seemed very much better; though when we arrived in Durban to stay with our children they were dismayed at the change in their father. It took two years before he was anything like his old self again.

Once home, we gave occasional circles, but only for immediate friends, not the public. Alec's confidence in sitters had been sadly shaken. He could never again be completely relaxed and at ease as in the days before the betrayal in the séance room. His health was not as good as previously. Spirit Friends had difficulty in materialising. When we first sat nothing happened, but we were asked to be patient as there would have to be a period of re-development. There did not seem to be enough power for materialisations to form completely, or as strongly, as before. Sometimes they could not build to their proper height. On other occasions only portions of their bodies took shape, perhaps an arm, leg, or face unrecognisable in incompleteness. Eventually, when a form did manage to build fully, there would be a long wait until the next materialisation. Before the incident when one Spirit returned to the cabinet another would step out almost immediately. There would be the minimum of delay.

I decided that Alec would give up sitting for materialisation and concentrate on voice phenomena only. At the next circle we sat around the room, instead of in two semi-circular rows, and extinguished the lights. We sat in complete darkness, which condition was necessary for the manifestation of voice.

When this voice circle opened who should leave the cabinet but the Scientist, fully materialised. He raised his arm and pulled the cord attached to the lights outside the cabinet and the room was bathed in a dull red glow.

"Sir," I explained, "we intend having a voice circle tonight."

"Oh," he said sharply, "well, if that is what you want," and he pulled the cord again and extinguished the lights and returned to the cabinet, somewhat put out.

It was an amusing circle. It was a constant battle of wills between the Spirit people who were determined to materialise, and me, equally determined that it should be a voice séance. They compromised by materialising in one place, but speaking so that their voices came through the trumpet elsewhere. Ginger too did his fair share of bantering in this manner and caused much laughter. I kept telling them that I wished this to be a voice circle, but still they came out materialised and put the lights on to show themselves. I began to get really cross, so I determined that at the next circle I would obstruct their efforts by removing the globes from their sockets and leaving them outside the room. This plan was put into operation, but they defeated me by bringing their own psychic blue-white lights with them. These showed the materialisations to even better advantage, every detail of their faces being absolutely clear.

White Wing came and explained to me that the scientists had worked hard to perfect this type of Spirit manifestation, and wanted to carry on the good work. He said that though Alec's health had deteriorated and the materialisations would not be as strong as previously, they would still bring comfort and enlightenment to many. The Guide added they would protect Alec, but insisted that care must be taken to ensure that only thoroughly reliable people would be included among the sitters.

When I told Alec what White Wing had said, he agreed reluctantly to carry on dedicating his life to this service. It was indeed just that, a life of service. With this knowledge in mind, Alec continued to give the occasional physical séance and still had excellent results in his healing circles. He never spoke about his mediumship. Even when asked about it he would say in all humility, "I take no credit for it. I know nothing about it."

The family in South Africa in 1966
(from left) Selma Peimer, Anthony, Louie, Dedoney and Bradley

Vidie did not like South Africa, and often suggested that we should return with her to settle in Britain. On the other hand, we loved the country of our adoption and we explained that we had come here expressly to be with our son and his family. We felt that at this stage in our lives we could not put 6,000 miles between us.

Ultimately, Vidie emigrated and took up residence in Guernsey, in the Channel Islands. We certainly missed her, although we did see her a couple of times when she visited South Africa, and also in 1969 when we again went to Britain to see our family and friends. That year, while we were in Guernsey with Vidie, we had a voice circle at which a young lad came through. It was her godson, Peter, who had died tragically at age 21 in a car crash, a short while before. Peter begged me to invite his parents to our circle when we returned to South Africa. He said that he was anxious to speak to them and comfort them. I promised that this would be arranged as soon as possible after our return.

We phoned Vidie to say goodbye the night before we left Britain on our homeward journey. Some sixth sense told her that this was a final goodbye. Her voice came sadly over the line: "This is really goodbye, my dears. I know we shall not meet again on this Earth." Then with a more cheerful note, "But I shall be on the other side to meet you when you come over." I could not hold back my tears as I murmured over the phone; "Goodbye dearest Vidie. You have always been a very good friend to us. God bless you."

On our return home, Peter's parents attended the first voice circle we gave. At this séance a Guide came through saying that there was a young man present, but that he was so overcome by emotion that he was finding difficulty in speaking. I felt sure that this must be Peter, so I said to his mother, "What was Peter's favourite song? Can you sing it, and we will all join in. This sometimes helps the Spirit to come through."

She thought hard, "He was always whistling a tune, but I can't remember the name of it. I know it, but I just can't start it." We were startled at this point by a melodious whistling coming from the cabinet. "That's it," the mother cried excitedly. "That was his song." The Spirit lad whistled the tune right through while we sat and listened, his mother sitting very still. Then she said quietly, "I remember it now so well. That was always his favourite tune," and she sighed in reminiscence.

The whistling of that tune had calmed the boy and Peter was now able to speak to his parents, giving them much comfort. They said it had been a wonderful experience for them. When I wrote and told Vidie the news she was delighted. Alec and I were most happy that Vidie had the satisfaction of knowing that her godson had been reunited with his parents before she herself passed into Spirit, December 1970. To prove that she was not parted from us irrevocably, she returned to speak to us at a voice circle in Durban in 1971.

Shortly after hearing of Vidie's death at the end of 1970, we had cause to suffer grave concern over our daughter-in-law, Doney. She had contracted a malignancy which was sapping her strength and vitality. When our children came to visit us in Johannesburg early in 1971, I could see a marked change in her and felt that she was not long for this world. Alec and I discussed her health. We thought that we were too far away from our little family, Johannesburg being over 400 miles away from Durban. We decided to move to Natal almost immediately to be near at hand if we should be needed.

It was suggested that we should all live together. A larger house was found in Westville where we could all be under one roof. We sadly bade farewell to Johannesburg and the many friends we had made there, and took up residence in our new home in Durban. It was a charming house, not far from the Peimer's old home, Wood Hall, which had passed to new owners on Selma Peimer's death in May 1968.

Alec and I were happy that at last we were together in a family unit. We cherished what little time we knew we had left with Doney, whose health was fast deteriorating. We gave her healing, but her allotted time on Earth was drawing to a close. It finally came to an end on 26th January 1973. After a painful terminal stage in her ailment, Doney passed into the Spirit World where she would no longer have any physical suffering. She came back to speak to us in voice circles subsequently held in Westville.

At our home in Westville we still had the occasional voice circle. These were always attended by our dear friends, the Vearys, and sometimes by several medical doctors whose acquaintances we had made since coming to Durban, one of whom was very kindly caring for Alec's health and well being.

Alec was reluctant to sit for séances any more, but he was always happy to hold the annual New Year's Eve circles. He felt these were important, because it was at these that we had an opportunity of meeting our Spirit friends who made a point of attending these special circles to exchange with us messages of goodwill and advice, making a good start for the New Year.

The special circles on 31st December 1971 and 1972 were as happy and jovial as all the previous ones we had in Johannesburg. They were followed by a little supper party given for our friends. Alec, who loved good company and especially a party, was always the amiable and perfect host once his trance state had worn off, which it did after half an hour.

But as New Year's Eve of 1973 approached the Vearys were disappointed. They were to be unable to be at that particular circle as their daughter and family were visiting from Canada, and they were having a special reunion of their own on that night. They regretfully told us that they would have to cancel. "Never mind," I consoled them. "There will be other circles, and we can be together again next year." Little did I know that was to be our last circle for all time!

A few days before New Year's Eve I had a phone call from a Mr Croxford. "You may not remember me Mrs Harris, but we met in Johannesburg when I brought my son to your husband for healing. I am sad to tell you that our boy was killed in a car crash last May." I offered my condolences.

He thanked me and continued: "Yes, it was a great tragedy. My poor wife was so very distressed. So I took her to London where we attended a meeting held by the well known clairvoyant medium, Joseph Benjamin. The hall was crowded, but my name was called, and the medium said that my son, Clive, was there. Mr Benjamin told us exactly how our boy had passed into the Spirit World and gave us a message from him. We were so thrilled with the evidence that we arranged to have a private sitting with him. At this Clive again came through and said that he wanted us to have a sitting with Mr Harris. I said, 'Son, Mr Harris does not give any more circles'. And Clive replied, 'We will arrange it'. Now I do not expect you to give us a circle, Mrs Harris. I am only phoning because we happened to be here on holiday. I just thought that you might like to hear what happened to my son. We are returning to Johannesburg almost immediately as our holiday is at an end."

Thinking quickly, I remembered that the Vearys had cancelled, and there would be a place for these reliable sitters in the coming New Year's Eve circle which was imminent. I suggested that he, his wife and daughter attend this special annual séance, and he accepted gladly. He was excited at the prospect, and decided that they would all go back home to Johannesburg, leave their luggage, and return to Durban immediately. Being high season, they would not be able to obtain accommodation anywhere in Natal, so they were prepared to sleep in their car, as nothing would make them forego this circle.

On New Year's Eve they drove the 400 miles from Johannesburg to Durban. When they arrived in Westville they enquired of a stranger if he knew where they might find accommodation for one night only. "Try the Westville Hotel," the man had said. "I know they have just had a cancellation." The family rushed to the hotel and secured the accommodation. "So Clive was right," said Mr Croxford, "Everything had been arranged."

What a lovely circle we had that night. All our beloved Friends spoke through the trumpet. White Wing was particularly inspiring. Then Clive materialised, in spite of it being a voice circle. He embraced his mother and sister, speaking gentle words of comfort to them and to their father. It was a moving experience for us to watch them being reunited with their boy.

After the circle closed we all filed out of the room, leaving Alec behind to come out of trance in his own time. Our doctor stayed with him in the darkened room, for until he was fully conscious he could not tolerate bright light. Suddenly, Alec groaned and complained of a pain in his chest. Our doctor called to another doctor in the lounge, and together they examined my husband and said that they suspected that he had an angina attack.

However, it passed off quickly, and Alec came out of the séance room for a social chat and refreshments as usual with the sitters, and my fears were lulled.

When the New Year dawned in 1974, Alec appeared to be listless and very tired, more so than usual after a séance. These symptoms persisted throughout the next five or six weeks. One evening as he sat in our cosy living room smoking quietly, deep in thought, he said, "You know, Lou, I'm not going to be with you for long."

I went to him and put my arm about him and lay my cheek against his. "Remember, darling, we are soon going to have our golden wedding. Forty six years we have been married. And we are going to celebrate that special fiftieth milestone together."

Alec looked thoughtfully at me for moment, then smiled, saying; "One of us has to go first. Better it's me than you. When I'm gone you will be able to carry on for sure."

Two weeks later, on 12th February 1974, I awoke suddenly in the early hours of the morning with a feeling that something was wrong. I reached out, switched on the light and glanced at Alec's bed. He was not in it, but sitting slumped on the edge, breathing heavily. Instantly alarmed, I hurried to him and asked him what was wrong.

"I have a queer tight feeling," he replied, adding that he had never experienced the same sensation before. To my anxious question whether he had any pain, he assured me that he was suffering none, for which I was thankful.

"I'll get the doctor," I said, reaching for the telephone and dialling quickly. When the calm voice came on the line I told him that something was seriously wrong with my husband, and begged him to come at once. I was relieved when he said he would come right away.

"The doctor will be here soon, Alec," I informed him, replacing the receiver, but he shook his head. "No," he said slowly, "he won't be in time."

I sat down next to him on the bed. Alec raised his head and looked at me for a long moment. Then he put his arms about me and held me in a close embrace, hugging me tightly to him. With a suddenness that took me by surprise Alec pressed his lips to mine and kissed me with desperate urgency, long and lovingly. Then his body went limp. I realised he had passed on.

I sat and held him to my breast, dazed and uncomprehending. I could not believe that last fond kiss Alec had given me was his farewell. Even with my knowledge of the Spirit World and its inhabitants, the shock of Alec's sudden passing was almost unbearable. I missed him, just as much as all those bereaved souls who had attended our remarkable circles over the years must have missed their loved ones. I wondered how I was going to live without him. Momentarily in my grief I had forgotten that he would never leave.

Twenty four hours later, at about the same time as he had passed over the night before, Alec returned to me. As I lay on my bed, I felt a man's hand, strong, warm, and well materialised, take hold of my arm and gently squeeze it in the old familiar loving way. My heart was eased. Soon the blessed sleep, which had evaded me, took me into soothing unconsciousness.

A few weeks later I had a remarkable experience. Again I was lying on my bed. I was on the point of entering the sleep state when I felt the weight of a body as someone lay beside me. I felt no fear, only a sense of keen expectancy. An arm reached over my waist; it was warm, strong and solid. A hand took hold of mine across my body, as it had so often done in the past. I knew beyond doubt that my Alec had come back.

Then I experienced a strange sensation. In a flash I found myself out of my physical body in an astral projection. I saw Alec standing in the room. His whole being seemed to be bathed in a mystic blue light. He appeared so much younger than when I had last seen him, no more than 30. I went to Alec. He placed his arms around me, murmuring tenderly, "I had to come, Lou .. I had to come."

I remember putting my arms around his neck, gazing up at his thick golden hair, the waves highlighted by the soft Spiritual light. "Oh, Alec," I said. "Isn't it wonderful to be together again?" Suddenly, I felt a strange trembling sensation. With a jerk that left me breathless I was back in my physical body.

I shall always remember the sweetness of that out-of-the-body encounter with my husband. It was certainly no dream. It gave me the comfort I so sorely needed.

Some months later, Clive's father phoned me to say that he had been to London again, and had a sitting with the famous medium Ena Twigg. As soon as they met she announced: "Alec Harris is here, and he has brought your son, Clive, with him. Alec is a highly evolved soul," she had said, "and he is looking after your son." I was as thrilled as this poor father at the wonderful news that my Alec was still involving himself in helping the bereaved.

I also had a letter from a lady in Cape Town, writing that she had been to London and had sat in a Leslie Flint circle. Alec, who had then only recently passed on, made his presence known to her and asked her to give his love to us all at home, and to all those he knew, but especially to me. He said that he had found it difficult to use the voice box and apologised for this.

My husband also came through in a friend's circle in Bulawayo, Rhodesia, as well as in Johannesburg, and again on two other occasions in our present home circle to speak to his grandson with words of encouragement and advice.

From personal experience, I can now appreciate just what it means to have communications from a 'dead' loved one. How much more rewarding is the sight of a loved face, the touch of a hand and the sound of a familiar voice.

Alec held sacred his gift of mediumship. Never once did he abuse it in 40 years. I realise now how blessed I was to have had the privilege of being chosen to help him with his great work.

Alec was a selfless man. Because of his great love for humanity, he dedicated his life to the service of his fellows, performing his demanding and often difficult work with humility, seeking only to be of service to others.

Ours was a happy marriage; our work brought us very close together. I look back over almost half a century of working with our beloved Spirit friends with a deep sense of gratitude that we were chosen to be so used. I sincerely pray that our psychic experiences, shared with so many others along the way, will convince many that truly there is no death.

Louie Harris joined Alec in the Spirit World in 1989 at the age of 89

Lightning Source UK Ltd.
Milton Keynes UK
UKOW04f0206060716

277789UK00015B/374/P